Microsoft System Center Virtual Machine Manager 2012 Cookbook

Over 60 recipes for the administration and management of Microsoft System Center Virtual Machine Manager 2012 SP1

Edvaldo Alessandro Cardoso

[PACKT] enterprise
PUBLISHING
professional expertise distilled

BIRMINGHAM - MUMBAI

Microsoft System Center Virtual Machine Manager 2012 Cookbook

First published: March 2013

Production Reference: 1140313

Published by Packt Publishing Ltd.
Livery Place
35 Livery Street
Birmingham B3 2PB, UK.

ISBN 978-1-84968-632-7

www.packtpub.com

Cover Image by Artie Ng (artherng@yahoo.com.au)

Credits

Author
Edvaldo Alessandro Cardoso

Reviewers
Steve Buchanan
Kristian Nese
Richard Skinner
Carmen M. Summers

Acquisition Editor
James Jones

Lead Technical Editor
Azharuddin Sheikh

Technical Editors
Jalasha D'costa
Ishita Malhi

Copy Editors
Brandt D'Mello
Insiya Morbiwala
Aditya Nair
Ruta Waghmare

Project Coordinator
Abhishek Kori

Proofreaders
Joel T. Johnson
Chris Smith

Indexer
Hemangini Bari

Production Coordinator
Arvindkumar Gupta

Cover Work
Arvindkumar Gupta

About the Author

Edvaldo Alessandro Cardoso is a virtualization and management enthusiast, author, and team leader. He is a subject matter expert in cloud computing and virtualization, and their management. He is strong team player, and pays attention to detail. His major strengths include strong leadership and hands-on skills, excellent communication skills, the ability to manage varied and conflicting demands to agreed standards and timelines. He has dutiful respect for compliance in all regulated environments. He also has supervisory skills, which includes hiring skills.

He has experience in managing, finding solutions, planning, organizing, and leading complex projects. All of these acquired in 23 years of experience in IT, in roles that span from an Application Developer through Network Manager, Network Security Manager, Systems Engineer, and Technical Consultant, working in segments spanning from government to health, education, and IT sectors.

His product skill set includes Microsoft infrastructure technologies such as Hyper-V, System Center, Windows Server, SQL Server, Active Directory, Exchange, SharePoint, IIS, and Forefront, and he also has sound knowledge of Quest Migration Manager, Linux Infrastructure, Networking, Security Solutions (such as VPN and Firewall), and VMware in complex and large scenarios. He also has a strong grasp of infrastructure and architecture solutions, IT management and industry-related datacenter processes, strategies, and industry regulations and requirements.

He has been a Microsoft Most Valuable Professional in virtualization since 2009, he is a well-known speaker at IT-related events such as TechEd, CNASI, Windows Road Shows, and User Groups. He has consistently been a presenter for more than 10 years.

He is an active member of Microsoft System Center TAP. He is also an Australian Computer Society (ACS) Certified Professional, a VMware Certified Professional, and also holds certifications in MCSE, MCSA, MCT. He was selected as Microsoft TechNet Brazil IT Hero in 2007. He was also awarded the Microsoft IT Heroes Happen award in Los Angeles in 2008. Furthermore, his virtualization project for a governmental institution in Brazil, while working as IT Manager, was selected as a business case by Microsoft.

He lead major virtualization, AD, and Exchange projects for large customers is APJ, closely collaborating and liaising with presales and sales teams to ensure order fulfillment, client satisfaction, and IT synergies.

As a key member of his team, he proactively shares expertise with peers around the globe, building and maintaining confidence of colleagues and customers, developing and nurturing deep expertise in key areas such as private cloud, migration and messages, and collaboration. He has also actively contributed to the development of materials and presentations related to his expertise, the development of best practices, and reusable content to ensure high-quality and consistent delivery of service projects across the globe.

He recently reviewed the book *Windows Server 2012 Hyper-V Cookbook*, published by Packt Publishing.

You can check out his blog at `http://virtualizationandmanagement.wordpress.com/` and follow him on Twitter at `@edvaldocardoso`.

About the Reviewers

Steve Buchanan is an infrastructure consultant. He has 13 years of experience in Information Technology around systems management, with a focus on the System Center product suite. Steve authored *Microsoft Data Protection Manager 2010* by Packt Publishing and is the contributing author of the upcoming *Microsoft Data Protection Manager 2012* book. Steve is a Microsoft System Center MVP and holds the following certifications: A+, Linux +, MCP, MCTS, MCSA, and MCITP: Server Administrator.

Steve's blog is located at www.buchatech.com.

Kristian Nese works for Microsoft both nationally and globally, and is a speaker and writer. He has experience with technologies such as virtualization and cloud computing, and is considered to be one of the best in this area.

He's the CTO at Lumagate, where he works with business development and systems management for their customers while keeping his consultants up to speed on what's hot and interesting.

Kristian has written and participated in the development of several books, such as *Cloud Computing* (in Norwegian), the *Microsoft Private Cloud Computing* book, and the *Windows Server 2012 Hyper-V Cookbook*.

Thanks to my girlfriend, Kristine, who let me spend time on this project while serving me food and beverage. You are the best, I love you.

And thank you Lukas, my son, for being the source of my inspiration through this life, I love you.

Richard Skinner has over ten years' experience in the field of IT. Since starting as a software developer, he has had a varied career covering many aspects of IT, including Windows desktop deployments, SQL Server database administration, SAN implementation, document management, SharePoint, and Hyper-V.

Carmen Summers is a Senior Program Manager at Microsoft Corporation, working in the Cloud & Datacenter Management System Center department. Carmen got her start in the industry while serving in the United States Air Force from 1991 to 2000. She has worked in the Information Technology and Service and Computer Software industries for over 18 years and has extensive Operations-related experience in various datacenter-related roles. Prior to joining Microsoft in 2007, she led the datacenter patching operations for a large scale IT services company that was responsible for patching over 40,000 servers monthly.

www.PacktPub.com

Support files, eBooks, discount offers and more

You might want to visit www.PacktPub.com for support files and downloads related to your book.

Did you know that Packt offers eBook versions of every book published, with PDF and ePub files available? You can upgrade to the eBook version at www.PacktPub.com and as a print book customer, you are entitled to a discount on the eBook copy. Get in touch with us at service@packtpub.com for more details.

At www.PacktPub.com, you can also read a collection of free technical articles, sign up for a range of free newsletters and receive exclusive discounts and offers on Packt books and eBooks.

http://PacktLib.PacktPub.com

Do you need instant solutions to your IT questions? PacktLib is Packt's online digital book library. Here, you can access, read and search across Packt's entire library of books.

Why Subscribe?

- Fully searchable across every book published by Packt
- Copy and paste, print and bookmark content
- On demand and accessible via web browser

Free Access for Packt account holders

If you have an account with Packt at www.PacktPub.com, you can use this to access PacktLib today and view nine entirely free books. Simply use your login credentials for immediate access.

Instant Updates on New Packt Books

Get notified! Find out when new books are published by following @PacktEnterprise on Twitter, or the *Packt Enterprise* Facebook page.

Table of Contents

Preface

Microsoft Virtual Machine Manager (VMM) is a management solution for the virtualized datacenter, enabling administrators to configure and manage their virtualization hosts, networking, and storage resources in order to create and deploy virtual machines and services to private clouds.

This book covers the features of VMM 2012 SP1 and Windows 2012, the architectural design, and deployment planning, and is full of tips, techniques, and solutions. It will guide you through creating, deploying, and managing your own private cloud with a mix of hypervisors such as Hyper-V, VMware ESXi, and Citrix XenServer.

This book is about designing and implementing a private cloud by using System Center Virtual Machine Manager 2012 SP1 and its integration components (WSUS and SQL), System Center Operations Manager, and System Center App Controller. It is perfect for presales, solutions architects, technical consultants, business solutions, technical advisors, administrators, and virtualization lovers aiming to gain knowledge about the System Center family of products.

I encourage you to spend some time on *Chapter 1, VMM 2012 Architecture*, in which I talk about the design of the solution as well the requirements based on deployment size and real- world implementation.

As someone who is passionate about virtualization and management, I really love this product. I have been working with it since its early stages back in 2007, and it is amazing to see how far the product has gone on to help with management tasks.

You will learn about VMM architecture and planning for real-word deployment, network virtualization, gateway integration, storage integration, resource throttling, availability options, and Operations Manager (SCOM) deployment and integration with VMM. You will also learn about App Controller (SCAC) deployment and integration with VMM to manage a private and public cloud (Azure), bare metal cluster deployment with VMM, creation and deployment of virtual machines from templates, and deployment of a High Available VMM management server. Apart from this, you will also learn about the management of Hyper-V, VMware, and Citrix XenServers from VMM, upgrading from SCVMM 2008 R2, WSUS integration for remediation, and many other features of VMM 2012 SP1.

What this book covers

Chapter 1, VMM 2012 Architecture, is designed to provide an understanding of the underlying VMM modular architecture, which is useful when troubleshooting VMM and improving implementation. Make sure you spend some extra time on this chapter.

Chapter 2, Installing SCVMM 2012, is designed to provide tips for shortening and automating processes while installing VMM 2012 and VMM 2012 SP1 and covers SQL installation, Active Directory containers for security and HA, and Run As accounts to automate and manage credentials through VMM.

Chapter 3, Installing the VMM Management Server, provides an understanding of how Virtual Machine Manager has become a critical part of the private cloud infrastructure. This chapter will walk you through the recipes to implement a Highly Available VMM server with useful tips and tricks.

Chapter 4, Configuring Fabric Resources in VMM, provides detailed recipes for the configuration and management of Fabric Resources, which are extremely powerful when configuring resources for hosts, virtual machines, and services. It provides information for the configuration and management of the virtualization host, networking, storage, and library resources. The recipes will allow you to get more out of this impressive feature and will help you to understand the logical flow, from preparing the infrastructure to making the infrastructure building blocks available to a private cloud.

Chapter 5, Deploying Virtual Machines and Services, provides information to help the Administrator create, deploy, and manage private clouds, virtual machines, templates, and services in System Center VMM 2012 and also provides you with recipes to assist you with getting the most out of deployment.

Chapter 6, Upgrading from SCVMM 2008 R2 SP1, provides recipes to allow you to smoothen the migration process from System Center 2008 R2 SP1 to System Center 2012 SP1, and includes tips and tricks for this purpose.

Chapter 7, Scripting in Virtual Machine Manager, provides a useful understanding of VMM PowerShell, which allows you to perform all VMM administrative functions by using commands or scripts. You will also find some useful sample scripts in this chapter.

Chapter 8, Managing VMware ESXi and Citrix XenServer Hosts, provides tips and techniques to allow you to integrate VMM directly with VMware vCenter Server, and also with Citrix XenServer, to manage and make their resources available for private cloud deployments. It also provides recipes to help you manage the day-to-day operations of VMware ESX/ESXi and Citrix XenServer hosts and clusters, such as the discovery and management of hosts and the ability to create, manage, store, place, and deploy virtual machines and templates, all from the VMM console.

Chapter 9, Managing Hybrid Clouds, Fabric Updates, Creating Clusters and New Features of SP1, provides recipes making use of more of the improvements provided in VMM 2012. The chapter also explores some of the key features of Service Pack 1, such as Linux VMs, availability options, and resource throttling. Additionally, it also provides recipes to integrate VMM with System Center App Controller 2012 SP1 for Hybrid Cloud Management.

Chapter 10, Integration with System Center Operations Manager 2012 SP1, provides tips and techniques to allow administrators to integrate SCOM 2012 with SCVMM when monitoring the private cloud infrastructure. You can download this chapter for free from our website, `www.packtpub.com`, using the following link:

```
http://www.packtpub.com/sites/default/files/downloads/6327EN_
Chapter10_Integration_with_System_Center_Operations_Manager_2012_SP1.
pdf
```

What you need for this book

This book is based on System Center 2012 SP1. In order to take full advantage of this book, you will need to have an understanding of Microsoft virtualization technologies (such as Hyper-V) as well as System Center Virtual Machine Manager 2012 SP1, System Center Operations Manager 2012 SP1, System Center App Controller 2012 SP1, SQL 2012, and Windows 2012 media.

Who this book is for

This book is well suited for presales, solutions architects, technical consultants, business solutions, technical advisors, administrators, and virtualization lovers.

Conventions

In this book, you will find a number of styles of text that distinguish between different kinds of information. Here are some examples of these styles, and an explanation of their meaning.

Code words in text are shown as follows: "The local agent installation information is logged in the `C:\ProgramData\VMMLogs` hidden folders."

Any command-line input or output is written as follows:

```
C:\>nslookup  xen-host1
C:\>ping  -a xen-host1
```

New terms and **important words** are shown in bold. Words that you see on the screen, in menus or dialog boxes for example, appear in the text like this: "clicking the **Next** button moves you to the next screen".

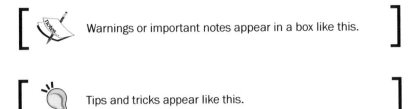

Warnings or important notes appear in a box like this.

Tips and tricks appear like this.

Reader feedback

Feedback from our readers is always welcome. Let us know what you think about this book—what you liked or may have disliked. Reader feedback is important for us to develop titles that you really get the most out of.

To send us general feedback, simply send an e-mail to feedback@packtpub.com, and mention the book title via the subject of your message.

If there is a topic that you have expertise in and you are interested in either writing or contributing to a book, see our author guide on www.packtpub.com/authors.

Customer support

Now that you are the proud owner of a Packt book, we have a number of things to help you to get the most from your purchase.

Errata

Although we have taken every care to ensure the accuracy of our content, mistakes do happen. If you find a mistake in one of our books—maybe a mistake in the text or the code—we would be grateful if you would report this to us. By doing so, you can save other readers from frustration and help us improve subsequent versions of this book. If you find any errata, please report them by visiting http://www.packtpub.com/submit-errata, selecting your book, clicking on the **errata submission form** link, and entering the details of your errata. Once your errata are verified, your submission will be accepted and the errata will be uploaded on our website, or added to any list of existing errata, under the Errata section of that title. Any existing errata can be viewed by selecting your title from http://www.packtpub.com/support.

Piracy

Piracy of copyright material on the Internet is an ongoing problem across all media. At Packt, we take the protection of our copyright and licenses very seriously. If you come across any illegal copies of our works, in any form, on the Internet, please provide us with the location address or website name immediately so that we can pursue a remedy.

Please contact us at `copyright@packtpub.com` with a link to the suspected pirated material.

We appreciate your help in protecting our authors, and our ability to bring you valuable content.

Questions

You can contact us at `questions@packtpub.com` if you are having a problem with any aspect of the book, and we will do our best to address it.

VMM 2012 Architecture

1

In this chapter will cover the following recipes:

- ▸ Understanding each component for a real-world implementation
- ▸ Designing the VMM server, database, and console implementation
- ▸ Planning for high availability
- ▸ Specifying the correct system requirements for a real-world scenario
- ▸ Licensing the System Center
- ▸ Troubleshooting VMM and supporting technologies

Introduction

This chapter has been designed to provide an understanding of the underlying **Virtual Machine Manager** (**VMM**) modular architecture, which is useful to improve implementation and when troubleshooting the VMM.

As a reference, this book is based on the System Center Virtual Machine Manager 2012 SP1 version.

The first version of VMM was launched in 2007 and was designed to manage virtual machines. The VMM 2012 SP1 version is a huge product change that will now give you the power to manage your own private cloud.

The focus of VMM 2012 is the ability to create and manage private clouds, retain the characteristics of public clouds by allowing tenants and delegated VMM administrators to perform functions, and abstract the underlying fabric to let them deploy the VM's applications and services. Although they have no visibility into the underlying hardware, there is a uniform resource pooling which allows you to add or remove capacity as your environment grows. VMM also supports private clouds across supported hypervisors, such as Hyper-V, Citrix, and VMware.

The main strategies of VMM 2012 are as follows:

- **Application focus**: VMM abstracts fabric (hosts servers, storage, and networking) into a unified pool of resources. It also gives you the ability to use Server App-V to deploy applications and SQL Server profiles to deploy customized database servers.

- **Service consumer**: One of the powerful features of VMM 2012 is its capability to deploy a service to a private cloud. These services are dependent on multiple VMs tied together (for example, web frontend servers, application servers, and backend database servers). They can be provisioned as simply as provisioning a VM, but all together.

- **Dynamic optimization**: This strategy will balance the workload in a cluster, while a feature called **power optimization** can *turn off* physical virtualization host servers when they are not needed. It can then turn them *back on* when the load increases. This process will automatically move VMs between hosts to balance the load.

- **Multivendor hypervisor support**: The list of managed hypervisors has been extended. VMM 2012 now manages Hyper-V, VMware, and Citrix XenServer, covering all of the major hypervisors on the market.

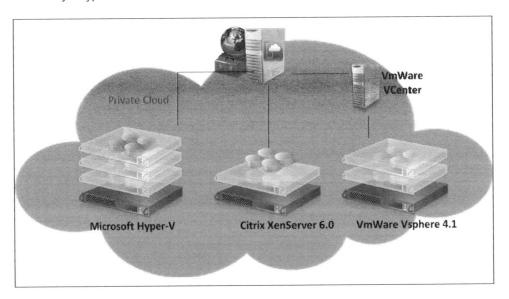

Knowing your current environment: Assessment

This is the first step. You need to do an assessment of your current environment to find out how and where the caveats are. You can use the Microsoft MAP toolkit (download it from `http://www.microsoft.com/en-us/download/details.aspx?id=7826`) or any other assessment tool to help you carry out a report assessment by querying the hardware, OS, application, and services. It is important to define what you can and need to address and, sometimes, what you cannot virtualize.

Currently, Microsoft supports the virtualization of all MS infrastructure technologies (for example, SQL, Exchange, AD, Lync, IIS, and File Server).

Designing the solution

With the assessment report in hand, it is recommended that you spend a reasonable amount of time on the solution design and architecture, and you will have a solid and consistent implementation. The following figure highlights the new VMM 2012 features for you to take into consideration when working on your private cloud design:

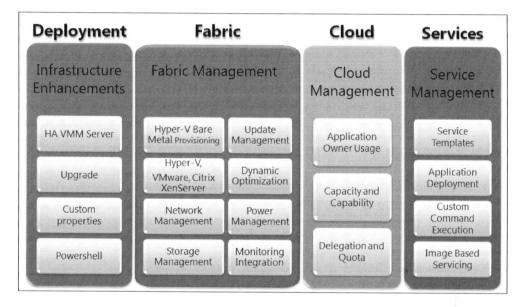

Creating the private cloud fabric

In VMM, before deploying VMs and services to a private cloud, you need to set up the **private cloud fabric**.

There are three resources that are included in the fabric in VMM 2012:

▶ **Servers**: These contain virtualization hosts (Hyper-V, VMware, and Citrix servers) and groups, PXE, update servers (that is, WSUS), and other servers.

▶ **Networking**: This contains the network fabric and devices configuration (for example, gateways, virtual switches, network virtualization); it presents the wiring between resource repositories, running instances, VMs, and services.

▶ **Storage**: This contains the configuration for storage connectivity and management, simplifying storage complexities, and how storage is virtualized. It is here that you configure the SMI-S and SMP providers or a Windows 2012 SMB 3.0 file server.

If you are really serious about setting up a private cloud, you should carry out a virtualization assessment and work on a detailed design document covering hardware, hypervisor, fabric, and management. With this in mind, the implementation will be pretty straightforward.

System Center 2012 will help you install, configure, manage, and monitor your private cloud from the fabric to the hypervisor and up to service deployment. It will also allow you to manage the public cloud (Azure).

> Refer to the *Designing the VMM server, database, and console* recipe in this chapter for further related information.

Understanding each component for a real-world implementation

System Center Virtual Machine Manager 2012 has six components. It is important to understand the role of each component in order to have a better design and implementation.

Getting ready

For small deployments, test environments, or a proof of concept, you can install all of the components in one server, but as is the best practice in the production environments, you should consider separating the components.

How to do it...

Let's start by reviewing each component of VMM 2012 and understanding the role it plays.

- ▶ VMM console

  This application connects to the **VMM management server** to allow you to manage VMM, to centrally view and manage physical and virtual resources (for example, hosts, VMs, services, the fabric, and library resources) and to carry out tasks on a daily basis, such as VM and services deployment, monitoring, and reporting.

  By using the VMM console from your desktop, you will be able to manage your private cloud without needing to remotely connect it to the VMM management server.

> It is recommended to install the VMM console on the administrator desktop machine, taking into the account the OS and prerequisites, such as a firewall and preinstalled software. See the *Specifying the correct system requirements for a real-world scenario* recipe in this chapter.

▶ The management server

The management server is the core of VMM. It is the server on which the Virtual Machine Manager service runs to process commands and control communications with the VMM console, the database, the library server, and the hosts.

Think of VMM management server as the heart, which means that you need to design your computer resources accordingly to accommodate such an important service. It is possible to run VMM 2012 as a highly available resource (clustered service or clustered VM).

 As is the best practice for medium and enterprise production environments, keep the VMM management server on a separate cluster from the production cluster, due to its crucial importance for your private cloud.

▶ Database

The database server runs SQL Server and contains all of the VMM data. It plays an important role when you have a clustered VMM deployment by keeping the shared data. The best practice is to also have the SQL database in a cluster.

 When running VMM in a cluster, you cannot install SQL Server in one of the VMM management servers. Instead, you will need to have it on another machine.

▶ VMM library

The VMM library servers are file shares, a catalog that stores resources, such as VM templates, virtual hard drive files, ISOs, scripts, and custom resources with a `.cr` extension, which will all be visible and indexed by VMM and then shared among application packages, tenants, and self-service users in private clouds.

The library has been enhanced to support services and the sharing of resources. It is a store for drivers for Bare Metal deployments, SQL data-tier apps, and web deploy packages.

In a distributed environment, you can group equivalent sets of resources and make them available in different locations by using resource groups. You can also store a resource in a storage group that will allow you to reference that group in profiles and templates rather than in a specific **virtual hard disk** (**VHD**). VMM will automatically select the local resource.

You can also have **application profiles** and **SQL profiles** to support the deployment of applications and databases to a VM after the base image is deployed. Application profiles can be server App-V packages, web applications, or a SQL data-tier.

▶ Self-Service Portal

It is a web-based Self-Service Portal, now removed from SC 2012 SP1, that lets self-service users launch and deploy **VMs** and services based on previous rules created by the **VMM** administrator.

 The Self-Service Portal's replacement is SC App Controller.

▶ VMM command shell

VMM is based on PowerShell. Everything you can do on the GUI, you can do by using PowerShell. VMM PowerShell extensions make available the cmdlets that perform all of the functions in VMM 2012.

 When working with complex environments, or if you need to automate some process, the PowerShell cmdlets will make your work easier. When doing any task on the GUI, save the PowerShell script for future use and automation.

How it works...

As you may have noticed, although **VMM** management is the core, each component is required in order to provide a better VMM experience. In addition to this, for a real-world deployment, you also need to consider implementing other System Center family components to complement your design. Every System Center component is designed to provide part of the private cloud solution. The Microsoft private cloud solution includes the implementation of VMM 2012 plus the following utilities:

▶ **System Center 2012 Unified Installer**: This is a utility designed to perform new, clean installations of all System Center 2012 components for testing and evaluation purposes only

▶ **System Center 2012 App Controller**: This provides a common self-service experience across private and public clouds that can help application owners to easily build, configure, deploy, and manage services

▶ **System Center 2012 Configuration Manager**: This provides comprehensive configuration management for the Microsoft platform that can help users with the devices and applications they need to be productive while maintaining corporate compliance and control

▶ **System Center 2012 Data Protection Manager**: This provides unified data protection for the Windows environment, delivering protection and restore scenarios from disk, tape, off premise, and from the cloud

- **System Center 2012 Endpoint Protection**: This is built on the System Center Configuration Manager and provides threat detection of malware and exploits as part of a unified infrastructure for managing client security and compliance to simplify and improve endpoint protection

- **System Center 2012 Operations Manager**: This provides deep application diagnostics and infrastructure monitoring to ensure the predictable performance and availability of vital applications, and offers a comprehensive view of the datacenter, private cloud, and public clouds

- **System Center 2012 Orchestrator**: This provides the orchestration, integration, and automation of IT processes through the creation of **runbooks** to define and standardize best practices and improve operational efficiency

- **System Center 2012 Service Manager**: This provides flexible self-service experiences and standardized datacenter processes to integrate people, workflows, and knowledge across enterprise infrastructure and applications

There's more...

When deploying System Center, there are some other systems and configurations you need to consider.

Domain controllers

Although the domain controller is not part of the System Center family and it is not a VMM component, it plays an important role in the deployment of a private cloud as **VMM** requires it to be installed on a domain environment.

> This requirement is for the System Center. You can have the managed hosts on a workgroup mode or even on a trusted domain other than the System Center domain. We will discuss this later in this chapter.

Windows Server Update Service (WSUS)

WSUS plays an important role with reference to the private cloud as it is used to update the Hyper-V hosts and library servers for compliance and remediation.

System Center App Controller

The App Controller provides a self-service experience through a web portal that can help you easily configure, deploy, and manage VMs and services across private and public clouds (Azure). For example, moving a VM from a private cloud to Azure, creating checkpoints, granting access, scaling out deployed services, and so on.

The App Controller is a replacement of the VMM Self-Service Portal in SC 2012 SP1.

System Center components scenarios

The following table will guide you through choosing which System Center component is necessary as per your deployment:

Scenarios	Enabling technologies				
	AppCtrl	Operations Manager	Orchestrator	Service Manager	VMM
Fabric provider					
Bare Metal deploy					√
Integration with network and storage			√		√
Host patching					√
Host optimization / power optimization					√
Monitoring of the fabric		√			√
Capacity reporting		√			√
Service provider					
Service templates (offerings)					√
Service and VM catalog	√			√	√
Life cycle (create, upgrade, retire)	√		√	√	√
Application and SLA monitoring		√			
SLA and capacity reporting		√		√	
Service consumer					
Request quote or capacity (cloud)			√	√	√
Request/deploy VM	√	√	√	√	√
Request/deploy service	√	√	√	√	√
Quota enforcement	√				√
Request approvals			√	√	

See also

▶ The *Planning for high availability* recipe in this chapter

▶ *Chapter 7, Scripting in Virtual Machine Manager*

▶ *Chapter 10, Integration with System Center Monitor 2012*

Designing the VMM server, database, and console

When planning a VMM 2012 design for deployment, consider the different VMM roles, keeping in mind that VMM is part of the Microsoft private cloud solution. If you are considering a private cloud, you will need to integrate VMM with the other System Center family components.

 By integrating VMM 2012 with Microsoft Server App-V, you can create application profiles that will provide instructions for installing Microsoft App-V applications, Microsoft Web Deploy applications and Microsoft SQL Server data-tier applications (DACs), and for running scripts when deploying a virtual machine as part of a service.

In VMM, you can create the hardware, guest operating system, SQL Server, and application profiles that will be used in a template to deploy virtual machines.

Getting ready

In VMM 2012, you can create a service as a set of related VMs that are configured and deployed together and managed as a single object (for example, a line of business applications that connect to SQL Server).

You can create a private cloud by combining hosts, even from different hypervisors (for example, Hyper-V, VMware, and Citrix), with networking, storage, and library resources.

To start deploying VMs and services, you first need to configure the fabric.

How to do it...

Create a spreadsheet with the server names and the IP settings, like seen in the following table, of every System Center component you plan to deploy. This will help you manage and integrate the solution:

Server name	Role	IP settings
Vmm-mgmt01	SCVMM Management Server 01	IP: 10.16.254.20/24
		GW: 10.16.254.1
		DNS: 10.16.254.2
Vmm-mgmt02	SCVMM Management Server 02	IP: 10.16.254.22/24
		GW: 10.16.254.1
		DNS: 10.16.254.1

Server name	Role	IP settings
Vmm-consol01	SCVMM Console	IP: 10.16.254.50/24
		GW: 10.16.254.1
		DNS: 10.16.254.2
Vmm-lib01	SCVMM Library	IP: 10.16.254.25/24
		GW: 10.16.254.1
		DNS: 10.16.254.2
w2012-sql	SQL Server 2012	IP: 10.16.254.40/24
		GW: 10.16.254.1
		DNS: 10.16.254.2

How it works...

The following rules need to be considered when planning a VMM 2012 SP1 deployment:

- The computer name cannot contain the character string "SCVMM" (for example, `srv-scvmm-01`) and cannot exceed 15 characters.

- Your VMM database must use a supported version of SQL Server to perform a VMM 2012 deployment. Express editions of Microsoft SQL Server are no longer supported for the VMM 2012 database. For more information, check the system requirements specified in the *Specifying the correct system requirements for a real- world scenario* recipe in this chapter.

- VMM 2012 does not support a library server on a computer that is running Windows Server 2003; it now requires Windows 2008 R2 as a minimum.

- VMM 2012 no longer supports Microsoft Virtual Server 2005 R2 Hosts. If you are upgrading from a previous version of VMM that has Virtual Server hosts, they will be removed from the VMM 2012 database. If you do not want these hosts to be removed automatically, remove the hosts manually before you start the upgrade process.

- Hosts running the following versions of VMware ESX and VMware vCenter Server are supported:
    - ESX 3.x
    - ESX 4.1
    - ESX 5.0, ESX 5.1

- Upgrading a previous version of VMM to a highly available VMM 2012 requires additional preparation. See *Chapter 5, Upgrading from SCVMM 2008* for this purpose.

- If you're planning for high availability of VMM 2012, be sure to install SQL Server on a separate server as it cannot physically be located on the same server as your VMM 2012 management server.

▸ The VMM management server must be a member of a domain. (This rule does not apply to the managed hosts, which can be on a workgroup.)

▸ The startup RAM for the VMM management server (if running on a VM with dynamic memory enabled) must be at least 2048 MB.

▸ VMM does not support **DFS Namespaces** (**DFSN**) or **DFS Replication** (**DFSR**).

▸ VMM does not support file servers configured with the "case-insensitive option" for Windows Services for Unix, as the network filesystem case control is set to `ignore`. Refer to the *Windows Services for UNIX 2.0 NFS Case Control* article available at `http://go.microsoft.com/fwlink/p/?LinkId=102944` to learn more.

▸ The VMM console machine must be a member of a domain.

There's more...

For a complete design solution, there are more items you need to consider.

Storage providers – SMI-S and SMP

Storage classifications enable you to assign user-defined storage classifications to discovered storage pools for **Quality of Service** (**QoS**) or chargeback purposes.

 You can, for example, assign a classification of Gold to storage pools that have the highest performance and availability, Silver for high performance, and Bronze for low performance.

In order to use this feature, you will need the SMI-S provider.

VMM 2012 SP1 can discover and communicate with SAN arrays through the **Storage Management Initiative** (SMI-S provider) and SMP provider.

If your storage is SMI-S compatible, you must install the storage provider on a separately available server (do not install **VMM** management server) and then add the provider to **VMM** management. If your storage is SMP compatible, it does not require a provider installation.

 Each vendor has its own SMI-S setup process. My recommendation is to contact the storage vendor to ask for an SMI-S provider compatible with SCVMM 2012, which is currently Version 1.4.

CIM-XML is used by VMM to communicate with the underlying SMI-S providers since VMM never communicates with the SAN arrays themselves.

By using the storage provider to integrate with the storage, VMM can create LUNs (both GPT and MBR) and assign storage to hosts or clusters.

VMM 2012 also supports the SAN snapshot and clone feature, allowing you to duplicate a LUN through a **SAN Copy-capable** template to provide for new VMs, if you are hosting those in a Hyper-V platform. You will need to provision outside of VMM for any other VMs hosted with VMware or Citrix hosts.

Bare Metal

This capability enables VMM 2012 to identify the hardware, install the operational system (OS), enable the Hyper-V role, and add the machine to a target-host group with streamlined operations in an automated process.

PXE capability is required and is an integral component of the server pool. The target server will need to have a **baseboard management controller** (**BMC**) supporting one of the following management protocols:

- **Data Center Management Interface** (**DCMI**) **1.0**
- **Systems Management Architecture for Server Hardware** (**SMASH**) **1.0**
- **Intelligent Platform Management Interface** (**IPMI**) **1.5** or **2.0**
- **HP Integrated Lights-Out** (**iLO**) **2.0**

Enterprise and hosting companies will benefit from the ability to provide new Hyper-V servers without having to install the operational system manually on each machine. By using BMC and integrating with **Windows Deployment Services** (**WDS**), VMM deploys the OS to designated hosts through the boot from the VHD feature.

Configuring security

To ensure that users can perform only assigned actions on selected resources, create tenants, self-service users, delegated administrators, and read-only administrators in VMM using the VMM console, you will need to create **Run As** accounts to provide necessary credentials for performing operations in VMM (for example, adding hosts).

Run As accounts and Run As profiles in VMM

Run As accounts and Run As profiles are very useful additions to enterprise environments. These accounts are used to store credentials that allow you to delegate tasks to other administrators and self-service users *without exposing sensitive credentials*.

By using **Windows Data Protection API** (**DPAPI**), VMM provides OS-level data protection when storing and retrieving the **Run As** account.

There are several different categories of **Run As** accounts:

▸ **Host computer**: This is used to provide access to Hyper-V, VMware ESX, and Citrix XenServer hosts

▸ **BMC**: This is used to communicate with BMC on the host computer, for out-of-band management

▸ **Network device**: This is used to connect to network load balancers

▸ **Profile**: This is to be used for service creation in the OS and application profiles as well as SQL and host profiles

▸ **External**: This is to be used for external systems such as System Center Operations Manager

Only administrators or delegated administrators can create and manage Run As accounts.

 During the installation of the VMM management server, you will be requested to use **distributed key management** (**DKM**) to store encryption keys in **Active Directory Domain Services** (**AD DS**).

Ports communications and protocols for firewall configuration

When designing the VMM implementation, you need to plan which ports you are going to use for communication and file transfers between VMM components. Based on the chosen ports, you will also need to configure your host and external firewalls. See the *Configuring ports and protocols on the host firewall for each SCVMM component* recipe in *Chapter 2, Installing SCVMM 2012*.

 Not all of the ports can be changed through VMM. Hosts and library servers must have access to the VMM management server on the ports specified during setup. This means that all firewalls, whether software based or hardware based, must be previously configured.

VM storage placement

The recommendation to get better performance is to create a big CSV volume instead of creating volumes based on the VHD purpose (for example, OS, data, and logs). The following figure shows both scenarios:

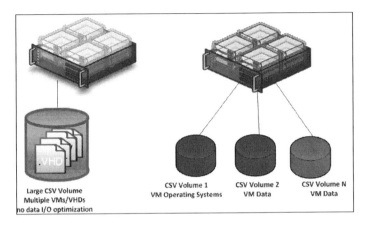

Large CSV Volume
Multiple VMs/VHDs
no data I/O optimization

CSV Volume 1
VM Operating Systems

CSV Volume 2
VM Data

CSV Volume N
VM Data

Management cluster

The best practice is to have a separate management cluster to manage the production, test, and development clusters.

In addition to this, although you can virtualize the domain controllers with Windows 2012, it is not the best practice to have all the domain controllers running on the management clusters, as the cluster and System Center components highly depend on the domain controllers.

The following figure shows a two-node management cluster, with System Center 2012 and SQL Server installed in separate VMs to manage the production cluster:

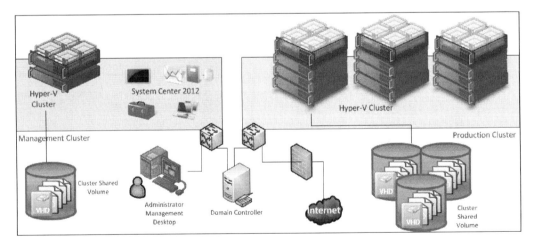

Small environment

In a small environment, you can have all the VMM components located on the same server. A small business may or may not have high availability in place as VMM 2012 is now a critical component for your private cloud deployment.

Start by selecting the VMM server's location, which could be a physical server or a virtual machine.

You can install SQL Server on the VMM server as well, but as VMM 2012 does not support SQL Express editions, you will need to install SQL Server first and then proceed with the VMM installation.

If you are managing more than 10 hosts in the production environment, my recommendation would be to have SQL Server running on a separate machine.

It is important to understand that when deploying VMM in production environments (real-world scenarios), the business will require a reliable system that it can trust.

The following figure illustrates a real-world deployment where all VMM 2012 components are installed on the same VM and SQL is running on a separate VM:

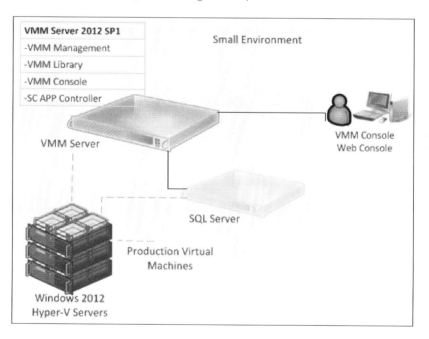

LAB environments

I would recommend up to 50 hosts in a lab environment with SQL Server and all VMM components installed on a single VM. It will work well, but I would not recommend this installation in a production environment.

Medium and enterprise environments

In a medium- or large-scale environment, the best practice is to split the roles across multiple servers or virtual machines. By splitting the components, you can scale out and introduce high availability to the System Center environment.

In the following design, you can see each component and what role it performs in the System Center Virtual Machine Manager environment:

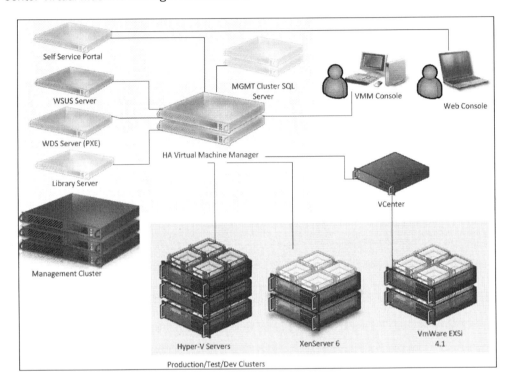

When designing an enterprise private cloud infrastructure, you should take into consideration some key factors such as business requirements, company policies, applications, services, workloads, current hardware, network infrastructure, storage, security, and users.

Private cloud sample infrastructure

Following is a sample of a real-world infrastructure that can support up to 3000 VMs and 64 server nodes running Windows 2012 Hyper-V.

The number of VMs you can run on an implementation like this will depend on some key factors. Do not take the following configuration as a mirror for your deployment, but as a starting point. My recommendation is to start understanding the environment, then run a capacity planner such as a MAP toolkit. It will help you gather information that you can use to design your private cloud.

I am assuming a ratio of 50 VMs per node cluster with 3 GB of RAM, configured to use **Dynamic Memory (DM)**.

- **Servers**
    - 64 servers (4 clusters x 16 nodes)
    - Dual processor, 6 cores: 12 cores in total
    - 192 GB RAM
    - 2 x 146 GB local HDD (ideally SDD) in Raid 1

- **Storage**

    Switch and host redundancy.
    - Fiber channel or iSCSI
    - Array with capacity to support customer workloads
    - Switch with connectivity for all hosts.

- **Network**

    A switch with switch redundancy and sufficient port density and connectivity to all hosts. It provides support for VLAN tagging and trunking. NIC Team and VLAN are recommended for better network availability, security, and performance achievement.

- **Storage connectivity**
    - If it uses a fiber channel: 2 (two) x 4 GB HBAs
    - If it uses ISCSI: 2 (two) x dedicated NICs (recommended 10 GbE)

- **Network connectivity**
    - If it maintains a 1 GbE connectivity: 6 dedicated 1 GbE (live migration, CSV, management, virtual machines' traffic)
    - If it maintains a 10 GbE connectivity: 3 dedicated NICs 10 GbE (live migration, CSV, management, virtual machines' traffic)

Hosting environments

System Center VMM 2012 SP1 introduced multitenancy. This is one of the most important features for hosting companies as they only need to install a single copy of System Center VMM, and then centralize their customer management, each one running in a controlled environment in their own domain.

See also

▶ The *Planning for highly availability* recipe

▶ The *Configuring ports and protocols on the host firewall for each VMM component* recipe in *Chapter 2, Installing SCVMM 2012*

▶ *Rapid Provisioning of Virtual Machines Using SAN Copy Overview*:

http://technet.microsoft.com/en-us/library/gg610594.aspx

▶ For more on Storage Management Initiative (SMI-S), refer to the following link:

http://www.snia.org/ctp/conformingproviders/index.html

▶ For more information on DPAPI architecture and security, visit the following link:

http://go.microsoft.com/fwlink/p/?LinkID=213089

Planning for high availability

High availability is important when your business requires minimum or no downtime, and planning for it in advance is very important.

Getting ready

Based on what we learned about each component, we now need to plan the **high availability** (**HA**) for each VMM component.

How to do it...

Start by planning the HA for the core component, followed by every VMM component of your design. It is important to consider hardware and other System Center components, as well the OS and software licenses.

How it works...

When planning for highly available VMM management servers, you should first consider where to place the VMM cluster. As per best practices, the recommendation is to install the VMM cluster on a management cluster. However, if you plan to install highly available VMM management servers on the managed cluster, you need to take into consideration the following points:

▶ Only one highly available VMM management server is allowed per failover cluster.

▶ Despite the possibility to have a VMM management server installed on all cluster nodes, only one node can be active at a time.

▶ To perform a planned failover, use **Failover Cluster Manager**. The use of the VMM console is not supported.

▶ In a planned failover situation, ensure that there are no running tasks on the VMM management server, as it will fail during a failover operation and will not automatically restart after the failover operation.

▶ Any connection to a highly available VMM management server from the VMM console will be disconnected during a failover operation, reconnecting right after.

▶ The failover cluster must be running Windows Server 2008 R2 or higher in order to be supported.

▶ The highly available VMM management server must meet system requirements. For information about system requirements for VMM, see the *Specifying the correct system requirements for a real-world scenario* recipe in this chapter.

▶ In a highly available VMM management deployment, you will need a domain account to install and run the VMM management service. You are required to use **distributed key management** (**DKM**) to store the encryption keys in Active Directory.

▶ A dedicated and supported version of Microsoft SQL Server should be installed. For supported versions of SQL Server for the VMM database, see the *Specifying the correct system requirements for a real-world scenario* recipe.

There's more...

The following sections are the considerations for SQL Server and the VMM library in an HA environment.

SQL Server

In an enterprise deployment of VMM, it is recommended that you have a SQL Server cluster to support the HA VMM, preferably on a cluster separated from the VMM cluster. VMM 2012 SP1 supports SQL Server **AlwaysOn Availability Groups**. The following link will show you a good example of how to set it up:

```
http://blogs.technet.com/b/scvmm/archive/2012/10/24/how-to-configure-
sql-2012-alwayson-availability-groups-in-system-center-2012-virtual-
machine-manager-service-pack-1.aspx
```

VMM library

As the best practice in an enterprise deployment, a highly available file server for hosting the VMM library shares is highly recommended as VMM does not provide a method for replicating files in the VMM library, and they need to be replicated outside of VMM.

As a suggestion, you can use the Microsoft Robocopy tool to replicate the VMM library files if necessary.

Specifying the correct system requirements for a real-world scenario

In a real-world production environment, you need to specify a system according to the design and business requirements.

Getting ready

When specifying the hardware for your private cloud deployment, take into consideration future growth needs. It is also important to apply the latest OS and software updates.

How to do it...

Use the following tables to carry out an extensive documentation of the hardware and software requirements for your deployment.

Create a document that outlines every solution component, describing the system requirements, before starting to implement.

How it works...

The following table shows the supported OS and servers for SC 2012 SP1:

Component	OS/Server supported	Version
VMM server	Windows Server 2012	64 bit (Standard, Datacenter)
	(Windows Server 2008 SP2/2008 R2/2008 R2 SP1 are not supported by VMM 2012 SP1)	
VMM database	SQL Server 2008 R2 SP1 or higher	Standard, Enterprise, Datacenter
	SQL Server 2012, SQL Server 2012 SP1	
VMM console	Windows Server 2008 R2 SP1	64 bit (Standard, Enterprise, Datacenter)
	Windows Server 2012	
	Windows 7 SP1	x86 and x64 Enterprise, Ultimate
	Windows 8	x86 and x64
VMM library	Windows Server 2008 R2 SP1	Standard, Enterprise, Datacenter
	Windows Server 2012	(full installation or Server Core installation)
SC App Controller	Windows Server 2008 R2 SP1	Standard, Enterprise, Datacenter
	Windows Server 2012	

For any procedure that uses `.vhdx`, the library server must be running on Windows Server 2012.

▶ Hardware requirements

Following are the hardware requirements to consider when specifying your VMM environment. The minimum values are the Microsoft-recommended values.

❑ Scenarios for up to 50 hosts, SMB environments, POC, and demos (all components installed on a single server)

Although for this type of scenario you can have SQL installed on the VMM management server, the recommendation is to have SQL Server installed on another server:

Hardware component	Minimum	Recommended
Processor	One Processor, 2 GHz (x64)	Dual processor, dual core, 2.8 GHz (x64) or higher
RAM	4 GB	6 GB [*2]
Hard disk space (recommended OS partition) [*4]	20 GB	40 GB or higher
Hard disk space (VMM components)[*1] [*4]	80 GB [*2]	150 GB [*2]
Hard disk space (VMM library) [*1] [*4]	As a minimum, I recommend 80 GB, taking into consideration some samples from real-world implementation, but it will vary depending on business requirements, on the number and size of the files stored, and especially when working with templates	
Roles	VMM management	
	VMM library	
	VMM console	
	VMM Self-Service Portal	
	VMM database (SQL Server full version—Standard or Enterprise) [*3]	

[*1] Excluding OS partition

[*2] With a full version of Microsoft SQL Server installed on the same server

[*3] The recommendation is to have SQL Server installed on another server

[*4] Recommended minimum total hard disk space for this deployment with full SQL: 270 GB

▶ Scenarios for up to 150 hosts

In this scenario, the recommendation is to have each component installed on a separate server, especially the VMM library server. Although (and this is not recommended) you can install SQL Server on the VMM management server as well.

VMM management server

Hardware component	Minimum	Recommended
Processor	Pentium 4, 2 GHz (x64)	Dual processor, dual core, 2.8 GHz (x64) or greater
RAM	2 GB	4 GB *2 / 6 GB *3
Hard disk space *1	2 GB *2/ 80 GB *3	40 GB *2 / 150 GB *3
*1 Excluding OS partition		
*2 Without a local VMM database (SQL Server installed)		
*3 With a local VMM database (Microsoft SQL Server installed on the same server)		

VMM database server

Hardware component	Minimum	Recommended
Processor	Pentium 4, 2.8 GHz	Dual core 64 bit, 2 GHz
RAM	2 GB	4 GB
Hard disk space*	80 GB	150 GB
* Excluding OS partition		

VMM console

Hardware component	Minimum	Recommended
Processor	Pentium 4, 550 MHz	Pentium 4, 1 GHz or higher
RAM	512 MB	1 GB
Hard disk space *	512 MB	2 GB
* Excluding OS partition		

VMM library server

The minimum and recommended requirements for a VMM library server will be determined by the quantity and size of the files that will be stored.

Hardware component	Minimum	Recommended
Processor	Pentium 4, 2.8 GHz	Dual core 64 bit, 3.2 GHz or higher
RAM	2 GB	2 GB
Hard disk space	As a minimum, I recommend 80 GB, taking into consideration the following table that contains some samples of real image sizes. However, the recommended size will vary depending on business requirements and on the number and size of files stored, especially when working with templates.	

ISOs

Image	ISO size	
en_windows_server_2008_r2_with_sp1_vl_build_x64_dvd_617403	2.94 GB	Windows 2008 R2
en_install_disc_windows_small_business_server_2011_standard_x64_dvd_611535	6.35 GB	SBS 2001
en_office_professional_plus_2010_x86_515486	650 MB	Office 2010

VMM Self-Service Portal

The hardware requirements for the VMM Self-Service Portal are based on the number of concurrent connections that are maintained by the web server.

❑ Scenarios for up to 10 concurrent user connections

Hardware component	Minimum	Recommended
Processor	Pentium 4, 2.8 GHz	Pentium 4, 2.8 GHz
RAM	2 GB	2 GB
Hard disk space*	512 MB	20 GB
* Excluding OS partition. Recommended OS partition: 40 GB.		

❑ Scenarios with more than 10 concurrent connections

Hardware component	Minimum	Recommended
Processor	Pentium 4, 2.8 GHz	Dual core 64 bit, 3.2 GHz or higher
RAM	2 GB	8 GB
Hard disk space *	10 GB	40 GB
* Excluding OS partition. Recommended OS partition: 40 GB.		

❑   Scenarios for more than 150 hosts

In this scenario, the recommendation is to have each component installed on a separate server.

Also, as per best practice:

▶   It is not recommended to run a local SQL Server when managing more than 150 physical hosts

▶   Add one or more servers as library servers

▶   Do not use the default library share on the VMM management server

VMM management server

Hardware component	Minimum	Recommended
Processor	Pentium 4, 2.8 GHz (x64)	Dual processor, dual core, 3.6 GHz or higher (x64)
RAM	4 GB	8 GB
Hard disk space*	10 GB	50 GB
* Excluding OS partition		

VMM database server

Hardware component	Minimum	Recommended
Processor	Dual-Core 64-bit, 2 GHz	Dual core 64 bit, 2.8 GHz
RAM	4 GB	8 GB
Hard disk space *	150 GB	200 GB
* Excluding OS partition		

VMM console

Hardware component	Minimum	Recommended
Processor	Pentium 4, 1 GHz	Pentium 4, 2 GHz or higher
RAM	1 GB	2 GB
Hard disk space *	512 MB	4 GB
* Excluding OS partition		

VMM library server

The minimum and recommended requirements for a VMM library server will be determined by the quantity and size of the files that will be stored.

Hardware component	Minimum	Recommended
Processor	Pentium 4, 2.8 GHz	Dual core 64bit, 3.2 GHz or higher
RAM	2 GB	2 GB
Hard disk space	As a minimum, I recommend: 80 GB*, taking into consideration the following table that contains some samples of real image sizes. However, the recommended size will vary depending on business requirements and on the number and size of files stored, especially when working with templates. * Excluding OS partition	

ISOs

Image	ISO size	
en_windows_server_2008_r2_with_sp1_vl_build_x64_dvd_617403	2.94 GB	Windows 2008 R2
en_install_disc_windows_small_business_server_2011_standard_x64_dvd_611535	6.35 GB	SBS 2001
en_office_professional_plus_2010_x86_515486	650 MB	Office 2010

VMM Self-Service Portal

The hardware requirements for the VMM Self-Service Portal are based on the number of concurrent connections that are maintained by the web server.

❑ Scenarios for up to 10 concurrent user connections

Hardware component	Minimum	Recommended
Processor	Pentium 4, 2.8 GHz	Pentium 4, 2.8 GHz
RAM	2 GB	2 GB
Hard disk space*	512 MB	20 GB
*Excluding OS partition. Recommended OS partition: 40 GB.		

❑   Scenarios with more than 10 concurrent connections

Hardware component	Minimum	Recommended
Processor	Pentium 4, 2.8 GHz	Dual core 64 bit, 3.2 GHz or higher
RAM	2 GB	8 GB
Hard disk space *	10 GB	40 GB
*Excluding OS partition. Recommended OS partition: 40 GB.		

▶   Software requirements

Following are the requirements for VMM management for SC 2012 SP1:

Software Requirement	Notes
Windows Remote Management (WinRM) 2.0	The WinRM service is set to start automatically (delayed start). If it is not configured in this way (manually modified or by GPO), you must configure and start it before installing VMM.
Microsoft .NET Framework 4.0, or Microsoft .NET Framework 4.5	Included in Windows Server 2012. Microsoft .NET Framework 4.5 is available at `http://go.microsoft.com/fwlink/p/?LinkId=267119`.
Windows Automated Installation Kit (AIK)	To install the Windows AIK, you need to download the ISO from `http://go.microsoft.com/fwlink/p/?LinkID=194654`, burn the ISO file to a DVD or map the ISO if VMM is a VM and then install the Windows AIK. **Important** Windows ADK replaced Windows Automated Installation (Windows AIK) as a VMM prerequisite in VMM 2012 SP1.
A supported version of SQL Server (if you're installing SQL on the VMM management server)	See the table for the supported OSes and servers for SC 2012 SP1.
SQL Server 2012 Command Line Utilities	The SQLCMD utility allows users to connect to, send Transact-SQL batches from, and output row set information from SQL Server 2005, SQL Server 2008, SQL Server 2008 R2, and SQL Server 2012 instances (`http://go.microsoft.com/fwlink/?LinkID=239650&clcid=0x409`)
Microsoft SQL Server Native Client	It contains runtime support for applications using native code APIs (ODBC, OLE DB, and ADO) to connect to Microsoft SQL Server 2005, 2008, 2008 R2, and SQL Server 2012. SQL Server Native Client is used to enhance applications that need to take advantage of new SQL Server 2012 features (`http://go.microsoft.com/fwlink/?LinkID=239648&clcid=0x409`)

The following table shows the requirement for the VMM console:

Software requirement	Notes
Windows PowerShell 2.0	Included in Windows Server 2008 R2 and Windows 7
At least Microsoft .NET Framework 3.5 Service Pack 1 (SP1)	On a computer running Windows 7, .NET Framework 3.5.1 will be installed by default
	On a computer running Windows Server 2008 R2, if the .NET Framework 3.5.1 feature is not installed (does not installed by default), the VMM setup wizard will install it

The following table shows the requirement for the VMM library:

Software requirement	Notes
Windows Remote Management (WinRM) 1.1 or 2.0	Version 1.1 is included in Windows Server 2008
	Version 2.0 is included in Windows Server 2008 R2
	By default, the WinRM (WS-Management) service is set to start automatically (delayed start). If it is not configured in this way (manually modified or by GPO), it must be configured and started before the setup can continue

See also

▶ Download the Windows Automated Installation Kit (AIK) available at the following link:

    http://go.microsoft.com/fwlink/p/?LinkID=194654

Licensing the System Center

System Center 2012 is licensed with two versions, Standard and Datacenter. The same capabilities across editions are differentiated only by virtualization rights. All System Center components are included in these two editions.

Getting ready

The license is now required only to manage endpoints. No additional licenses are required for management consoles and they are available exclusively with Software Assurance.

How to do it...

As part of the private cloud design solution, you need to define which license you will need, based on your solution design and business requirements.

How it works...

Each license covers up to two physical processors. ECI requires a 25-license minimum initial purchase. A two-processor license targets the most common hardware configuration:

System Center 2012 Editions	Datacenter	Standard
Recommendation	For highly virtualized environments	For lightly- or non-virtualized environments
Virtualization rights	Unlimited	Two operational systems
Capabilities	All SC components and all workload types	All SC components and all workload types
License type	This covers up to two physical processors	This covers up to two physical processors

Troubleshooting VMM and supporting technologies

This recipe will take you through the process of troubleshooting VMM and its supporting technologies for a successful VMM deployment.

Getting ready

Having an understanding of the core technologies that VMM depends on in order to work correctly is the initial step to troubleshooting VMM:

- WS Management (WinRM)
- WMI
- BITS
- DCOM
- WCF

Troubleshooting is never an easy task, but VMM 2012 provides tools and ways to help you find and remediate an issue.

How to do it...

Following are some techniques you can use to troubleshoot:

▶ **Event logs**

A good starting point is to look at the event logs. Look for OS- and VMM-related errors or failures. A problem with the operational system (OS) or one of its core services could result or lead to a problem in VMM.

For example, if you are running SQL Server on the same server and it did not start, VMM management service will not start either and VMM operations will fail as a direct result of this. You can easily find this by looking for errors in the system or application logs, errors that would indicate, in this example, that the service is not running (for this example, you can also check `Services.msc`).

▶ **VM manager log**

When looking for VMM errors, it is recommended that you to look at the VM Manager log as well. To do so, perform the following steps on the VMM server running Windows 2012:

1. On the **Server Manager** window, click on **Tools**.

2. Select **Event Viewer**, expand **Applications and Services logs**, and then select the **VM Manager** log.

▶ **VMM installation-related troubleshooting logs**

VMM records information about for the VMM agent installation. However, if the installation logging is not sufficient to determine the cause of failure, you can enable tracing by using the **VMM MPS Reports tool** and then restart the installation.

▶ **VMM server setup logging**

Installation logs are written, by default, to the `C:\ProgramData\VMMLogs` hidden folder.

▶ **VMM agent installation logging**

When installing an MSI package, such as installing the VMM agent manually, you can enable logging using the following syntax:

```
msiexec /I <MSIPackageName.msi> /L*V <path\logfilename>.log
```

For example, using the syntax, we can come up with something like the following command:

```
msiexec /I "C:\setup\vmmAgent.msi" /L*V vmmagent.log
```

The local agent installation information is logged in the `C:\ProgramData\VMMLogs` hidden folders.

Look for the logfile `vmmAgent.msi_<m-d-yyy_hh-mm-dss>.log`.

 In logs, it is common to see errors shown as **Carmine** errors. Carmine was a VMM project name code during its development process.

▶ **Troubleshooting WinRM**

To check if WinRM has remote access, check if:

❑ The SID in **RootSDDL** maps to the **Virtual Machine Manager Servers** local group on each Hyper-V host

❑ The local group contains the account that VMM management service runs as a service

How it works...

A good understanding of what a successful installation log contains from a POC or a pilot environment is important to identify possible issues, especially if it appears when deploying VMM on a production environment, as you can then compare both logs.

There's more...

Run the following command on the Hyper-V host:

```
winrm id
```

This should produce an output similar to the following output:

```
IdentifyResponse
ProtocolVersion = http://schemas.dmtf.org/wbem/wsman/1/wsman.xsd
ProductVendor = Microsoft Corporation
ProductVersion = OS: 6.1.7201 SP: 0.0 Stack: 2.0
```

If the result shows an error, run the following command for a quick configuration of WinRM:

```
winrm qc
```

If prompted, answer `Yes`. You will receive a response like the following:

```
WinRM already is set up to receive requests on this machine.

WinRM is not set up to allow remote access to this machine for
management.

The following changes must be made:
Enable the WinRM firewall exception

Make these changes [y/n]?

WinRM has been updated for remote management.

WinRM firewall exception enabled.

WinRM can now be tested again by typing 'winrm id' as before
```

Now check the listener:

```
winrm enum winrm/config/listener
```

Run the following command on the VMM management server:

```
winrm id -r:http://HyperVHost.yourdomain.local:5985  -u:YOURDOMAIN\
AdminUser
```

The result will be similar to the following result:

```
IdentifyResponse

ProtocolVersion = http://schemas.dmtf.org/wbem/wsman/1/wsman.xsd

ProductVendor = Microsoft Corporation

ProductVersion = OS: 6.1.7201 SP: 0.0 Stack: 2.0
```

Otherwise you will receive the following error:

```
Error number: -2144108526 0x80338012

The Client cannot connect to the destination specified in the request
```

This could indicate communication issues, so check your network, host firewall, and connectivity.

Most WinRM-related events appear in the system or application event logs. The **Service Control Manager** often contains the error, as the WinRM service has terminated or restarted for some reason.

During the VMM installation, you will get the following error:

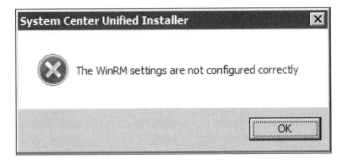

To avoid this scenario, conduct the following checks:

- ▶ Make sure you installed all of the prerequisites
- ▶ Check the firewall rules and make sure the ports are configured correctly
- ▶ Open the command prompt (**Run as Administrator**) and type the following command:

```
winrm qc -q
winrm set winrm/config/service/auth @{CredSSP="True"}
winrm set winrm/config/winrs @{AllowRemoteShellAccess="True"}
winrm set winrm/config/winrs @{MaxMemoryPerShellMB="2048"}
```

Verifying WMI providers

You can check if the WinRM can communicate with OS WMI providers by running the following command:

```
winrm enum wmi/root/cimv2/Win32_ComputerSystem -r:http://servername:5985
[-u:YOURDOMAIN\AdminUser]
```

By running the following command, you can check if the WinRM can communicate with Hyper-V WMI providers:

```
winrm enum wmi/root/virtualization/msvm_computersystem
  -r:http://servername:5985 [-u:YOURDOMAIN\AdminUser]
```

Also, to check if the WinRM can communicate with the VMM agent WMI provider, run the following command:

```
winrm invoke GetVersion wmi/root/scvmm/AgentManagement
  -r:servername [-u:YOURDOMAIN\AdminUser] @{}
```

If you are using VMM services, do not remove and re-add the host. Instead, evacuate the host before removing or, on the host, uninstall and then re-install the agent manually, then reassociate it in VMM.

Troubleshooting tools

Following are the troubleshooting tools available for use:

▶ **Windows Management Instrumentation Tester** (wbemtest.exe)

The wbemtest.exe gives you the ability to query WMI namespaces on local or remote servers.

Connecting to a namespace locally indicates that it is properly registered and accessible via the WMI service. By connecting to a remote server additionally, it also indicates that WMI connectivity between the two machines is working.

For more information about wbemtest, refer to the following website:

http://technet.microsoft.com/en-us/library/cc785775.aspx

▶ **WMI Service Control Utility**

This tool configures and controls the WMI service, allowing namespace permissions to be modified.

To open this tool, at the command prompt type the following command:

`winmgmt.msc`

Then perform the following steps:

1. Right-click on **WMI Control (Local)**.
2. Select **Properties**.
3. Click on the **Security** tab and then select **Root**.
4. Click on the **Security** button to check the permissions.

Background Intelligent Transfer Service (BITS) troubleshooting

BITS transfers files between machines, providing information about the operation's progress. The transfer can be asynchronous.

In VMM, BITS is used for encrypted data transfer between managed computers. Encryption is done by using a self-signed certificate generated when the Hyper-V host is added to VMM.

You can use **BITSadmin** to verify that BITS is working properly outside of VMM.

BITSadmin can be downloaded at http://msdn.microsoft.com/en-us/library/aa362813(VS.85).aspx.

You can also find some examples of BITSadmin at `http://msdn.microsoft.com/en-us/library/aa362812(VS.85).aspx`.

Data collection tools

The following tools are used to collect data surrounding VMM issues:

- ▶ **VMM tracing tools**

  VMM tracing tools provide the ability to manage, collect, and view various traces and diagnostic information in a VMM environment:

  Gathering trace information

  When you face an issue and need to report it to Microsoft, you can gather the trace by performing the following steps:

  1. In the VMM server, open the command prompt with administrative rights and type the following command:

     ```
     logman create trace

     VMMDebug -v mmddhhmm -o %SystemDrive%\VMMlogs\
     DebugTrace_%computername%.ETL -cnf 01:00:00 -p
     Microsoft-VirtualMachineManager-Debug
     ```

  2. Start the trace collection by executing the following command:

     ```
     logman start VMMDebug
     ```

  3. Next, try to reproduce the issue, and at the end stop the trace collection by executing the following command:

     ```
     logman stop VMMDebug
     ```

  4. Send the ETL file located in `%SystemDrive%\VMMlogs\DebugTrace_%computerna;me%.ETL` to Microsoft.

  5. Delete the debug information by executing the following command:

     ```
     logman delete VMMDebug
     ```

- ▶ **The VMM TraceViewer utility**

  After gathering the trace, you can use **TraceViewer** on the traces. This tool converts the ETL binary trace logs into CAR files that can be viewed in both the TraceViewer and other trace parsing tools, and provides basic trace parsing.

  To convert the ETL file:

  1. In the TraceViewer, drag the trace file into the open pane.

  2. Provide the location to where you want to save the CAR file. Once the file has been saved, TraceViewer will open the converted ETL file for analysis.

  You can download the tool from `https://connect.microsoft.com/site799/Downloads`.

See also

▸ The *Configuring ports and protocols on the host firewall for each SCVMM component* recipe in *Chapter 2, Installing SCVMM 2012*

2

Installing SCVMM 2012

In this chapter, we will cover:

- ▸ Creating service accounts
- ▸ Deploying a Microsoft SQL Server for VMM implementation
- ▸ Installing VMM dependencies
- ▸ Configuring distributed key management
- ▸ Installing a VMM management server
- ▸ Installing the VMM console
- ▸ Connecting to a VMM management server by using the VMM console
- ▸ Creating a Run As account's credentials in VMM
- ▸ Configuring ports and protocols on the host firewall for each SCVMM component

Introduction

Based on what we learned in the previous chapter, you now know that in order to start our System Center Virtual Machine Manager 2012 deployment, we should create the install accounts and deploy the SQL database.

As discussed, VMM is required to be an Active Directory member server.

In addition, it is up to business requirements and your design to decide where you will deploy the SQL database. However, as previously stated in *Chapter 1, VMM 2012 Architecture*, you should always have SQL installed on a separate server. In this way, you are safe to grow and you will have the scalability and high availability (if installing a SQL Cluster) on the database side.

For the purpose of this chapter, we will be referring to the following infrastructure:

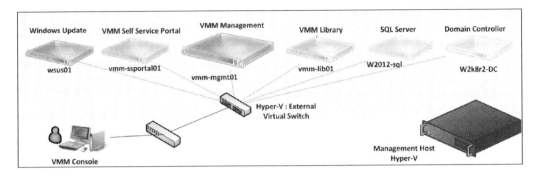

Creating service accounts

Let's start our private cloud deployment. First, we need to create a service account.

In order to install, configure, and manage SQL, and Virtual Machine Manager (VMM) and its components, we need to create the user and service accounts. My recommendation is to keep the account names alike, but the naming convention is up to your business to decide.

Getting ready

To perform this recipe, you need to have domain administrator rights or delegate permissions assigned to your account. You will also need to connect to the domain controller w2kr8-DC (in our infrastructure) by using **Remote Desktop Connection** (**RDC**), or use the **Remote Administrative Tools** (**RSAT**) to open the Active Directory users and computers.

 If you do not have the domain admin rights or delegate permissions to execute the following recipe, ask the domain administrator to do it.

We are also using LAB.local as our domain. Replace it with your own domain.

How to do it...

Carry out the following steps to create a service account:

1. Create the following accounts and groups; you may name them according to your naming convention:

    i. SCVMM Service user account: LAB\vmm-svc

    ii. SCVMM Run As user account: LAB\vmm-admin

    iii. SCVMM administrators' security group: LAB\vmm-admins

    iv. SQL Service user account: LAB\sql-svc

    v. SQL Server system administrators' user account: LAB\sql-admin

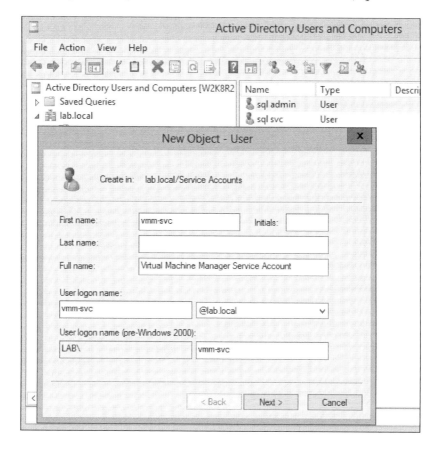

 I normally create these accounts under a previously created OU: Service Accounts

2. After creating the accounts, double-click on **vmm-admins**.

> Make sure that in these accounts the **Password never expires** and **User cannot change password** options are checked. Also make sure there is no GPO Appling that changes these settings.

3. Select the **Members** tab and then click on **Add**.

4. Enter vmm-svc and click on **OK.**

5. Log in to the VMM management server (vmm-mgmt01) with an account that has local administrator rights (for example, **LAB\Administrator**).

6. Launch **Computer Management** (on Server 2008) and open the **Start** menu. Right-click on **Computer** and then click on **Manage**.

7. Expand **System Tools**, select **Local Users and Groups**, double-click on **Administrators**, and then add **vmm-admins**.

8. Repeat steps 5 to 7 for all of the VMM servers: **vmm-console**, **vmm-lib01**, and **vmm-ssportal01**.

9. Log in to the SQL Server (w2012-sql) with an account that has local administrator rights (for example, **LAB\Administrator**).

10. Launch **Computer Management** (on Server 2008) and open the **Start** menu. Right-click on **Computer** and then click on **Manage**.

11. Expand **System Tools**, select **Local Users and Groups**, double-click on **Administrators**, and then add **sql-svc** and **sql-admin**.

> You can use the domain policy to assign those accounts to the local Administrators group on the VMM and SQL servers. For more information, see http://social.technet.microsoft.com/wiki/contents/articles/7833.how-to-make-domain-user-as-a-local-administrator-for-all-pcs.aspx.

How it works...

These accounts will be used to install, configure, and manage SQL Server. They will be used to install, configure, and manage VMM 2012 as well, to configure VMM to communicate with SQL and other System Center components.

It will be used by VMM to manage the Hyper-V hosts as well.

There's more...

At the VMM management server installation, on the **Configure service account and distributed key management** page, you will be required to provide an account for the Virtual Machine Manager service account. The account could be either the local system or a domain account (recommended):

- ▶ The domain account that you create specifically to be used for this purpose, as per best practice, must be a member of the local `Administrators` group on the computer.

- ▶ You are required to use a domain account for the VMM service if you want to use shared ISO images with Hyper-V VMs.

- ▶ You are required to use a domain account if you want to use a disjointed namespace.

- ▶ You are required to use a domain account if you want to install a highly available VMM management server.

- ▶ Changing the account identity of the Virtual Machine Manager service after the VMM installation is completed is not supported. If you need to change it, you must uninstall VMM and then select the **Retain data** option to keep the SQL Server database and the data, and then reinstall VMM by using the new service account.

Deploying a Microsoft SQL Server for VMM implementation

In this recipe, we will see how to install SQL Server 2012.

For more information about SQL Server versions supported by Virtual Machine Manager 2012, see the *Specifying the correct system requirements on a real-world scenario* recipe in *Chapter 1, VMM 2012 Architecture*.

Getting ready

Assuming that you have already installed the operational system according to the SQL Server requirements of the SQL version you are installing, connect to the SQL Server (for example, **vm2012-sql**) machine.

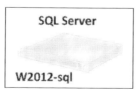

SQL 2012 and SQL 2012 SP1 are only supported by VMM 2012 SP1.
SQL AlwaysOn is also supported. See `http://blogs.technet.`
`com/b/scvmm/archive/2012/10/24/how-to-configure-`
`sql-2012-alwayson-availability-groups-in-system-`
`center-2012-virtual-machine-manager-service-pack-1.`
`aspx for how to setup` for more information.

Before starting, make sure the machine is a member of the domain, and refer to the following Microsoft articles for hardware and software requirements for SQL Server:

- SQL 2012 and SQL 2012 SP1:

  `msdn.microsoft.com/en-us/library/ms143506.aspx`

- SQL 2008 R2:

  `http://technet.microsoft.com/en-us/library/ms143506(v=sql.105).`
  `aspx`

There are three ways to install SQL 2012: through a wizard, a configuration file, or the command prompt. The following recipe will guide you through the process of installing SQL 2012 by using the configuration file method. By using this method, after you have deployed the proof of concept, you will use the same file to replicate the SQL installation onto production or test sites.

How to do it...

The following configuration will install SQL server 2012 with the following components: Database Engine, Replication, Full Text, Reporting Services, and client tools.

1. Log in as **LAB\SQL-admin** or another account that has SQL system admin rights.

2. Create a folder named `Setup` in `C:\`.

3. Open Notepad and copy the following on a new file:

```
;SQL Server 2012 Configuration File
[OPTIONS]
; Setup work flow: INSTALL, UNINSTALL, or UPGRADE.
ACTION="Install"
; Language.
ENU="True"
; Display progress only, no user interaction.
QUIETSIMPLE="True"
; Include product updates: True and False or 1 and 0.
UpdateEnabled="True"
; Features: SQL, AS, RS, IS, MDS, and Tools.
FEATURES=SQL,RS,Tools
```

```
; Detailed Setup log to show on the console.
INDICATEPROGRESS="False"
; 32-bit.
X86="False"
; Installation folder for shared components.
INSTALLSHAREDDIR="C:\Program Files\Microsoft SQL Server"
; Installation folder for the WOW64 shared components.
INSTALLSHAREDWOWDIR="C:\Program Files (x86)\Microsoft SQL Server"
; Named instance. MSSQLSERVER is the default
INSTANCENAME="MSSQLSERVER"
; Instance ID
INSTANCEID="MSSQLSERVER"
; Data collected can be sent to Microsoft. True and False or 1 and
0.
SQMREPORTING="False"
; Reporting Services Mode
RSINSTALLMODE="DefaultNativeMode"
; Installation directory.
INSTANCEDIR="C:\Program Files\Microsoft SQL Server"
; Agent account name
AGTSVCACCOUNT="LAB\sql-svc"
; Service start mode.
AGTSVCSTARTUPTYPE="Automatic"
; Startup type for Integration Services.
ISSVCSTARTUPTYPE="Automatic"
; Account for Integration Services: Domain\User or system account.
ISSVCACCOUNT="LAB\sql-svc"
; Startup type for the SQL Server service.
SQLSVCSTARTUPTYPE="Automatic"
; Level to enable FILESTREAM feature at (0, 1, 2 or 3).
FILESTREAMLEVEL="0"
; Windows collation or an SQL collation to use for the Database
Engine.
SQLCOLLATION="SQL_Latin1_General_CP1_CI_AS"
; Account for SQL Server service: Domain\User or system account.
SQLSVCACCOUNT="LAB\sql-svc"
; Windows account(s) to provision as SQL Server system
administrators.
SQLSYSADMINACCOUNTS="LAB\sql-svc" "LAB\sql-admin"
; Provision current user as a Database Engine system
administrator.
ADDCURRENTUSERASSQLADMIN="true"
; Specify 0 to disable or 1 to enable the TCP/IP protocol.
TCPENABLED="1"
; Specify 0 to disable or 1 to enable the Named Pipes protocol.
```

```
NPENABLED="0"
; Startup type for Browser Service.
BROWSERSVCSTARTUPTYPE="Automatic"
; Account the report server NT service should execute under.
RSSVCACCOUNT="LAB\sql-svc"
; Startup mode of the report server service : Manual, Automatic,
Disabled
RSSVCSTARTUPTYPE="Automatic"
; FTSVCACCOUNT
FTSVCACCOUNT="NT Service\MSSQLFDLauncher"
IAcceptSQLServerLicenseTerms="True"
```

4. Save the file as `SQLConfigurationFile.ini` in `c:\setup`.

    Now that you have created the configuration file, let's proceed with the installation of SQL 2012 by using the file.

5. Open the command prompt with administrative rights (**Run as administrator**).

6. Navigate to "SQL Server Source Media path" and type the following:

    ```
    Setup.exe /SQLSVCPASSWORD="P@ssword" /AGTSVCPASSWORD="P@
    ssword" /ASSVCPASSWORD="P@ssword" /ISSVCPASSWORD="P@ssword" /
    RSSVCPASSWORD="P@ssword" /ConfigurationFile=c:\setup\
    SQLConfigurationFile.INI
    ```

7. Press *Enter* for the installation to start.

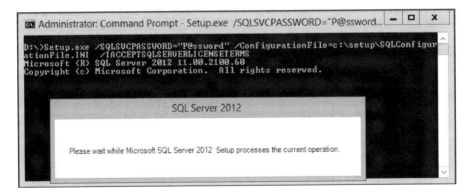

8. You should see a window showing the installation progress (as shown in the previous screenshot). The installation will proceed without user input.

How it works...

The configuration file is a text file with parameters and descriptive comments, which can be useful to standardize SQL deployments. It is processed in the following order:

1. The values in the configuration file replace the defaults values.
2. Command-line values replace the default and the configuration file values.

For security reasons, is recommended to specify the passwords at the command prompt instead of in the configuration file.

The SQL parameter will install the SQL Server Database Engine, Replication, Full Text, and Data Quality Services. The RS parameter will install all Reporting Services components and the Tools parameter will install the client tools.

In this sample configuration file, LAB is the domain and you need to replace it with your own domain.

The following table enlists service accounts and passwords parameters:

SQL component	Account parameter	Password parameter	Startup type
SQL Server Agent	/AGTSVCACCOUNT	/AGTSVCPASSWORD	/AGTSVCSTARTUPTYPE
Analysis Services	/ASSVCACCOUNT	/ASSVCPASSWORD	/ASSVCSTARTUPTYPE
Database Engine	/SQLSVCACCOUNT	/SQLSVCPASSWORD	/SQLSVCSTARTUPTYPE
Integration Services	/ISSVCACCOUNT	/ISSVCPASSWORD	/ISSVCSTARTUPTYPE
Reporting Services	/RSSVCACCOUNT	/RSSVCPASSWORD	/RSSVCSTARTUPTYPE

There's more...

Generating the configuration file by using SQL 2012 Wizard (optional). To do this, carry out the following steps:

1. Browse to the SQL Server installation media.
2. Select and double-click on Setup.exe.
3. Follow the SQL setup wizard through to the **Ready to Install** page, writing down the configuration file path on the **configuration file path** section.
4. At this point, you can click on **Cancel** to cancel the setup, as we are just looking to generate the configuration file.

5. Browse through the configuration path folder for the generated INI file, as seen here:

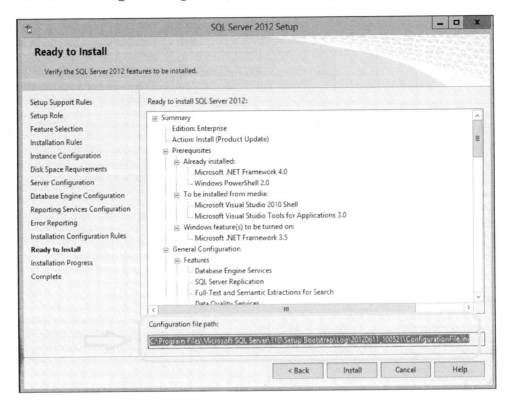

See also

▸ *SQL Server Failover Cluster Installation*:

http://msdn.microsoft.com/en-us/library/hh231721

▸ *Install SQL Server 2012 from the Installation Wizard (Setup)*:

http://msdn.microsoft.com/en-us/library/ms143219

▸ *Install SQL Server 2012 from the Command Prompt*:

http://msdn.microsoft.com/en-us/library/ms144259.aspx

▸ *Configure Windows Service Accounts and Permissions*:

http://msdn.microsoft.com/en-us/library/ms143504

► *Run DQSInstaller.exe to Complete Data Quality Server Installation*:

`http://msdn.microsoft.com/en-us/library/hh231682`

► *Configure the Windows Firewall to Allow SQL Server Access*:

`http://msdn.microsoft.com/en-us/library/cc646023.aspx`

Installing VMM dependencies

Before installing a VMM, we need to ensure that the server meets the minimum system requirements and that all of the prerequisite software are installed. For more information, check the software requirements specified in the *Specifying the correct system requirements for a real-world scenario* recipe in *Chapter 1, VMM 2012 Architecture*.

The previous versions of Windows Server introduced Windows PowerShell support, and Windows Server 2012 improved with over 2,300 cmdlets to manage the platform.

You can use Windows PowerShell to automate all of the IT tasks around cloud datacenter deployment and management, starting with deploying your cloud infrastructure servers, through on-boarding virtual machines to that infrastructure, and ending with monitoring your datacenter environment and collecting information about how it performs.

Getting ready

Virtual Machine Manager 2012 has automated almost all of the prerequisites, but you will need to install the Windows **Assessment and Deployment Kit** (**ADK**) and SQL features (if you are not running SQL on the management server).

 I also recommend that you install the Telnet client feature as it is very useful when testing or troubleshooting on all servers.

To download the Windows Assessment and Deployment Kit, go to `http://go.microsoft.com/fwlink/?LinkId=246387`.

How to do it...

To install, carry out the following steps:

1. Download and run the `adksetup.exe` file.

2. Select **Install the Assessment and Deployment Kit on this computer** and click on **Next**.

3. On the **Customer Experience Improvement Program** page, select **Yes** to join the Customer Experience program and click on **Next**. Then click on **Accept**.

4. Select **Deployment Tools** and **Windows PreInstallation Environment (Windows PE)**, as shown in the following screenshot, and click on **Install**:

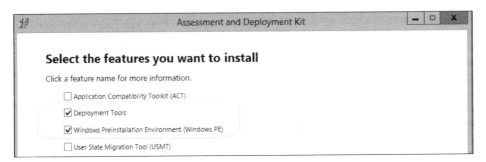

 For complete installation options, go to `http://go.microsoft.com/fwlink/?LinkId=234980`.

How it works...

The **Windows Assessment and Deployment Kit** (**Windows ADK**) for Windows 8, which is a collection of tools that you can use to customize, assess, and deploy Windows operating systems to new computers, is a prerequisite for VMM 2012 SP1 and is used for Bare Metal deployment of Hyper-V servers.

It includes Windows Preinstallation Environment, Deployment Imaging, Servicing and Management, and Windows System Image Manager.

Right after starting the installation, at the **Assessment and Deployment** kit page, select **Deployment Tools** and **Windows Preinstallation Environment (Windows PE)** and then follow the wizard to complete the installation.

There's more...

There are more items that you need to install, which will be seen in the following sections.

SQL Server Connectivity Feature Pack components

Download SQL Server Connectivity Feature Pack and then run the downloaded file to install that package. Note though that you need the feature pack for the SQL version that the VMM database is running on.

▸ **SQL Server 2012 Command Line Utilities**: The SQLCMD utility allows users to connect to, send Transact-SQL batches from, and output row set information from SQL Server 2005, SQL Server 2008, SQL Server 2008 R2, and SQL Server 2012 instances. Visit the following site for more information:

```
http://go.microsoft.com/fwlink/?LinkID=239650&clcid=0x409
```

▸ **Microsoft SQL Server Native Client**: This contains runtime support for applications using native code APIs (ODBC, OLE DB, and ADO) to connect to Microsoft SQL Server 2005, 2008, 2008 R2, and SQL Server 2012. SQL Server Native Client is used to enhance applications that need to take advantage of new SQL Server 2012 features. Visit the following site for more information:

```
http://go.microsoft.com/fwlink/?LinkID=239648&clcid=0x409
```

The Telnet client

Install the Telnet client, as it is very useful when testing and troubleshooting:

1. On the Windows 2012 start screen, right-click on the tile for Windows PowerShell. Next, on the app bar, click on **Run as administrator**.

2. Type the following command and hit *Enter*:

```
Install-WindowsFeature TelnetClient
```

See also

▸ The *Installing the Windows ADK* article available at `http://go.microsoft.com/fwlink/?LinkId=234980`

Configuring distributed key management

Distributed key management (DKM) is used to store VMM encryption keys in **Active Directory Domain Services (AD DS)**.

When installing VMM, for security reasons (recommended, as it encrypts the information on AD) and when deploying HA VMM (required), choose to use DKM on the **Configure service account and distributed key management** page.

Why do we need the DKM? By default, using the **Windows Data Protection API** (**DPAPI**), VMM encrypts some data in the VMM database (for example, the Run As account credentials and passwords), and this data is tied to the VMM server and the service account used by VMM. However, with DKM, different machines can securely access the shared data.

Once an HA VMM node fails over to another node, it will start accessing the VMM database and use the encryption keys conveniently stored under a container in AD to decrypt the data in the VMM database.

Getting ready

The following are some considerations for using distributed key management in VMM 2012:

- ▶ When installing a highly available VMM management server, DKM is required.

- ▶ The VMDK container should be created in AD by starting with the VMM setup, if you do not have domain administrator rights when installing VMM.

- ▶ You must create the VMDK container and the Virtual Machine Manager Service account in the same domain as the VMM management server.

- ▶ The installation account requires **Full Control** permissions to the VMDK container in AD DS. Also, in the **Apply to** drop-down menu, choose the **This object and all descendant objects** option.

- ▶ On the **Configure service account and distributed key management** page, you must specify the location of the container in AD DS (for example, CN=VMMDKM, DC=lab, DC=local).

 If you do not have the domain admin rights, or delegate permissions to execute the following recipe, ask the domain administrator to do it.

How to do it...

1. Log in as domain administrator on your domain controller (for example, **W2k8r2-DC**) or from the administrator desktop if you have installed RSAT.

2. Type adsiedit.msc on the **Run** window.

3. When the **ADSI Edit** window opens, right-click on **adsiedit** and select **Connect to**.

4. Click on **Select a well known Naming Context** and select **Default naming context**.

5. Click on **OK** and expand **Default naming context**.

6. Expand **DC=lab,DC=local**.

7. Right-click on **DC=lab,DC=local** and select **New**, and then select **Object**.

8. Select **container** and click on **Next>**, as show here:

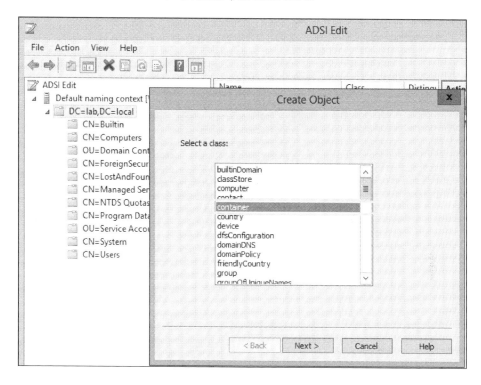

9. On the **Value** textbox, type VMMDKM and click on **Next.**

10. Click on **Finish** and close the **ADSI Edit** window.

11. In the **Active Directory Users and Computers** window, in the top menu, click on **View** and then select **Advanced Features**.

12. Right-click on the **VMMDKM** container and click on **Properties**.

13. Click on the **Security** tab and click on **Add**.

14. Type the name of the VMM Administrators group: lab\vmm-admins.

15. Check the **Read**, **Write**, and **Create all child objects** options.

16. Click on **Advanced**.

17. Select **VMM Admins** and click on **Edit**.

18. In the **Apply to** drop-down menu, select **This object and all descendant objects**.

19. Click on **OK**.

How it works...

You can configure the DKM before installing VMM by using **ADSI Edit** or during the VMM setup when you will be asked to enter the location in AD that you would like to use for storing the encryption keys. The location is the distinguished name of the container.

If you choose to create the DKM during the VMM setup, the user running the VMM installation (for example, **lab\vmm-admin**) needs to have the following access rights on the location that you specify during setup:

- ▸ **Read**
- ▸ **Write**
- ▸ **Create all child objects**

 If creating DKM under the root level, you will need those rights at the domain level.

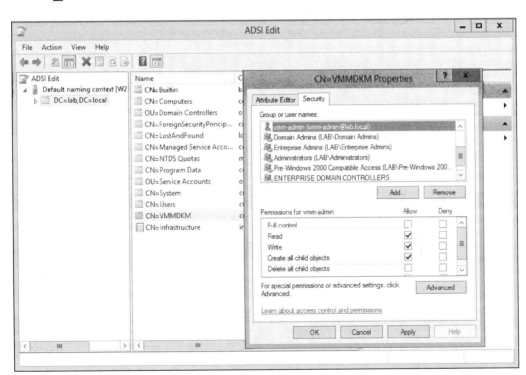

If the user running the setup has the right to create a container in AD DS, VMM setup will check if there is a DKM container and then do either of the following:

> ▸ If there is a DKM container already created in AD, VMM setup creates a new container under **VMMDKM** and gives the necessary permissions to the VMM service account for this new container

> ▸ If there is no DKM container in AD, the VMM setup will create the container

 Note that the VMM service account is also selected on this wizard page. For HA VMM installations, the local system account is disabled.

See also

> ▸ *KB: System Center 2012 Virtual Machine Manager Setup fails to create child objects for DKM*:
>
> `http://blogs.technet.com/b/scvmm/archive/2012/06/18/kb-system-center-2012-virtual-machine-manager-setup-fails-to-create-child-objects-for-dkm.aspx`

> ▸ *Configuring Distributed Key Management in VMM*:
>
> `http://go.microsoft.com/fwlink/p/?LinkID=209609`

Installing a VMM management server

As discussed in *Chapter 1, VMM 2012 Architecture*, the VMM management server is the core of VMM. In this recipe, we will install the VMM management component. Again, it is important to look at your design first to find out where you are going to deploy this component. This should be the first component to install.

Getting ready

Before you start the installation of the VMM management server, ensure that your SQL server is up and running.

From the VMM server, run the following at the command prompt:

`Telnet SQL-Server 1433`

If you get a black screen, the communication is established. If you receive the message **Could not open connection to the host**, the connection has failed and you need to look at SQL services or the firewall rules of your SQL Server and proceed with the VMM installation. You can close the black screen.

Get your computer updated by running Windows update and restarting it if requested, before continuing with the VMM installation.

Ensure that:

> ► The server meets the minimum system requirements.

> ► You have created the domain account that will be used by the Virtual Machine Manager Service (for example, **lab\vmm-svc**). *Do not log in with this account.* The VMM service account will be used in the **VMMDKM** wizard page.

> ► The installation account (for example, **lab\vmm-admin**) is a member of the local `Administrators` group. The account you are going to use for VMM is required to be a member of the local `Administrators` group on the computer you are installing VMM in. Add `LAB\vmm-svc` as well, which is the account we created previously to be the SCVMM service account.

> ► You have closed any open applications and that there is no pending restart on the server.

> ► The computer is a member of the domain. In our case, we are using `LAB.LOCAL` as the domain.

> ► You have created a DKM container in AD DS before installing VMM. Otherwise, if the user account running setup (`LAB\vmm-admin`) has the right to create the VMMDKM container in AD DS, you don't need to have created it previously.

If the setup does not complete successfully, check the logs in the `%SYSTEMDRIVE%\ProgramData\VMMLogs` folder.

How to do it...

Carry out the following steps to install VMM management server:

1. Log in as **LAB\vmm-admin** or with an account that has administrator rights.

2. Browse to the VMM setup folder, right-click on **setup**, and then select **Run as administrator**.

3. On the Setup page, click on **Install** and on the **Select features to install** page, select **VMM Management server**, and then click on **Next**, shown as follows:

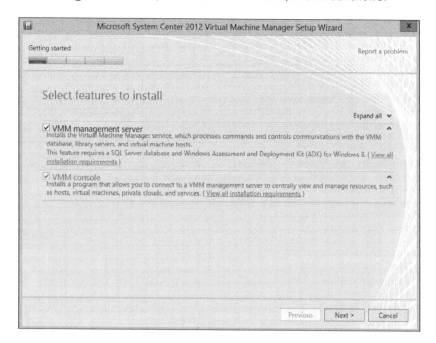

The VMM Self-Service Portal is not available for installation with VMM 2012 SP1 as it was replaced by System Center App Controller. See the *Deploying SC App Controller 2012 SP1 for Hybrid Cloud Management* recipe in *Chapter 9, Managing Hybrid Clouds, Fabric Updates, Creating Clusters, and SP1 new features*.

The VMM console option will be selected and installed when you select **VMM management server**.

4. On the **Product registration information** page, type the key and then click on **Next**.

5. On the **Please read this license agreement** page, tick the **I have read, understood, and agree with the terms of the license agreement** checkbox and then click on **Next**.

6. On the **Customer Experience Improvement Program** page, choose **Yes** to participate or **No**, and then click on **Next**.

7. On the **Microsoft Update** page, tick the checkbox **ON** (recommended) to look at the Microsoft Update for latest updates, and then click on **Next**.

8. On the **Installation location** page, provide the path for the installation and then click on **Next**.

If you plan to install all VMM 2012 components on the same server, my recommendation is to keep the operational system (OS) partition (C:) only for the OS. In this case, you should select another drive for the VMM program files.

9. The server will now be scanned to check if the requirements are met and a page will be displayed showing us which requirement has not been met and how to resolve the issue.

10. As we planned our installation and had all prerequisites already installed, the **Database configuration** page will be directly displayed.

11. On the **Database configuration** page, specify the name of the server that is running SQL Server. In our case, it is **w2012-sql.lab.local**, as seen here:

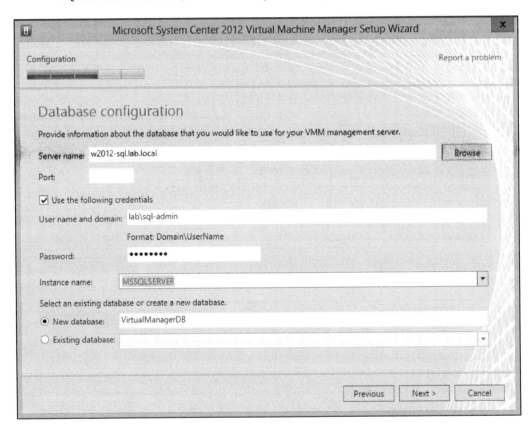

If the SQL Server is running on the same server, which is not a recommended approach, you can type localhost or the name of the computer (for example, vmm-mgmt01.lab.local).

12. You don't need to specify the port used for SQL communication, unless *all* of the following conditions are true for SQL:

- The SQL Server is running on another server (recommended)
- The SQL Server Browser service is not started
- Not using the default port of 1433

13. In the **Instance name**, provide the SQL Server instance, or select the default, **MSSQLSERVER**.

If the **Instance** name does not show the SQL instances to select, confirm if the **SQL Server Browser** service is running and check the inbound firewall rules on the SQL Server.

14. Agree to create a new database (new VMM installation) or to use an existing database (for example, a recover situation) and click on **Next**.

15. On the **Configure service account and distributed key management** page, select the account for Virtual Machine Manager Service.

16. If the selection is **Domain Account**, type in the user domain account, in the format domain\user, and the password and click on **Next**.

You will not be able (as it is not supported) to change the account after the VMM installation is completed. See the *Creating service accounts* recipe in this chapter.

17. In the **Distributed Key Management** section, select **Store my keys in Active Directory** if you have decided to use DKM (recommended approach), shown as follows:

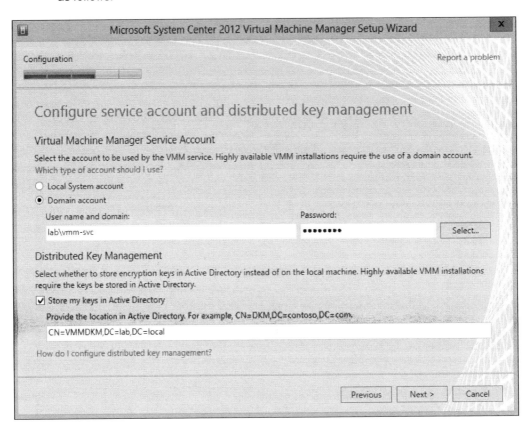

It is strongly recommended that you select to store in Active Directory, and it is required when installing a highly available VMM server.

18. On the **Port configuration** page, leave the default port numbers or provide a unique value for each feature, and then click on **Next** as seen here:

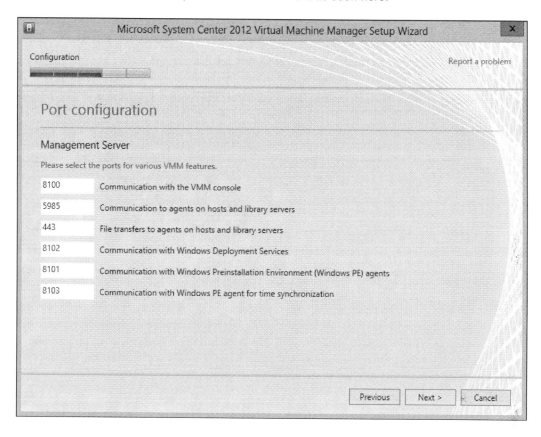

 Document and plan the ports before choosing, as you cannot change the ports without reinstalling VMM.

19. On the **Library configuration** page, you can select the **Create a new library share** option if you want to create a new library share or you can select the **Use an existing library share** option if you want to use the existing library share, depending upon your requirements. Click on **Select** to specify the share location.

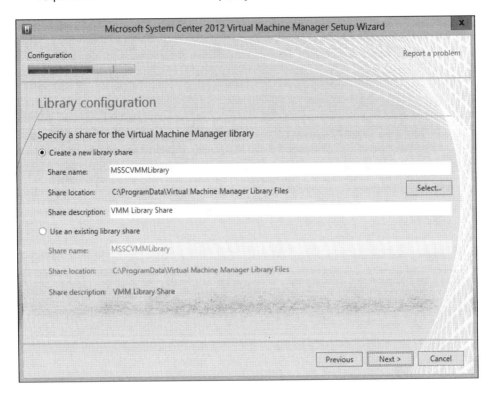

20. Click on **Next** to continue.

21. On the **Installation summary** page, review your selections. Click on **Previous** if you want to change any selections.

22. Click on **Install** to start the installation and an installation progress bar will be displayed.

23. On the **Setup completed successfully** page, click on **Close**.

How it works...

The installation of VMM Management Server 2012 is straightforward because it has enhancements added that simplifies the installation process. When you click on **Install** on the main Setup page, this version will install some of the prerequisites for you, if they are necessary. In addition, if you are installing VMM on a cluster node, you will be prompted to make it highly available. For more info, see *Chapter 3, Installing a Highly Available VMM Management Server*.

If the user account running the **VMM** setup (LAB\vmm-admin) has the right to create the VMMDKM container in AD DS, you don't necessarily need to have created it previously; although, it is recommended because of the following:

▶ VMM setup checks if the VMMDKM container is present in AD. If it is present, it will create a new container under VMMDKM.

▶ If the VMMDKM container does not exist, the setup will try to create it.

When creating the container, VMM will give the **VMM** service domain account's (informed on the same page) selected permissions to it.

 When installing HA VMM, you cannot select the local system account, as it is not supported in this case.

If your account does not have the CREATE permissions option on the SQL database server, or if you are not a database administrator, you can ask them to previously create the VMM Database. Alternatively, you can provide an account with permissions to create a database on SQL Server during the installation process by selecting the **Use the following credentials** checkbox and then providing the username and password.

During installation, you will be required to create the VMM library. The default share is MSSCVMMLibrary and the folder is located at %SYSTEMDRIVE%\ProgramData\Virtual Machine Manager Library Files, which is a hidden folder.

 You will be able to add additional library shares or servers on the VMM console by using the VMM command shell, after the installation.

See also

▶ The *Designing the VMM server, database, and console implementation* recipe in *Chapter 1, VMM 2012 Architecture*

Installing the VMM console

After installing **VMM** management server, we need to install the **VMM** Console to manage VMM from your desktop.

The VMM console is the GUI interface to the **VMM** management server. For example, you will be using it to manage the cloud, fabric, storage, and resources.

Getting ready

Before you start the installation of the VMM console, ensure that the VMM management server is up and running. Also, check if your machine has all the prerequisites for the VMM console installation.

 Consult the logfiles in the `%SYSTEMDRIVE%\ProgramData\ VMMLogs` folder. Check `ProgramData` if you find issues at the time of installation.

Make sure you log in with an account that is a member of the local `Administrators` group before starting the installation.

How to do it...

Carry out the following steps:

1. Log in as **lab\vmm-admin** or with administrator rights.

2. Browse to the VMM setup folder, right-click on **setup**, and then select **Run as administrator**.

3. On the Setup page, click on **Install**.

4. On the **Select features to install** page, select only **VMM console**, and then click on **Next**, as shown:

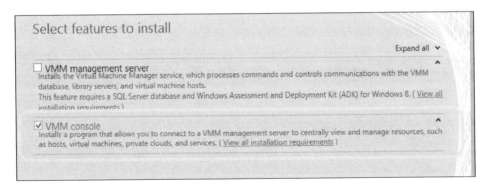

5. On the **Please read this license agreement** page, tick the **I have read, understood, and agree with the terms of the license agreement** checkbox and then click on **Next**.

6. On the **Join the Customer Experience Improvement Program (CEIP)** page, choose **Yes** to participate or **No**, and then click on **Next**.

7. On the **Microsoft Update** page, tick the checkbox **ON** (recommended) to look at the Microsoft Update for latest updates, and then click on **Next**.

8. On the **Installation location** page, provide the path for the installation and then click on **Next**.

9. On the **Port configuration** page, type the port that VMM console will use to communicate with the VMM management server, and then click on **Next**.

 You already configured this port setting during the installation of the VMM management server. The default port setting is 8100.

10. On the **Installation summary** page, click on **Previous** if you want to change any selections or click on **Install** to proceed with the installation.

 To open the VMM console at the end of the installation, select **Open the VMM console when this wizard closes**.

11. On the **Setup completed successfully** page, click on **Close**.

How it works...

The installation process will install VMM console on your desktop machine. By doing this, you will be able to connect and perform all VMM-related activities remotely from your computer.

The installation process will scan the computer to make sure the requirements are met, and a page will be displayed showing any prerequisites that have not been met.

Connecting to a VMM management server by using the VMM console

The VMM console is the GUI interface to the VMM management server. You will be using it, for example, to manage virtual machines, services, private cloud, fabric, storage, and resources.

You can use the following recipe to configure the VMM console to connect to a VMM management server.

The VMM console will enable you to manage VMM remotely from your desktop without the need of RDP into the VMM server.

How to do it...

Carry out the following steps:

1. In the **Server name** box that is in the **Connect to Server** dialog box of the **Virtual Machine Manager Console** window, type in the name of the VMM management server (for example, **vmm-mgmt01:8100**, where 8100 is the default port).

2. To connect, click on **Specify credentials** and then type the user credentials (for example, **lab\vmm-admin**) or click on **Use current Microsoft Windows Identity**.

3. Click on **Connect**.

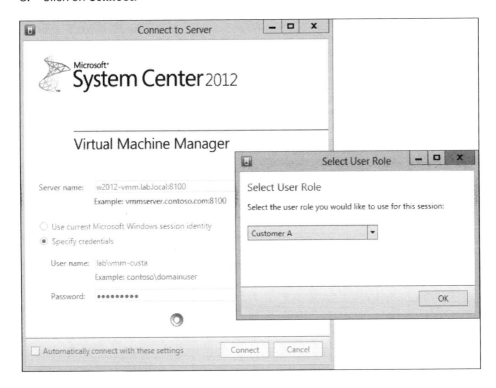

How it works...

You can use the logged Windows login credentials to connect to VMM if the user is allowed to connect, or you can specify an account.

You will need to specify the user credentials on a multitenant environment, or if the user account is not on the same domain as the VMM management server.

If the account has multiples user roles (for example, Tenant Administrator and Self-Service user), you will be prompted to select the user role with which you can log in.

See also

▸ The *Creating user roles in VMM* recipe in *Chapter 5, Deploying Virtual Machines and Services*

Creating a Run As account's credentials in VMM

This recipe will guide you through the process of configuring security in VMM, by using Run As accounts.

In VMM 2012, the credentials that a user enters for any process can be provided by a Run As account.

Only administrators or delegated administrators have the rights to create and manage Run As accounts.

If within their scope, read-only administrators will be able to read a user's account name related to the Run As account.

How to do it...

Carry out the following steps:

1. In Windows, click on the Start menu and click on the VMM console.
2. On the VMM 2012 console, on the left-bottom side, click on the **Settings** workspace.
3. In the **Home** tab, on the top ribbon, click on **Create Run As Account**.
4. In the **Create Run As Account** dialog box, type in the name for the Run As account (for example, `Hyper-V Host Administration Account`).
5. Optionally, enter a description for the account.

6. Provide the user account that will be used by the Run As account in the **User name** field (for example, **lab\vmm-admin**).

 You can use a domain user or group or a local credential.

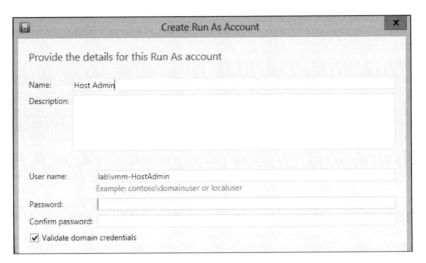

7. Type in the password.

 Unselect **Validate domain credentials** if you are sure that the user and the password are correct.

8. Click on **OK** to create the account.

How it works...

Creating a Run As account starts by creating the account on the Active Directory that will be used for the association.

A Run As account is an account securely stored in **VMM** that will be used to perform VMM administrative tasks such as adding hosts, clusters, and performing Bare Metal deployments. By using the Run As account, you will not need to provide a username and password while performing tasks that require credentials.

There is no limit to the number of Run As accounts you may have.

There's more...

Administrators and delegated administrators can create, delete, and make a Run As account unavailable temporarily in VMM. They can do the last by disabling the account and then enabling it to have it available again.

> Delegated administrators can only perform these actions within their scope.

Disabling a Run As account

Carry out the following steps to disable a Run As account:

1. In the VMM 2012 console, on the left-bottom side, click on the **Settings** workspace.
2. On the **Settings** pane, click on **Security**, and then click on **Run As Accounts**.
3. On the **Run As Accounts** main pane, click on the enabled Run As account to be disabled.
4. In the **Home** tab, on the top ribbon, click on **Disable** and then you will see the **Enabled** status changing to a red **X**.

> The account will be unavailable until you enable it again.

Enabling a disabled Run As account

Carry out the following steps to enable a Run As account:

1. In the VMM 2012 console, on the left-bottom side, click on the **Settings** workspace.
2. On the **Settings** pane, click on **Security** and then click on **Run As Accounts**.
3. On the **Run As Accounts** main pane, click on the disabled Run As account to be enabled.
4. In the **Home** tab, on the top ribbon, click on **Enable**; you will see the status changing to **Enabled**.

Deleting a Run As account

Use the following steps to delete a Run As account that is not being used by any VMM running task:

1. In the VMM 2012 console, on the left-bottom side, click on the **Settings** workspace.

2. On the **Settings** pane, click on **Security**, and then click on **Run As Accounts**.

3. On the **Run As Accounts** main pane, click on the Run As account to be deleted.

4. In the **Home** tab, on the top ribbon, click on **Delete** and then click on **Yes** to confirm the removal.

Configuring ports and protocols on the host firewall for each SCVMM component

When designing the VMM implementation, you need to plan which ports you are going to use for communication and file transfers between the VMM components. Based on the chosen ports, you also need to configure the host firewall and external firewalls to enable those ports.

Getting ready

Take note of the following ports to create the firewall exceptions. Depending on your environment, you will need to configure the following exceptions on the host firewall, as well on your external firewall (for example, if you have a DMZ in place).

 Some ports cannot be changed through VMM.

The following table lists the default port settings and the place to change, if it is possible:

Connection from and to	Protocol	Default port	To change the port settings
SFTP file transfer from VMware ESX Server 3.0 to VMware ESX Server 3.5 hosts	SFTP	22	Cannot be changed.
The VMM management server to the P2V source agent (control channel)	DCOM	135	Cannot be changed.
The VMM management server to Load Balancer	HTTP/HTTPS	80/443	Load balancer configuration provide.
The VMM management server to the WSUS server (data channel)	HTTP/HTTPS	80/8530 (non-SSL) and 443/8531 (with SSL)	These ports are the IIS port bindings with WSUS. They cannot be changed from the VMM.
The VMM management server to the WSUS server (control channel)	HTTP/HTTPS	80/8530 (non-SSL) and 443/8531 (with SSL)	These ports are the IIS port bindings with WSUS. They cannot be changed from the VMM.

Connection from and to	Protocol	Default port	To change the port settings
The BITS port for VMM transfers (data channel)	BITS	443	During VMM setup.
The VMM library server to the hosts (file transfer)	BITS	443 (Maximum value: 32768)	During VMM setup.
VMM host-to-host file transfer	BITS	443 (Maximum value: 32768)	Cannot be changed.
VMware Web Services communication	HTTPS	443	VMM console.
SFTP file transfer from the VMM management server to VMware ESX Server 3i hosts	HTTPS	443	Cannot be changed.
OOB Connection – SMASH over WS-Man	HTTPS	443	On BMC.
The VMM management server to the in-guest agent (VMM to the virtual machine data channel)	HTTPS (using BITS)	443	Cannot be changed.
The VMM management server to the VMM agent on the Windows-Server-based host (data channel for file transfers)	HTTPS (using BITS)	443 (Maximum value: 32768)	Cannot be changed.
OOB connection IPMI	IPMI	623	On BMC.
The VMM management server to the remote Microsoft SQL Server database	TDS	1433	Cannot be changed.
Console connections (RDP) to virtual machines through Hyper-V hosts (VMConnect)	RDP	2179	VMM console.
The VMM management server to the Citrix XenServer host (customization data channel)	iSCSI	3260	On XenServer in transfer VM.
Remote Desktop to virtual machines	RDP	3389	On the virtual machine.
The VMM management server to the VMM agent on the Windows-Server-based host (control channel)	WS-Management	5985	During VMM setup.

Connection from and to	Protocol	Default port	To change the port settings
The VMM management server to the in-guest agent (VMM to the virtual machine control channel)	WS-Management	5985	Cannot be changed.
The VMM management server to the VMM agent on the Windows-Server-based host (control channel – SSL)	WS-Management	5986	Cannot be changed.
The VMM management server to the XenServer host (control channel)	HTTPS	5989	On the XenServer host, in `/opt/cimserver/cimserver_planned.conf`.
The VMM console to the VMM management server	WCF	8100	During VMM setup.
The VMM console to the VMM management server (HTTPS)	WCF	8101	During VMM setup.
The Windows PE agent to the VMM management server (control channel)	WCF	8101	During VMM setup.
The VMM console to the VMM management server (NET.TCP)	WCF	8102	During VMM setup.
The WDS provider to the VMM management server	WCF	8102	During VMM setup.
The VMM console to the VMM management server (HTTP)	WCF	8103	During VMM setup.
The Windows PE agent to the VMM management server (time sync)	WCF	8103	During VMM setup.
The VMM management server to Storage Management Service	WMI	Local call	Cannot be changed.
The VMM management server to the Cluster PowerShell interface	PowerShell	n/a	Cannot be changed.
Storage Management Service to SMI-S provider	CIM-XML	Provider-specific port	Cannot be changed.
The VMM management server to the P2V source agent (data channel)	BITS	User-defined	P2V cmdlet option.

References:

▸ *SCVMM 2012 Ports Communications for Firewall Configuration* available at `http://social.technet.microsoft.com/wiki/contents/articles/4581.scvmm-2012-ports-communications-for-firewall-configuration.aspx`

▸ *Technical Documentation Download for System Center 2012 – Operations Manager,* available at `http://www.microsoft.com/en-au/download/details.aspx?id=29256`

How to do it...

Carry out the following steps:

1. On the server where you need to configure the firewall exceptions, click on **Start**. Next, click on **Administrative Tools**, and then click on **Windows Firewall with Advanced Security**.

2. In the **Windows Firewall with Advanced Security on Local Computer** pane, click on **Inbound Rules**.

3. In the **Actions** pane, under **Inbound Rules**, click on **New Rule**.

4. In the **New Inbound Rule Wizard** window, under **Rule Type**, click on **Port**, and then click on **Next**.

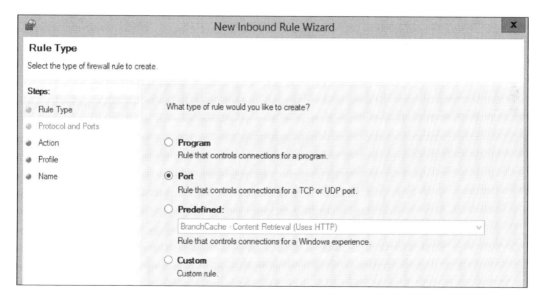

5. In **Protocol and Ports**, click on **TCP**.

6. Click on **Specific local ports** and type the port number (for example, 8100); then click on **Next**.

7. On the **Action** page, click on **Next**.

8. On the **Profile** page, click on **Next**.

9. On the **Name** page, type the description (for example, **VMM console TCP 8100**).

10. Click on **Finish** to create the rule.

 Repeat steps 3 to 10 for each port number you need to configure.

11. Close **Windows Firewall with Advanced Security**.

See also

▶ *Configure the Windows Firewall to Allow SQL Server Access:*

   http://msdn.microsoft.com/en-us/library/cc646023.aspx

3
Installing the VMM Management Server

In this chapter, we will cover:

- ▸ Installing a highly available VMM management server
- ▸ Installing a VMM management server on an additional node of a cluster
- ▸ Connecting to a highly available VMM management server by using the VMM console
- ▸ Deploying a highly available library server on a file server cluster
- ▸ Uninstalling a highly available VMM management server

Introduction

Understanding how Virtual Machine Manager has become a critical part of the private cloud infrastructure is very important. This chapter will walk you through the recipes to implement a **highly available** (**HA**) VMM server, especially useful in enterprise and datacenter environments.

VMM plays a critical role in managing the private cloud and datacenter infrastructure, which means that keeping the VMM infrastructure 100 percent available is crucial to preserving the services' continuity, provision and to monitor VMs to respond to fluctuations in usage.

Before VMM 2012, it was not possible to have an HA VMM management server, which resulted in an unavailable service if a VM stopped responding or if the host server restarted, failed, or needed to be shut down for maintenance or patching.

VMM 2012 now allows you to deploy the VMM server on a failover cluster resulting in highly available services. You can then plan the failover for maintenance purposes, for example, and it will automatically, in case of a failure, fail over to a running node to ensure that the VMM service remains online.

Keep in mind that the **VMM** library needs to be made accessible by all cluster nodes as the **VMM** server requires access to the library irrespective of which cluster node it is running on. This can be achieved by placing the **VMM** library files on a clustered file server.

Installing a highly available VMM management server

This recipe will provide the steps to install a high available **VMM** management server.

The HA **VMM** installation is very similar to the standalone installation, and it is integrated into the usual standalone installation.

To install **VMM** in an HA, you just need to start the installation of **VMM** management in one of the nodes of the cluster and then select **Install**.

Important SCVMM 2012 high available VMM notes:

- ▸ It is a fault tolerant service feature, but it does not mean that it will increase the scale or performance.
- ▸ Of a maximum of 16 nodes, only one VMM management node will be active at any time.
- ▸ Connecting to a node name is not allowed. You will have to type the HA VMM service cluster name in the VMM console login when prompted for a VMM server name and port number.
- ▸ To run a VMM planned failover, say for server patching, use the failover cluster UI and not the VMM console.
- ▸ In SP1, high availability with **N_Port ID Virtualization** (**NPIV**) is not supported although VMM does support **virtual fiber channel** configured for VMs in Windows 2012 Hyper-V.

Designing and planning the failover cluster is the first thing to do before beginning the installation of a highly available **VMM** management server. You can install a **VMM** management server on a physical cluster or on a guest cluster.

The best practice—and my recommendation—for production hosting and datacenter operations would be to install the **VMM** management server on a cluster with dedicated physical servers as you will be running critical solutions.

The following figures show the architecture design for a guest cluster:

▸ **A typical configuration**: iSCSI connectivity to the storage

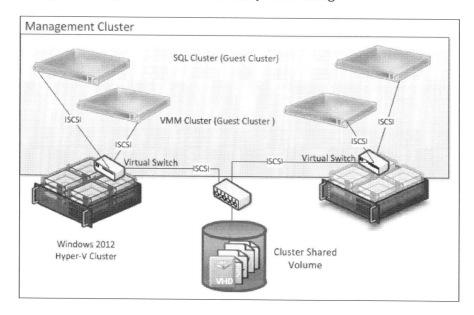

▸ **Virtual fiber channel**: New in Windows 2012, if your storage is fiber channel and does support NPIV, you can use it to create a guest cluster by using virtual fiber channel connectivity directly with the storage

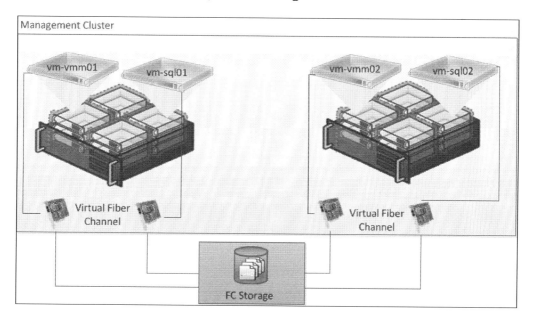

> VMM 2012 SP1 does not support NPIV, but you can still deploy it by using the Hyper-V Manager console.

Getting ready

Get your computer updated by running Windows update and restarting it if requested before continuing with the VMM installation.

Ensure that:

- The server meets the minimum system requirements:
  - The failover cluster is created and configured.
  - The SQL Server is deployed and ready. The recommendation and best practice is to have a clustered SQL Server.
  - The **Distributed key management** (**DKM**) container is created earlier on Active Directory or an installation account with permission on the Active Directory container.

- The domain account that will be used by the VMM service (for example, `Lab\vmm-svc`) is created. *Do not log in with this account*. The VMM service account will be used in the VMMDKM wizard page. For HA VMM installations, the local system account is disabled.

- The installation account (for example, `Lab\vmm-admin`) is a member of the local `Administrators` group on the computer that you are installing VMM on. Add the `Lab\vmm-svc` account as well, which is the account we previously created to be the SCVMM Service Account.

- You have closed any open applications and there is no pending restart on the server.

- The computer is a member of the domain. In our case, we are using `LAB.LOCAL` as the domain.

- You installed all the VMM prerequisites.

> If setup is not completed successfully, check the log files for details. The log files are present in the `%SYSTEMDRIVE%\ProgramData\VMMLogs` folder.
> Note that the `ProgramData` folder is a hidden folder.

How to do it...

Carry out the following steps to install an HA VMM management server:

1. Log in as `lab\vmm-admin` or with an account that has administrator rights.

2. Browse to the VMM installation media, right-click on `setup`, and select **Run as administrator**.

3. On the main **Setup** page, click on **Install** and the install process will detect whether it is running on a cluster node and will then ask if you want to make it highly available.

4. Click on **Yes** to start the HA VMM installation.

> If you click on **No**, VMM will be installed as a standalone VMM server.

5. Click to select **VMM management server** and click on **Next>**:

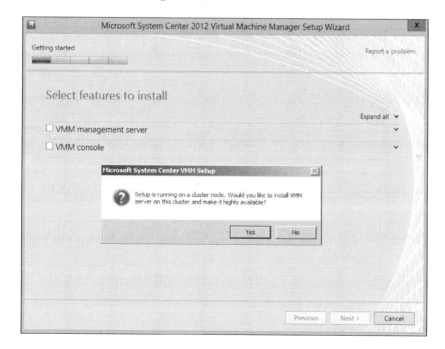

> The VMM Self-Service Portal is not available to install in VMM 2012 SP1 as it was replaced by System Center App Controller.
>
> Also note that the **VMM console** is automatically selected when you select a VMM management server.

6. On the **Product registration information** page, type the VMM key and click on **Next**.

7. On the **Please read this license agreement** page, accept the license and click on **Next**.

8. On the **Join the Customer Experience Improvement Program (CEIP)** page, choose **Yes** or **No** and click on **Next**.

9. On the **Microsoft Update** page, select **On (recommended)** to use Microsoft Update and click on **Next**.

10. On the **Installation location** page, provide the path for the installation and then click on **Next**.

 It is recommended that you keep the OS partition (C:) only for the operating system and allot another drive for the VMM program files.

11. The server will now be scanned to check whether the requirements are met. A page will be displayed showing which requirement has not been met and how to resolve the issue.

12. As we have planned our installation and have had all prerequisites already installed, the **Database configuration** page will be displayed.

 As per best practice, and for a full high availability deployment of VMM, it is recommended that you use a clustered SQL Server. See the *Planning for high availability* recipe in *Chapter 1, VMM 2012 Architecture*.

13. On the **Database configuration** page, specify the name of the server that is running SQL Server. In our case, it is **w2012-sql.lab.local**:

 You cannot have SQL Server on the same machine that will run the high available VMM management server. SQL Server needs to be available from both cluster nodes.

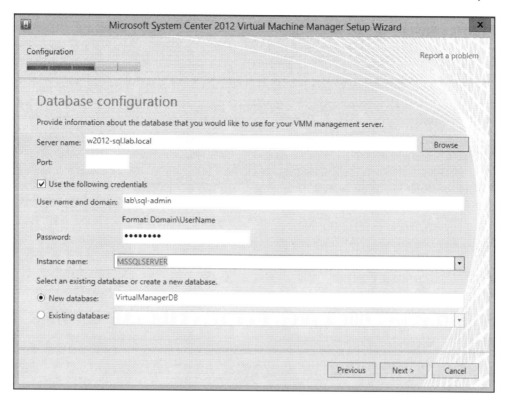

14. You don't need to specify the port used for SQL communication unless *all* of the following conditions are true for SQL:

    ❑ The SQL Server is running on another server (recommended).

    ❑ The SQL Server Browser service is not started.

    ❑ You are not using the default port of 1433.

15. In the **Instance name** field, provide the SQL Server instance or select the default, **MSSQLSERVER**.

> If the **Instance name** field does not show the SQL instances to select, check whether **SQL Browser service** is running on the SQL Server and the inbound firewall rules on the SQL server are running as well.

16. Specify whether to create a new database or to use an existing database and click on **Next**.

17. In the **Cluster Configuration** page, specify the cluster name, and if required, the network configuration (if the IP is provided by DHCP servers, for example, the network configuration will not be requested):

 The cluster name is an AD object name. Make sure the cluster name is a unique name.

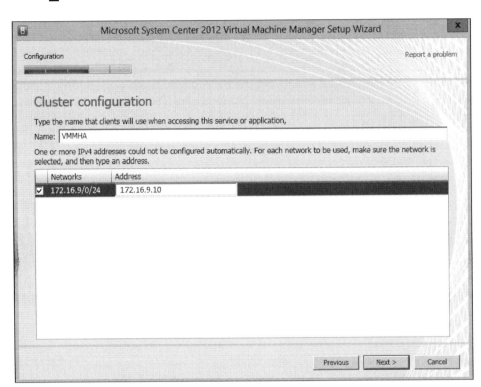

18. On the **Configure service account and distributed key management** page, provide the domain account for the VMM service.

 Create a dedicated domain account for VMM as a service account (for example, **LAB\vmm-svc**).

It is important to know that you will not be able (as it is not supported) to change the account after the VMM installation is completed. See the *Creating service accounts* recipe in *Chapter 2, Installing SCVMM 2012.*

19. In the **Distributed Key Management** section, select **Store my keys in Active Directory** as it is required by the HA VMM deployment:

 You are required to enter it as the distinguished name of the DKM container (for example, `CN=VMMDKM,DC=lab,DC=local`).

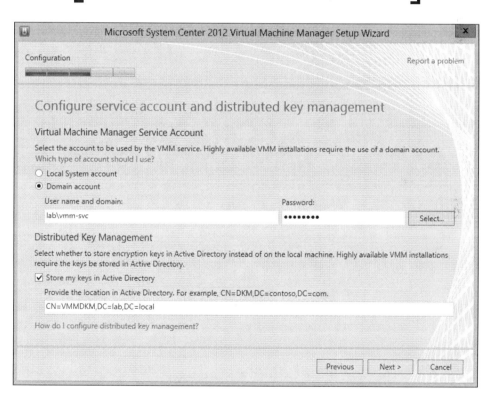

20. On the **Port configuration** page, leave the default port numbers or provide a unique value for each feature, as seen in the screenshot below, and then click on **Next**.

 Document and plan the ports before choosing as you cannot change the ports without reinstalling VMM.

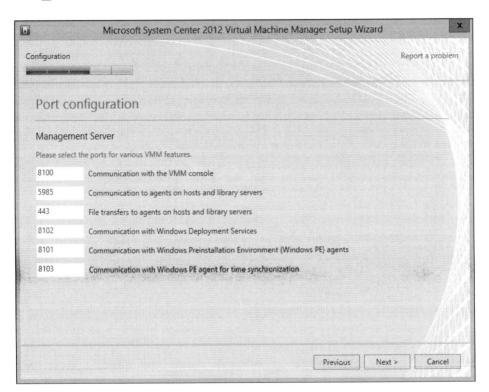

21. On the **Library configuration** page, click on **Next**.

 The setup does not create a default library share on an HA VMM installation, as you cannot have a VMM library running on the VMM management cluster.

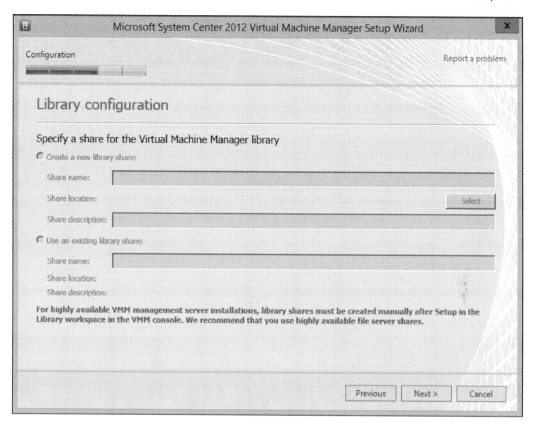

22. On the **Installation summary** page, review your selections. Click on **Previous** if you want to change any selections.

23. Click on **Install** to start the installation and the installation progress will be displayed.

24. On the **Setup completed successfully** page, click on **Close**.

 As the installation finished successfully, you can now install VMM in the other cluster nodes.

How it works...

The installation of VMM management server is straightforward with enhancements added that simplifies the installation process. The 2012 version will install *some* of the prerequisites for you, if that's necessary. When you click on **Install** on the main **Setup** page, the setup process will prompt you to install the missing prerequisites.

As we are installing VMM management server on a cluster node, you will be prompted to make the VMM management server highly available. Click on **Yes** to install an HA VMM, or **No** to install it as a standalone VMM running on a cluster.

If the user account running the VMM setup (in our case, LAB\vmm-admin) has the right to create the VMMDKM container in AD DS, you don't need to create it previously as the VMM setup checks and creates the VMMDKM container. The DKM allows users and processes running on diverse servers to share data securely. On an HA VMM, if a VMM management service fails over to another node on the cluster, the active node will access the VMM database using the encryption keys stored in the DKM container to decrypt the data that is being held securely encrypted in the VMM database.

If your account does not have the **CREATE** permissions on the SQL database server, or you are not a database administrator, you can ask them to previously create the VMM database. Alternatively, you can provide an account with permissions to create a database on the SQL Server during the install process by selecting the **Use the following credentials** checkbox and then providing the username and password.

When performing an HA VMM installation, although the **Library Configuration** page does appear, click on **Next** as it will not create the default VMM library and you will be required to create an HA library after the installation is complete by using the VMM console.

There's more...

When carrying out a planned failover for VMM, make sure you know of the following points:

▶ Any connection from the VMM console to the VMM management server from will be lost in a failover operation but will reconnect after the failover as the connection is made through the VMM cluster service name and not to a particular node. Keep that in mind and communicate to the VMM admin/users beforehand.

▶ Active running jobs will fail in a failover operation. You will need to restart it manually if it does support restart, otherwise you will need to start the job/task from the beginning.

Finally, the following are some best practices for highly available VMM management server deployment:

▶ Use a SQL Server cluster for database high availability

▶ Give preference, if deploying a highly available production environment, to have the SQL Server cluster on a distinct cluster other than the VMM cluster

▶ Use a file server to host the library shares

See also

▸ *Windows Server 2012 Scale-Out File Server for SQL Server 2012 – Step-by-step Installation* (http://blogs.technet.com/b/josebda/archive/2012/08/23/windows-server-2012-scale-out-file-server-for-sql-server-2012-step-by-step-installation.aspx)

▸ The *Configuring distributed key management in VMM* recipe in *Chapter 2, Installing SCVMM 2012*

▸ *What's New in Failover Clustering* (http://technet.microsoft.com/en-us/library/hh831414.aspx)

▸ *Introduction of iSCSI Target in Windows Server 2012* (http://blogs.technet.com/b/filecab/archive/2012/05/21/introduction-of-iscsi-target-in-windows-server-2012.aspx)

Installing a VMM management server on an additional node of a cluster

Now that we have our first node running, we are going to deploy the second node of the VMM cluster. This recipe will guide you on how to add the additional VMM nodes to an existing VMM management cluster.

You can install VMM management servers on up to 16 nodes on a cluster, but keep in mind that *only one* VMM management service will be active at a time.

The VMM console, in case of a failover, will reconnect automatically to the VMM management server as you are using the cluster service name to connect.

Getting ready

Before we start the installation of an additional node for VMM 2012, close any connections (VMM console, PowerShell, any web portal) to the primary VMM management node. Also, make sure there are no pending restarts on the current and primary VMM management node.

How to do it...

Carry out the following steps in order to add another VMM node to the VMM cluster:

1. On an additional node of your cluster, log in as `lab\vmm-admin` or with administrator rights.

2. Browse to the VMM installation media, right-click on **setup**, and select **Run as administrator**.

3. On the main **Setup** page, click on **Install**, and on the **Select features to install** page, select **VMM management server**, as shown in the following screenshot:

> The VMM console option will be selected and installed when you select **VMM management server**.

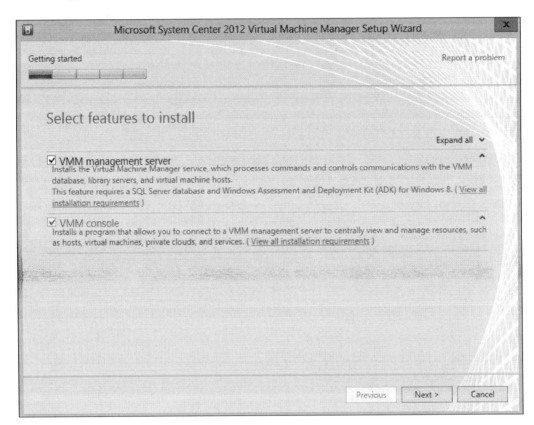

4. Click on **Yes** when the **Highly available VMM already installed** window pops up (seen below), to proceed with the installation, and then click on **Next**.

5. On the **Product registration information** page, type the VMM key and click on **Next**.

6. On the **Please read this license agreement** page, accept the license, and click on **Next**.

7. On the **Join the Customer Experience Improvement Program (CEIP)** page, choose **Yes** or **No** and click on **Next**.

8. On the **Microsoft Update** page, select **On (recommended)** to use the Microsoft Update and click on **Next**.

9. On the **Installation location** page, provide the path for the installation and then click on **Next**.

 It is recommended that you keep the OS partition (C:) only for the operating system and to have another drive for the VMM program files.

10. The server will now be scanned to check if the requirements are met and a page will be displayed showing which requirement has not been met and how to resolve the issue.

11. In the **Database configuration** page, click on **Next**.

 Because we are installing an additional VMM management server on a cluster node and they both share the same SQL database, this page is only informational.

12. On the **Configure service account and distributed key management** page, provide the password for **Virtual Machine Manager Service**.

13. On the **Port configuration** page, click on **Next**.

14. On the **Library configuration** page, we click on **Next**, as we cannot have a VMM library running on the VMM management cluster.

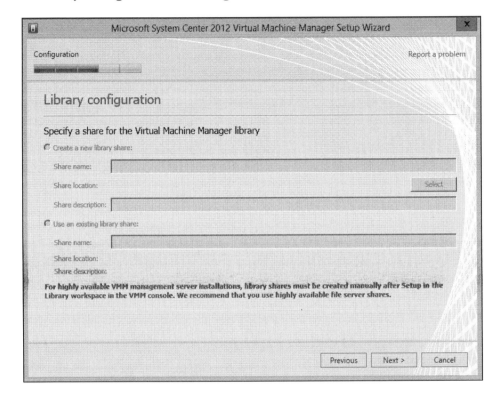

15. On the **Installation summary** page, review your selections. Click on **Previous** if you want to change any selections.

16. Click on **Install** to start the installation, and an installation progress bar will be displayed.

17. On the **Setup completed successfully** page, click on **Close**.

How it works...

With VMM 2012, you can now deploy the management server on a cluster.

The installation of an additional node of VMM management server on a cluster is straightforward, with enhancements added that simplifies the installation process.

To start, make sure you have the required hardware and software. Remember that SC 2012 SP1 only supports Windows 2012. Check *Chapter 1, VMM 2012 Architecture*, for more information about the hardware and software required for VMM.

The 2012 version will install *some* of the prerequisites for you, if that's necessary. When you click on **Install** in the main **Setup** page, the setup process will prompt you to install the missing prerequisites.

The setup process will detect that you are running on a cluster, and then you will be prompted to choose whether you want to add the installation server to the existing highly available VMM management server or not. Click on **Yes** to confirm the additional node.

On the database page, because you have already informed the SQL Server of whether you want to add the installation server or not during the first VMM node deployment, you will not be prompted to inform it again and the page will be a read-only page.

As for the VMM library, you cannot have a VMM library running on the VMM management cluster. The page will be only for informational purposes.

See also

  ▶ The *Planning for high availability* recipe in *Chapter 1, VMM 2012 Architecture*

  ▶ The *Specifying the correct system requirements for a real-world scenario* recipe in *Chapter 1, VMM 2012 Architecture*

Connecting to a highly available VMM management server by using the VMM console

The VMM console is the GUI interface of the VMM management server. You will be using it to manage the cloud, fabric, storage, and resources, for example.

You can use this recipe to configure the VMM console to connect to a highly available VMM management server.

Getting ready

Best practice recommends installing the VMM console on a machine other than the clustered VMM servers. It is recommended that you install it on the management desktop, and from there, connect to the HA VMM cluster as this will prevent a connection loss in case of failure in one of the VMM management nodes.

Review the *Installing the VMM console* recipe in *Chapter 2, Installing SCVMM 2012*, for information about installing the VMM console and *Chapter 1, VMM 2012 Architecture*, for system prerequisites.

The VMM console will enable you to manage VMM remotely from your desktop without needing to use RDP into the VMM server.

How to do it...

Carry out the following steps to connect to an HA VMM management server:

1. On a computer on which the VMM console is installed, start the Virtual Machine Manager console.

2. On the login screen, in the **Server name** box (shown below), type the VMM cluster service name, followed by a colon and the port (for example, vmmha:8100).

 The default port for VMM console connection is 8100.

3. To connect, click on **Specify credentials** and then type the user's credentials (for example, type the username `lab\vmm-admin`) or select **Use current Microsoft Windows session identity**.

 You will need to specify the user credentials on a multitenant environment or if the user account is not on the same domain as VMM management server.

4. Click on **Connect**.

5. If the account has multiple user roles (for example, **Tenant Administrator** or **Self-Service User**), you will be prompted to select the user role with which to log in. In this case, select the role, **Customer A** and click on **OK**.

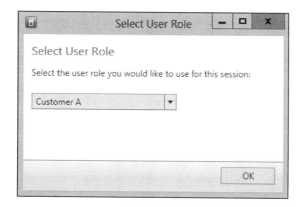

How it works...

After installing the VMM on a cluster, to manage it by using the GUI you will need to use the VMM console to connect to the VMM management server.

It is preferable to install the VMM console on the administrator desktop and then follow this recipe to connect to the HA VMM management service by providing the VMM cluster service name (mentioned at the installation of the first VMM cluster node on the **Cluster configuration** page). *Do not type a particular VMM computer server name.*

The VMM console will reconnect automatically to the HA VMM service by using the VMM cluster service name.

See also

▶ The *Installing the VMM console* recipe in *Chapter 2, Installing SCVMM 2012*

Deploying a highly available library server on a file server cluster

Following the deployment of a VMM management server in a cluster and knowing that VMM 2012, when installed in a high availability mode, does not automatically create the VMM library, we now need to deploy the VMM library. Since we are talking about a high available deployment, the VMM library will have to be HA as well.

In this recipe, we will go through a deployment of a file server cluster to be used as the VMM library. You you can use an existing file server cluster as the library as long as it meets the system requirements for SC 2012 SP1.

VMM 2012 SP1 includes support for designating network file shares on Windows 2012 servers as the storage location for the VMM library.

Getting ready

As a start, make sure your hardware meets the VMM library requirements, as discussed in *Chapter 1, VMM 2012 Architecture*, plus note the following points:

- The hardware must meet the qualifications for Windows Server 2012.
- The storage should be attached to all nodes in the cluster if you are using shared storage.
- The device controllers or appropriate adapters for the storage must be one of these types: **iSCSI**, **Fibre Channel (FC)**, **Fibre Channel over Ethernet (FCoE)**, or **Serial Attached SCSI (SAS)**.
- The cluster configuration (servers, network, and storage) should pass all of the cluster validation tests.
- VMM does not support a clustered file share for the VMM library running on the VMM cluster. You need to deploy the cluster file share on another cluster.

The following figure is a sample design scenario for a highly available VMM library over SMB 3.0 file server deployment:

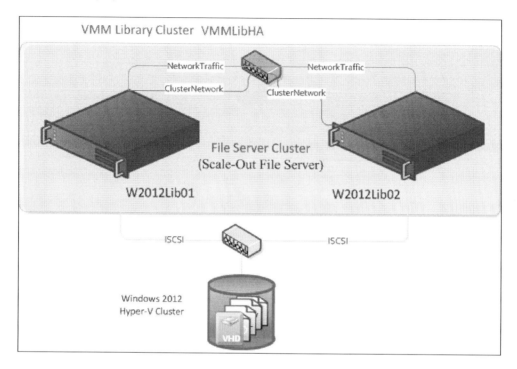

How to do it...

Let's start by setting the file server cluster. Carry out the following steps in order to deploy the HA VMM library.

 For this recipe, I am using two dedicated physical servers for the file server cluster. However, you can set up a Hyper-V guest cluster as well.

First, we will have a look at how to install, validate, and configure the Failover Clustering feature by using PowerShell:

1. Log in on the first cluster node.

2. Open the Windows PowerShell command prompt with administrator rights and type the following command:

```
Add-WindowsFeature -name File-Services,Failover-Clustering -
IncludeManagementTools
```

3. Validate and create the cluster by using PowerShell:

```
Test-Cluster -Node w2012Lib01, w2012Lib02


New-Cluster -Name vmmLibHA -Node w2012Lib01, w2012Lib02
```

 w2012Lib01 and w2012Lib02 are the physical servers' names, and vmmLibHA is the cluster name.

4. Configure the cluster networks in such a way as to use the `ClusterNetwork` network and to exclude the `NetworkTraffic` one, as shown in the following configuration:

```
(Get-ClusterNetwork | ? Address -like 10.16.1.*).Name =
"ClusterNetwork"

(Get-ClusterNetwork | ? Name -notlike Internal*).Name =
"NetworkTraffic"

(Get-ClusterNetwork ClusterNetwork).Role = 3

(Get-ClusterNetwork NetworkTraffic).Role = 1


# Confirm the configuration was successful

Get-ClusterNetwork | Select *
```

 NetworkTraffic and ClusterNetwork are the network names which were previously renamed. You can use any denomination, but remember, for consistency, to rename the cluster networks to match the network names used previously.

5. Add storage by using the following PowerShell command:

```
Add-ClusterSharedVolume
```

This command is used in the following manner:

```
Get-ClusterResource | ? OwnerGroup -like Available* | Add-
ClusterSharedVolume
```

The following screenshot is an example of adding storage using a PowerShell command:

```
                                        Administrator: Windows PowerShell

PS C:\Windows> Get-ClusterResource *disk* | Add-ClusterSharedVolume

Name                                    State
----                                    -----
Cluster Disk 2                          Online
Cluster Disk 3                          Online
```

6. You can also use the GUI to perform these tasks. For more information, refer to `http://technet.microsoft.com/en-us/library/hh831478.aspx`.

Next, we will need to configure the file server. You will carry out the following steps after installing and configuring the failover cluster:

1. In the **Failover Cluster Manager** page, select the main node on the tree, and in the **Actions** menu on the right pane, click on **Configure Role**.
2. When the **High Availability Wizard** starts, click on **Next** to continue.
3. In the **Select Role** page, select **File Server** and click on **Next**.
4. In the **File Server Type** page, select **File Server for General Use**.
5. In the **Client Access Point** page, type the name of the clustered file server (for example, VMMLibFS) and the IP Address (for example, `10.1.2.100`) if needed and click on **Next**.
6. In the **Select Storage** page, select the disks to assign to this clustered file server and click on **Next**.
7. On the **Confirmation** page, click on **Next**.
8. On the **Summary** page, click on **Finish**.

Next, we will create a file share on the cluster shared volume by carrying out the following steps:

1. In the **Failover Cluster Manager** window, click on the cluster, expand it, and click on **Roles**.
2. Select the file server, right-click on it, and then click on **Add File Share**.
3. On the **Select the profile** page, select **SMB Share – Applications** and click on **Next**.
4. On the **Share location** page, click on the volume to create the CSV file and click on **Next**.
5. On the **Share name** page, type the share name (for example, VMMLibShare) and click on **Next**.

6. On the **Configure share settings** page, select **Enable continuous availability** and click on **Next**.

7. On the **Specify permissions to control access** page, click on **Customize permissions** to grant full control on the share and the security filesystem to the **SYSTEM** account, **Administrators** and all **VMM administrators**.

8. Click on **Next**.

9. On the **Confirm selections** page, click on **Create** and then click on **Close**.

Next, we will see how to add a VMM library share by performing the following steps:

1. Start the VMM console.

2. On the login screen, in the **Server name** box, type the VMM cluster service name followed by a colon and the port (for example, vmmha:8100).

3. In the bottom-left pane, click on the **Library** workspace.

4. Click on the **Home** tab, and then click on the **Add Library Server** option in the ribbon, as shown in the following screenshot:

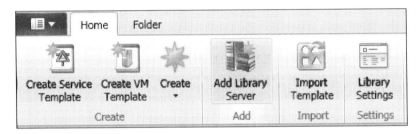

5. In the **Add Library Server** wizard, type a domain account that has administrative rights on the library servers (for example, LAB\vmm-admin) and click on **Next**.

 As discussed in *Chapter 2, Installing SCVMM 2012*, as best practice, it is recommended that you use a Run As account, which you can create by clicking on **Browse**. For more information, see the *Creating Run As account credentials in VMM* recipe.

6. On the **Select Library Servers** page, type the library server domain name (for example, LAB.local) and then click on **Add**.

7. In the **Computer name** box, type the name of the HA file server cluster (for example, `vmmLibHA`) or click on **Search** to find it in AD.

8. In the **Add Library Shares** page, select the library shares from the file server cluster to add to VMM (for example, **VMMLibShare**).

9. If you select **Add Default Resource**, the default library resources will be added to the share that is used for services. In addition, it will add the `ApplicationFrameworks` folder to the library share.

10. We click on **Next** and then, in the **Summary** page, click on **Add Library Servers** to add the selected servers and shares.

How it works...

This recipe guided us through the steps of how to set up a Windows 2012 file server cluster and how to add a VMM library server to VMM management.

VMM does not offer replication for physical files stored in the VMM library or metadata for objects stored in the VMM database. As a recommendation, you should use file server cluster for high availability.

In a clustered file server, when you take the associated file server resource offline, all shared folders in that resource go offline. This means that all shared folders will be affected.

You can set up the file server cluster on a physical server or on a Windows 2012 cluster, by using Hyper-V guest cluster options.

When adding a library server to VMM management, VMM automatically installs the agent on the new library server.

The minimum required permission to the local system (**SYSTEM**) is full control permissions for share and NTFS filesystem level (this is the default setting).

 Make sure you assign the correct access control permissions and assign full control share and NTFS permissions to the **Administrators** group.

See also

▸ The *Failover Clustering Overview* article (`http://go.microsoft.com/fwlink/p/?LinkId=243991`)

Uninstalling a highly available VMM management server

When you have a highly available VMM server, to uninstall the high availability completely you will need to uninstall the VMM management server from each node in the cluster.

Before uninstalling VMM management server, ensure that any connections to VMM management server are closed.

How to do it...

Carry out the following steps to remove an additional node of a VMM:

1. On a VMM highly available server node, in the `Programs and Features` folder (**Control | Panel | Programs**), click on **Microsoft System Center 2012 Virtual Machine Manager** and click on **Remove features**.
2. On the **Select features to remove** page, click on the **VMM management server** and click on **Next**.
3. On the **Database options** page, click on **Next**.
4. On the **Summary** page, click on **Uninstall** and then click on **Close**.

How it works...

The preceding steps show you how to remove a VMM server installed as an HA VMM server, in which you need to be a member of the local **Administrators** group, or have equivalent rights on the VMM server node that you are removing.

Beforehand, make sure the node is not currently the owner of the HA VMM service in the Failover Cluster Manager, moving it to another node in case it is the owner, and then proceed with the removal.

You can, during the removal steps, select the VMM console to be removed as well.

There's more...

We can uninstall the last node of a highly available VMM management server by using the following steps:

1. On a VMM highly available server node, in the `Programs and Features` folder (**Control | Panel | Programs**), click on **Microsoft System Center 2012 Virtual Machine Manager** and click on **Remove features**.

2. In the **Select features to remove** page, click on the **VMM management server** and click on **Next**.

3. Click on **Yes** when prompted to uninstall the last node of the highly available VMM management server and click on **Next**.

4. On the **Database options** page, choose whether you want to retain or remove the VMM database.

> By selecting **Retain database**, keep in mind that this database can only be reused for an HA VMM deployment.

5. Click on **Next**.

6. On the **Summary** page, click on **Uninstall** and then click on **Close**.

4
Configuring Fabric Resources in VMM

In this chapter, we will cover:

- ▶ Creating host groups
- ▶ Setting up a VMM library
- ▶ Networking – configuring logical networks with VMM
- ▶ Networking – VM networking and gateways with VMM
- ▶ Networking – configuring ports and switches with VMM
- ▶ Configuring storage with VMM
- ▶ Provisioning a physical computer as a Hyper-V host – Bare Metal host deployment
- ▶ Adding and managing Hyper-V hosts and host clusters with VMM

Introduction

This chapter is all about configuring the fabric resources infrastructure that you can use in your private cloud deployment. The following design shows the VMM components' infrastructure deployed as VMs on a Hyper-V cluster. You can use this as an example for your deployment. Note that, on this design, there is no guest-cluster implementation; VMM are neither implemented as HA, and nor as SQL:

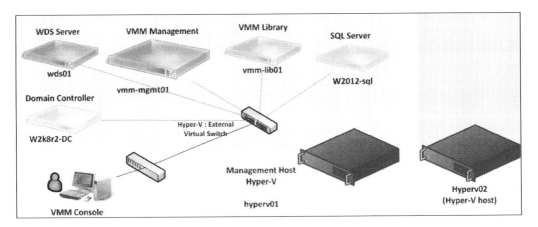

VMM 2012 fabric resources are powerful when configuring resources for private clouds, hosts, VMs, and services. This chapter will give you the necessary guidance to deploy physical servers as Hyper-V hosts and to configure and manage networking, storage, and VMM library resources. These recipes will empower you to get more out of this feature and help you understand the steps required to create the necessary infrastructure for your private cloud deployment.

The fabric resources are the infrastructure needed in order to manage the private cloud, hosts, VMs, or services. The following recipes will guide you when creating those resources.

The following figure illustrates the fabric resources that can be managed by VMM:

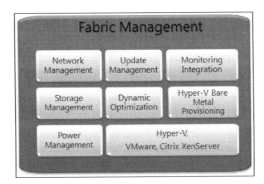

Creating host groups

Based on site location \ or resource allocation, host groups are designed to group virtual machine hosts.

Getting ready

When you have a host group structure, the following settings and resources will be allocated at the host group level:

- Placement rules
- Host reserve settings (CPU, memory, disk I/O, disk space, and network I/O)
- Dynamic optimization and power optimization settings
- Network resources
- Storage capacity allocation
- PRO configuration
- Custom properties

A host group will also allow you to:

- Assign the groups to delegated administrators and to the read-only administrators roles, and then members of these user roles will be able to view and/or assign fabric resources
- Create a private cloud, assign host groups to it, and then allocate resources from the assigned host groups to that private cloud

 For this recipe, we will create a host group based on site location and system capabilities. You should create it based on your solution design.

How to do it...

Carry out the following steps:

1. Connect to the VMM 2012 console by using the VMM admin account previously created (lab\vmm-admin), and then on the left bottom pane, click on **Fabric** to open the **fabric workspace**.
2. In the left-hand pane called **Fabric**, expand **Servers**, right-click on **All Hosts**, and then click on **Create Host Group**.
3. Type the name for the host group, for example, Sydney.

The following steps will help you create a child host group:

1. In the **Fabric** pane, expand the parent host group for which you want to create the child, right-click on it, and then click on **Create Host Group**.

2. Type the name for the host group, for example, Hyper-V.

3. Repeat steps 1 and 2 to create your host group structure.

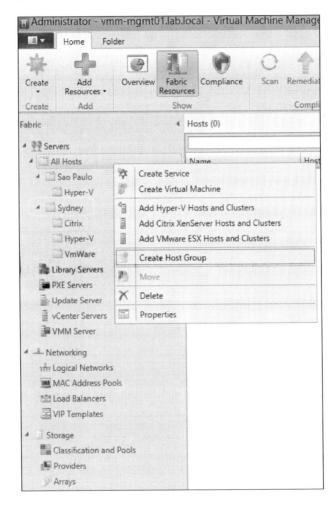

How it works...

By default, child host groups inherit settings from the parent host group, but it is possible to override those settings in the host properties.

Optionally, you can create a host group by clicking on **All Hosts**, and then on the **Folder** tab, by clicking on **Create Host Group**. VMM will create a new host group initially named **New host group**, with the host group name highlighted. Right-click on that, click on **Rename**, and type in the name you want for the host group.

For guidance, you can create the host group structure based on location, hardware capabilities, applications, server roles, type of hypervisors, business unit, or delegation model.

There's more...

With the host group created, you can then configure its properties.

Moving a host group to another location

1. In the VMM 2012 console, in the **Fabric** workspace, on the left, expand **Servers** and then expand **All Hosts**.

2. Carry out one of the following actions:

   1. Drag-and-drop the host group to its new location in the tree

   2. Click to select the host group and then:

      i. Click on the **Folder** tab.

      ii. Click on **Move** in the top ribbon.

      iii. Click to select the target parent host group.

      iv. Click on **OK**.

Configuring host group properties

1. In the VMM 2012 console, in the **Fabric** pane, expand **Servers**, expand **All Hosts**, and then click on the host group to configure.

2. In the **Folder** tab, click on **Properties**, on the ribbon, as shown in the following screenshot:

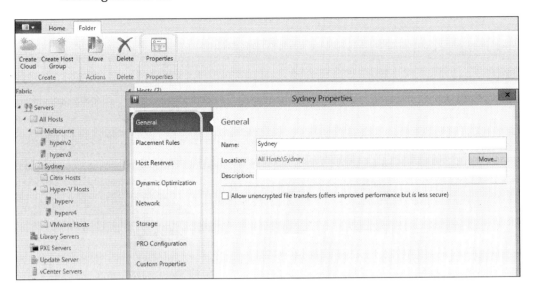

3. Click on the **General** tab and provide the host group name. Optionally, type a description and click on **Allow unencrypted file transfers**; this will improve the transfer performance but will be less secure.

4. Click on the **Host Reserves** tab if you want to configure reserve values (**CPU**, **Memory**, **Disk I/O**, **Disk space**, and **Network I/O**).

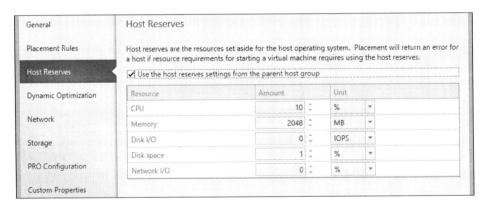

5. Click on the **Placement Rules** tab if you want to specify custom placement rules for this host group.

By default, a host group inherits the placement settings from its parent host group.

6. Click on the **Dynamic Optimization** tab to configure dynamic optimization (aggressiveness and thresholds) and power optimization settings.

7. Click on the **Network** tab to view the associated network resource type and optionally configure the **Inherit network logical resources from parent host groups** setting.

8. Click on the **Storage** tab to view and allocate **storage pools** and **storage units**.

9. Click on **PRO Configuration** (if VMM is integrated with OpsMgr) to configure the host PRO monitor.

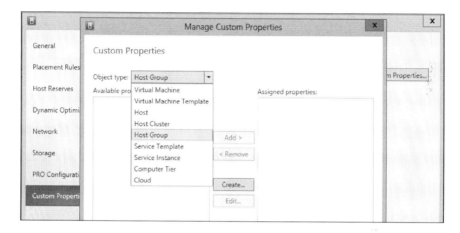

10. Click on the **Custom Properties** tab (as shown in the preceding screenshot) to assign custom properties for **Virtual Machine**, **Virtual Machine Template**, **Host**, **Host Cluster**, **Host Group**, **Service Template**, **Service Instance**, **Computer Tier**, and **Cloud**.

See also

▸ The _How to Allocate Logical Units to a Host Group in VMM_ article at
  http://technet.microsoft.com/en-us/library/gg610686.aspx

▸ The _How to Allocate Storage Pools to a Host Group in VMM_ article at
  http://technet.microsoft.com/en-us/library/gg610635.aspx

▸ The _Configuring Dynamic Optimization and Power Optimization in VMM_ article at
  http://technet.microsoft.com/en-us/library/gg675109.aspx

Setting up a VMM library

A default VMM library is configured when you install a VMM management server. However, you can add more VMM libraries later on.

In VMM 2012, the library can store file-based resources, custom resources, templates and profiles, equivalent objects, private cloud libraries, self-service user content, stored virtual machines and services, orphaned resources and update catalogs, and baseline files.

 It is strongly recommended that you use the Windows 2012 server for the Library Server OS as the VHDX does require Windows Server 2012.

This recipe will guide you through the process of configuring the VMM library.

Getting ready

The following table shows the configuration that we are going to use in this recipe:

Resource	Name
VMM management server	vmm-mgmt01.lab.local
Library share added during VMM management server installation	vmm-mgmt01\MSSCVMMLibrary
Library server and share in Sydney office	vmm-lib01\VMMSYD-Library
Second library share in Sydney office	vmm-lib01\ISO-Library
Library server and share in Seattle office	vmm-lib02\VMMSEA-Library

During the VMM setup, you can accept the default MSSCVMMLibrary library, provide a new name to be created, or specify an existing share.

The library server must be on the same domain as VMM, or in a two-way trusted domain.

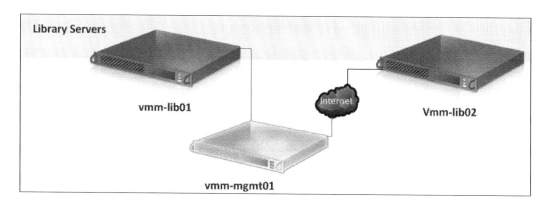

Library Servers

vmm-lib01   Vmm-lib02

vmm-mgmt01

How to do it...

Carry out the following steps to add a library server:

1. Connect to the VMM 2012 console by using the VMM admin account previously created (lab\vmm-admin) or use an account with VMM administrator rights.

2. On the bottom-left pane, click on **Library** to open the library workspace.

3. Click on the **Home** tab, and then click on the **Add Library Server** button on the ribbon shown in the following screenshot:

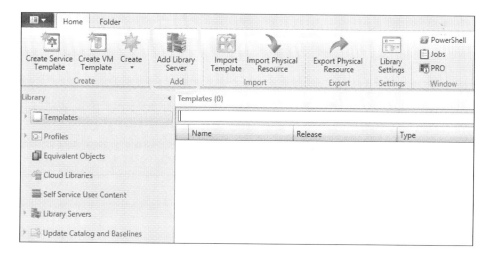

4. When the **Add Library Server** wizard opens, in the **Enter Credentials** page, type a domain account that has administrative rights on the library servers, for example, LAB\vmm-admin, and then click on **Next**.

 You can specify a Run As account. Create one by clicking on **Browse**, or manually type the user credentials in the format *domain\username*.

5. In the **Select Library Servers** page, in the **Domain** box, type the library server domain name, for example, LAB.local, and then click on **Add**.

6. In the **Computer name** box, type the name of the library server, for example, vmm-lib01, or click on **Search** to find for the library server in Active Directory.

 Although not recommended, if you are sure about the name, you can click on **Skip Active Directory name verification**. By skipping the name verification, you need to manually certify the computer is a domain member.

7. In the **Add Library Shares** page, select the library shares to add, for example, **VMMSYD-Library**.

8. By selecting the **Add Default Resources** checkbox, the default library resources will be added to the share that is used for services. In addition, it will add the ApplicationFrameworks folder to the library share.

9. Click on **Next**, and on the **Summary** page, click on **Add Library Servers** and add the selected servers and shares.

10. In the **Jobs** dialog box, confirm that the library server was successfully added; then close it.

How it works...

The preceding steps guided us through the process of adding a library server and library shares to an existing VMM 2012 installation.

When adding a library server to VMM, it automatically installs the agent on the new library server.

The minimum required permission is the local system account with full control permission in the file share and NTFS filesystem (the **Security** tab), which is the default setting.

 Make sure you assign the correct access control permissions and assign Full Control share and NTFS permissions to the local **Administrators** group.

There's more...

You can also add library shares or file-based resources to a library share.

Adding a library share

1. Connect to the VMM 2012 console by using the VMM admin account previously created (`lab\vmm-admin`) or use an account with VMM administrator rights.

2. In the library workspace, on the **Library** pane to the left, expand **Library Servers**. Next, select the library server that has a library share to be added.

3. Click on the **Library Server** tab on the ribbon, and then click on **Add Library Shares** (or right-click on the library server and then on **Add Library Shares**).

4. On the **Add Library Shares** page, select the library share and then click on **Next**.

5. On the **Summary** page, confirm the settings and click on **Add Library Servers**.

6. In the **Jobs** dialog box, confirm that the library was successfully added; then close it.

Adding file-based resources to a VMM library share

Carry out one the following steps to add file-based resources to an existing VMM library share and then manually refresh it.

 When you add files to a VMM library share, they will not show up until VMM indexes them in the next library refresh.

▸ In Windows Explorer, copy the new files to the library share. You can also use **Robocopy** or any other copy method. For more information about using Robocopy, see `http://technet.microsoft.com/en-us/library/cc733145(v=ws.10).aspx`.

▸ Using the VMM console in the library workspace:

   1. In the left-hand pane, expand **Library Servers** and then select the library server. Right-click on the library share, click on **Explore**, and start copying the files to the library share.

   2. Click on the **Home** tab, and then click on **Import Physical Resource** or **Export Physical Resource** to import/export file-based resources between library shares.

 To manually refresh the VMM library, right-click on the library server or library share and then click on **Refresh**.

You can change the library refresh interval by going to the library workspace, in the left-hand pane, under **Library Settings**. The default and the minimum value is one hour.

Creating or modifying equivalent objects in the VMM library

You can mark (create) a similar file type library object in different sites as an equivalent object. This will enable VMM to use any instance of the object when deploying it.

If you have a VHD file that is stored in a library share, for example, in Sydney as well in Sao Paulo, and if you mark it as an equivalent object, when you create a new VM template and then specify that VHD for the template, VMM will interpret that as a global object instead of a site-specific object. This allows you to create single templates across multiple locations.

To mark resources as equivalent, they must be of the same file type (same family name, release value, and namespace).

The following section will guide you through creating and modifying library resources as equivalent objects in VMM.

Marking (creating) objects as equivalent

1. In the VMM console, in the library workspace and in the **Library** pane to the left, click on **Library Servers** (or if connected using a self-service user, expand **Self Service User Content**, and click on the data path).

2. In the **Physical Library Objects** main pane (or the **Self Service User Objects** pane if connected as a self-service user), click on **Type** on the column header to sort the library resources by type.

3. Next, to select the resources to mark as equivalent, carry out one of the following steps:

    ❑   Select the first resource to mark, press and hold the *Ctrl* key, and then click on the other resources that you want to mark as equivalent

    ❑   Select the first resource to mark, press and hold the *Shift* key, and then click on the last resource

4. Right-click on the objects and then click on **Mark Equivalent**, as shown in the following screenshot:

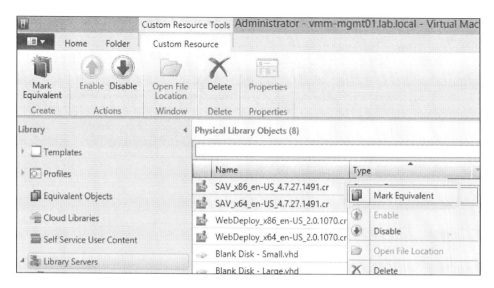

5. In the **Equivalent Library Objects** dialog, type the family name in the **Family** list (for example, W2012 STD) and a release value (string) in the **Release** list (for example, Aug 2012).

6. Click on **OK** and verify that the objects show in the **Equivalent Objects** pane. They will be grouped by family name.

 The namespace will automatically be assigned by VMM; a Global namespace if created by an administrator, or a namespace that matches the self-service user name if created by an a self-service user.

Modifying equivalent objects

If you need to modify equivalent objects, carry out the following steps:

1. In the library workspace, in the **Library** pane to the left, click on **Equivalent Objects**.

2. In the **Equivalent Objects** main pane, expand the family name and the release value, right-click on the equivalent object, and then click on **Properties**.

3. In the **General** tab, add/modify the values.

 Delete the family name and release values if you require to remove an object from an equivalent objects set.

4. Click on **OK** to confirm.

See also

▶ The *How to Import and Export File-Based Resources To and From the Library* article at `http://go.microsoft.com/fwlink/p/?LinkId=227739`

Networking – configuring logical networks in VMM

Networking in VMM 2012 includes enhancements such as logical networks, network load balance integration, and network virtualization which enables administrators to efficiently provision network resources for a virtualized environment.

In this recipe, we will go through the logical network configuration.

Getting ready

A logical network linked to a network site is a user-defined group of IP subnets, VLANs, or IP subnet/VLAN pairs that is used to organize and simplify network assignments. It can be used to label networks with different purposes, for traffic isolation, and to provision networks for different types of **service-level agreements** (**SLAs**).

As VMs move across Hyper-V servers, make sure that the virtual network switches are named exactly the same in all Hyper-V servers (as they are associated with VMs). In addition, if you plan to use the Hyper-V host as part of a cluster node, make sure that you have at least two external virtual network switches per node. For more information about virtual switches, see `http://technet.microsoft.com/en-us/library/hh831823.aspx`.

To make a logical network available to a host, you must associate the logical network with a physical network adapter on the host.

 You cannot associate a logical network with a Hyper-V internal or private VSwitch.

The following tables shows the configuration that I will be using for our deployment:

Physical NIC	Hyper-V VSwitch	IP address pool	Can it be associated with a logical network?
Intel(R) 82577LM Gigabit #1	vExternal	10.1.10.0/24	Yes
Intel(R) 82577LM Gigabit #2	vIntranet	10.1.20.0/24	Yes
Hyper-V Virtual Ethernet Adapter	vInternalHost	10.1.30.0/24	No

Create the following logical networks, and then associate them with the virtual switch:

Host group	Logical network	Associated Hyper-V Virtual Switch	Site name
Sydney	ExternalAccess	vExternal	Internet-Sydney
Sydney	Intranet	vIntranet	Intranet-Sydney

[Some other possible examples of logical networks would include DMZ, backend, frontend, backup, cluster, and extranet.]

How to do it...

Carry out the following steps to create a logical network and an associated network site:

1. Connect to the VMM 2012 console by using the VMM admin account previously created (`lab\vmm-admin`), and then, on the bottom-left pane, click on **Fabric** to open the fabric workspace.

2. Click on the **Home** tab on the ribbon, and then click on **Fabric Resources**.

3. Expand **Networking** in the **Fabric** pane to the left, and then click on **Logical Networks**.

4. On the **Home** tab, click on **Create Logical Network**.

5. When the **Create Logical Network Wizard** window opens, type the logical network name on the **Name** page. For example, type `Intranet`.

6. You may type an optional description for the logical network, for example, `internal network traffic`.

7. Click on **Next**, and then click on **Add** on the **Network Site** page.

8. For **Host groups that can use this network site**, select the host group(s) to make available for this logical network. For example, **Sydney**, as shown in the following screenshot:

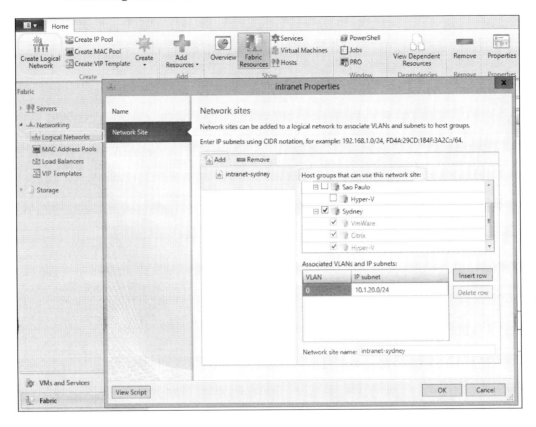

9. Under **Associated VLANs and IP subnets**, click on **Insert row**.

10. In the **VLAN** column, type the VLAN information, if any.

Leave it blank if there is no VLAN, or type `20`, for example, to create VLAN 20.

11. Under **IP subnet**, type the IP address, for example, `10.1.20.0/24`.

12. In the **Network Site Name** box, type the network site name, for example, `Intranet-Sydney` and then click on **Next**.

13. In the **Summary** page, click on **Finish**.

14. Repeat steps 5 to 13 to create all of the necessary logical networks (for example, `External`).

How it works...

The recipe describes the process of creating a logical network, associating it with a site (normally a physical location), and IP subnet and VLANs (if any).

For VMM to automatically assign static IP addresses, you can create IP address pools from an IP subnet associated with a network site.

When you add a Hyper-V host to VMM, if the physical network adapter is not associated with a logical network, VMM will then automatically create and associate a logical network that matches the DNS suffix of the connection (first one). Refer to *How to Configure Global Network Settings* at `technet.microsoft.com/en-us/library/gg610695.aspx`.

Certify that you have at least one physical network adapter available for communication between the host and the VMM management server when associating a logical network with a physical network adapter.

There's more...

Now, let's create the IP address pool for the **logical network** (**LN**), and then associate the LN to a physical network adapter.

Creating an IP address pool

Carry out the following steps to create an IP address pool for the logical network:

1. Open the **Fabric** workspace, and then click on the **Home** tab on the ribbon.

2. Click on **Fabric Resources**, expand **Networking** in the **Fabric** pane to the left, and then click on **Logical Networks**.

3. In the **Logical Networks and IP Pools** main pane, click on the logical network to create the IP address pool (**intranet**, in our example).

4. On the **Home** tab on the ribbon, click on **Create IP Pool**.

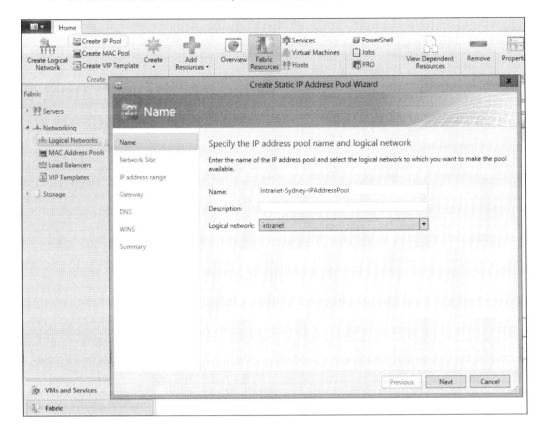

5. When **Create Static IP Address Pool Wizard** opens, on the **Name** page and type the name and description (optional) for the IP address pool, for example, `Intranet-Sydney-IPAddressPool`.

6. On the **Network Site** page, click on **Use an existing network site**.

7. Enter the correct IP address range and click on **Next**.

8. Enter the correct gateway and metric and click on **Next**.

9. Enter the correct DNS server address and DNS Suffix (if any) and click on **Next**.

10. Enter the correct WINS (if any) and click on **Next**.

11. On the **Summary** page, review the settings and click on **Finish**.

 You can specify one or more IP addresses from the address range in the IP subnet to use to create a **virtual IP** (**VIP**) address or to reserve one for other purposes.

Associating the VMM logical network with the physical adapter

Carry out the following steps to associate the VMM logical network with the physical adapter on the hypervisor host:

1. In the **Fabric** workspace, on the **Fabric** pane to the left, expand **Servers | All Hosts**, and then expand the host group, for example, **Hyper-V**.

2. In the **Hosts** main pane, select the host to configure, for example, **hyperv02**.

 In order to proceed with this step, you should have added the Hyper-V server to the host group first. See the *Adding and managing Hyper-V hosts and host clusters with VMM* recipe in this chapter.

3. In the **Host** tab on the ribbon, click on **Properties** (or right-click on the host and click on **Properties**).

4. In the **Host Name Properties** dialog box, click on **Hardware | Network Adapters** and select the physical network adapter to be associated.

 Wireless network adapters will not be displayed as this technology is not supported.

5. On the **Logical network connectivity** page, select the logical network(s) to associate with the physical adapter, for example, **intranet**.

6. Click on **Advanced** to configure the connection mode for the physical switch; you can chose **Trunk mode** or **Access mode** (default).

7. Click on **OK**.

 Repeat these steps on every host of the host group that's using the same logical network.

See also

▶ *How to Create IP Address Pools for Logical Networks in VMM*:

    http://go.microsoft.com/fwlink/p/?LinkID=212422

▶ *How to Configure Network Settings on a Hyper-V Host in VMM*:

    http://go.microsoft.com/fwlink/p/?LinkID=212537

▶ *How to Configure Global Network Settings in VMM*:

    technet.microsoft.com/en-us/library/gg610695.aspx

Networking – VM network and gateways with VMM

A VM network is created on top of a logical network, enabling you to create multiple virtualization networks. Network virtualization and gateway devices are new features in VMM 2012 SP1, which is only available on Windows Server 2012 Hyper-V hosts. The types of VM networks in VMM 2012 SP1 are as follows:

▶ **Isolation** (network virtualization):

Without the VLAN constraints, isolation enables VM deployment flexibility as the VM keeps its IP address independent of the host it is placed on, removing the necessity of physical IP subnet hierarchies or VLANs.

It allows you to configure numerous virtual network infrastructures (they can even have the same **customer IP address** (**CA**)) that are connected to the same physical network. A likely scenario is either a hosting environment, with customers sharing the same physical fabric infrastructure, or an enterprise environment with different teams that have different objectives also sharing the same physical fabric infrastructure or even on a software house having test, stage, and production environments sharing the physical infrastructure. There are many other different scenarios where the network virtualization will enable each virtual network infrastructure to work as unique, but in fact it will be running on a shared physical network.

▶ **No Isolation**

In No Isolation mode, the VM network will act as the associated logical network and you only have one VM network configured with no isolation per logical network.

▶ **VLAN-based**

If your environment makes use of a VLAN for network isolation, you can use VMM to manage it.

▶ **External networks implemented through a vendor network-management console**

If you have configured the network through a vendor management software console, you can use VMM to import the data settings (for example, for logical networks, network sites, and VM networks) by installing the vendor-specific virtual switch extension manager.

If running a multitenant environment, such as a hosted datacenter with multiple customers, the feature will give you a powerful advantage.

Network virtualization in Windows Server 2012 is designed to remove the constraints of VLAN and hierarchical IP address assignment for virtual machine provisioning. This enables flexibility in virtual machine placement because the virtual machine can keep its IP address regardless of which host it is placed on. Placement is no longer limited by physical IP subnet hierarchies or VLAN configurations.

▶ **Gateways**

The likely scenario for this implementation is when you want to configure a VPN tunnel directly on your gateway device and then connect it directly to a VM, by selecting **Remote Networks** when creating the VM network. Note though that a gateway device software provider is required on the VMM management server. In the VMM model, the Hyper-V Network Virtualization gateway is managed via a PowerShell plugin module (which will communicate policy to the gateway). You will need to request from your vendor a PowerShell plugin module to install on the VMM server.

Getting ready

Network virtualization only works on Windows Server 2012 Hyper-V hosts and VMM 2012 SP1.

Make sure you've created the logical network in VMM before you start creating the VM Network as VMM will use it to assign the **provider addresses** (**PAs**).

VMM 2012 SP1 uses the IP address pools that are associated with a VM network to assign customized addresses to virtual machines by using network virtualization.

IP address virtualization uses **Network Virtualization with Generic Routing Encapsulation** (**NVGRE**).

For our deployment, we have two customers with the same IP range sharing the same logical network:

Logical network	Associated Hyper-VSwitch	VM network	Customer IP address
Internet	vExternal	VM-CustA	172.16.2.0/24
Internet	vExternal	VM-CustB	172.16.2.0/24

How to do it...

Carry out the following steps to create network virtualization.

First, we will have a look at enabling the Windows Network Virtualization Filter driver.

On each host (running Windows 2012 Hyper-V), on the properties of the physical network adapter associated with the virtual switch, check **Windows Network Virtualization Filter driver** and click on **OK** to apply and close:

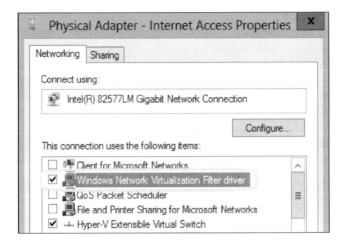

Next, we will look at enabling the DHCP virtual switch extension

You can use a DHCP server to provide an IP address on a VM network environment, but first you need to enable the DHCP server switch extension on the virtual switch on each host.

Carry out the following steps if you want to use the DHCP server to give out an IP address:

1. On each host (running Windows 2012 Hyper-V), browse to the VMM setup folder (for example, `D:\amd64\Setup\msi\DHCPExtension`) and double-click on `DHCPExtn` to install DHCPv4 Server Switch Extension.

2. In Hyper-V Manager, select the host, and then on the left-hand panel, in the **Actions** menu, click on **Virtual Switch Manager...**.

3. Select and expand the virtual switch (for example, **Internet-VSwitch**), and then click on **Extensions**. In the **Switch extensions** section, click on **Microsoft VMM DHCPv4 Server Switch Extension**, and then click on **OK** to apply and close.

Next, we will look at configuring the VM network with Isolation. Carry out the following steps to create a subnet:

1. In the VMM 2012 console, click on **VMs and Services** in the bottom-left area to open the **VMs and Services** workspace, and then click on the **Home** tab on the ribbon.

2. Click on **Create VM Network**, and in **Create VM Network Wizard**, type the name for the VM network (for example, VM-CustA) and an optional description.

3. In the **Logical network** list, select a previously created logical network (following our sample infrastructure, select **Internet**).

4. On the **Isolation** page, click on **Isolate using Hyper-V network virtualization** and click on **Next**.

 If you select **No isolation**, the **VM Subnets and Gateway** page configuration will not appear.

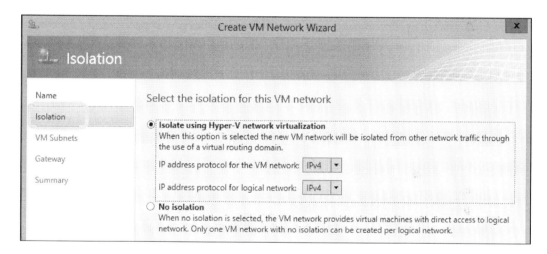

5. On the **VM Subnets** page, click on **Add** and type a name for the VM subnet, for example, VM-Network-Internal-Servers.

6. In the **Subnet** box, type an IP subnet address (for example, 172.16.2.0/24) followed by the **Classless Inter-Domain Routing** (**CDIR**) notation.

7. On the gateway page, you can choose **No connectivity** if the VMs will have data flow only on this VM network. You can select **Remote networks** if the VMs will have data flow through a VPN tunnel (requires the selection of a VPN gateway device and the configuration of VPN settings), or **Local networks** if the VMs are to have data flow to other VMM networks (requires a gateway device provider software and configuration).

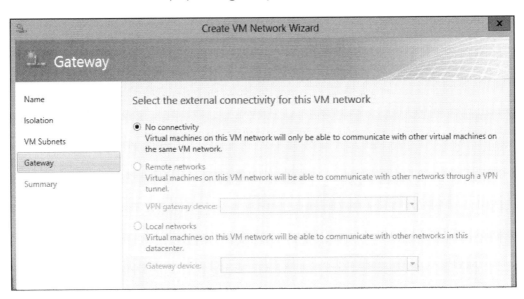

8. Click on **Next**, and then on the **Summary** page, click on **Finish**.

To create an IP Pool, select the VM network (for example, **VM-intranet**), right-click on it and click on **Create IP Pool**, and then follow the steps provided in the *Creating an IP address pool* subsection of the *Networking – configuring logical networks in VMM* recipe in this chapter.

How it works...

By using Windows Server 2012 virtual networking enhancement, VMM creates the necessary IP address mappings for the VMs.

You are required to set up the logical network first since VMM uses it to assign **provider addresses** (**PA**). It will then be visible to the physical network (for example, to hosts, physical switches, gateways). However, it will not be visible to a virtual machine, which will have **customized addresses** (**CA**) assigned by VMM from an IP address pool associated with a virtual network (VM network).

In network virtualization, each virtual machine will be assigned two IP addresses:

> ▶ **Customer IP address (CA)**: This address is visible to the VM and is used to communicate with the virtual machine

> ▶ **Provider IP address (PA)**: This address is not visible to the VM and is only used by the Hyper-V server to communicate with the VM it hosts

The mechanism that can be used to virtualize the IP address of a VM is called **Network Virtualization with Generic Routing Encapsulation** (**NVGRE**), in which all of the VM's packets are encapsulated with a new header before they get transmitted on the physical network.

 Because the VMs on a specific host can share the same PA, IP encapsulation offers better scalability.

You can assign customer addresses through the DHCP server (it requires DHCPv4 Server Switch Extension), or by using static IP addresses. Then when creating an IP address pool for a VM subnet, it will automatically provision IP addresses by either of the mechanisms.

New in VMM 2012 SP1, it can create a VM network through a gateway (VPN tunnel), if the gateway device has the required software provider.

There's more...

If you have a gateway device that does support VMM 20012 SP1, check the following section.

Adding a gateway device for VM network support

Carry out the following steps to configure a gateway device to provide support for the VM network. Note that it is required that you previously installed the gateway provider on the VMM management server.

1. In the **Fabric** workspace, on the **Fabric** pane, under **Networking**, click on **Gateways**. On the **Home** tab, click on **Add resources**.

2. Click on **Gateway**, and then in the **Add Gateway Wizard** window, type the gateway name and description (optional) and click on **Next**.

3. On the **Credentials** page, provide the Run As account and click on **Next**.

4. On the **Manufacturer and Model** page, select the provider manufacturer and model and click on **Next**.

5. On the **Logical Network** page, type the gateway IP address, select the associated logical network, and click on **Next**.

6. On the **Connection String** page, type the gateway connection string in accordance with vendor predefined syntax (for example, `gateway.lab.local`) and click on **Next**.

7. On the **Provider** page, select the provider and click on **Next**.

> To carry out a simple validation check, click on **Test**.

8. On the **Summary** page, click on **Finish**.

See also

▶ *Hyper-V Network Virtualization Overview*:

    http://go.microsoft.com/fwlink/p/?LinkId=243484

▶ *Network Virtualization technical details*:

    http://technet.microsoft.com/en-us/library/jj134174.aspx

▶ *Hyper-V Network Virtualization Gateway Architectural Guide*:

    http://technet.microsoft.com/en-us/library/jj618319.aspx

Networking – configuring ports and switches with VMM

With this new VMM 2012 SP1 feature, you can configure port profiles and logical switches. They work as containers for network adapter capabilities and settings, and by using them, you can apply the configuration to selected adapters instead of configuring those settings on each host network adapter.

How to do it...

Carry out the following steps to create native port profiles for uplinks:

1. In the VMM console, in the **Fabric** workspace and on the **Fabric** pane, under **Networking**, click on **Native Port Profiles**.
2. On the **Home** tab on the ribbon, click on **Create**, and then click on **Native Port Profile**.
3. In the **Create Native Port Profile Wizard** window, on the **General** page, type the port profile and optionally a description.
4. Select **Uplink port profile**, and click on **Next**. On the **Network configuration** page, select the network site (which could be more than one).

5. Optionally, to enable network virtualization support for it, click on **Enable Windows Network Virtualization** (requires a logical network with the **Allow new VM networks created on this logical network to use network virtualization** setting checked).

6. Click on **Next**, and then on the **Summary** page, click on **Finish**.

How it works...

Profiles are useful features that can be used to apply settings or capabilities to an entire datacenter instead of configuring each adapter's settings.

After creating a native port profile, the profile will need to be assigned to a logical switch. Make it available through the assigned logical switch which can then be selected to be applied to a network adapter in a host. This will make the network consistent across the Hyper-V hosts.

There's more...

VMM 2012 SP1 now supports native port profiles, port classifications, and virtual switch extensions. Let's configure them.

Creating a native port profile for VM adapters

Carry out the following steps to create native port profiles:

1. In the VMM console, in the **Fabric** workspace and on the **Fabric** pane, under **Networking**, click on **Native Port Profiles**.

2. On the **Home** tab on the ribbon, click on **Create** and then click on **Native Port Profile**.

3. In the **Create Native Port Profile Wizard** window, on the **General** page, type the port profile and optionally a description.

4. Click on **Virtual network adapter port profile**, and then click on **Next**.

5. On the **Offload Settings** page, select the settings you want to enable (if any), such as **virtual machine queue**, **IPsec task offloading** and **Single-root I/O virtualization**, and click on **Next**.

6. In the **Security Settings** page, select the settings you want to allow/enable (if any), such as **MAC spoofing**, **DHCP guard**, **router guard**, **guest teaming**, and **IEEE priority tagging**, and click on **Next**.

7. On the **Bandwidth Settings** page, if SR-IOV is not enabled and you want to configure the bandwidth settings, specify **Minimum bandwidth (Mbps)** or **Minimum bandwidth weight**, and **Maximum bandwidth (Mbps)**.

8. On the **Summary** page, click on the **Finish** button.

Creating a port classification

Carry out the following steps to create port classifications:

1. In the VMM console, in the **Fabric** workspace, on the **Fabric** pane, click on **Networking** and then click on **Port Classifications**.

2. On the **Home** tab on the ribbon, click on **Create** and then click on **Port Classification**.

3. In the **Create Port Classification Wizard** window, type the port classification name and optional description and click on **OK**.

Adding a virtual switch extension manager

Carry out the following steps to add a virtual switch extension. Note that it is required that you previously installed the provider on the VMM management server.

1. In the **Fabric** workspace, on the **Fabric** pane, under **Networking**, click on **Switch Extension Managers**, and then on the **Home** tab, click on **Add resources**.

2. Click on **Virtual Switch Extension Manager**, and then in the **Add Virtual Switch Extension Manager Wizard** window, type the gateway name and description (optional) and click on **Next**.

3. On the **Credentials** page, provide the Run As account and click on **Next**.

4. On the **Manufacturer and Model** page, select the provider manufacturer and model and click on **Next**.

5. On the **Connection String** page, type the connection string, in accordance with the vendor predefined syntax (for example, `vmswitch.lab.local`) and click on **Next**.

6. Select a Run As account by clicking on **Browse**, clicking on **OK**, and then on **OK** again to confirm the settings.

7. On the **Host Groups** page, select at least one host group that will have the virtual switch extension manager available and click on **Next**.

8. On the **Summary** page, click on **Finish**.

Creating a logical switch

Carry out the following steps to create logical switches:

1. In the VMM console, in the **Fabric** workspace, on the **Fabric** pane, click on **Logical Switches**.

2. Right-click on it and then click on **Create Logical Switch**.

3. In the **Create Logical Switch Wizard** window, type the logical switch name and an optional description.

4. If the network adapter has SR-IOV support and you want to enable it, click on **Enable Single Root I/O Virtualization (SR-IOV)**.

5. If you are using the virtual switch extensions select the extensions on the **Extensions** page, making sure they are in order as to be processed, and click on **Next**.

6. On the **Uplink** page, select the uplink mode, **Team** or **No Uplink Team**, and then click on **Add** to add port profiles that will be available and click on **Next**.

7. On the **Virtual Port** page, click on **Add** to add port classifications, that are associated or not to a VM network adapter port profile and click on **Next**.

8. On the **Summary** page, click on **Finish**.

Configuring the network adapter for VMs and host management

Carry out the following steps to configure the network adapter:

1. In the **Fabric** workspace, on the **Fabric** pane, expand **Servers | All Hosts** and select a host group; then select a host in the **Hosts** main pane.

2. Right-click on the host and click on **Properties**, and then click on the **Hardware** tab.

3. In **Network Adapters**, select the physical network adapter to configure. For VMs, click on **Available for placement**. For management, click on **Used by management**.

> If a logical switch and an uplink port profile were previously configured for the network adapter, when you click on **Logical network connectivity**, the result connectivity will display.

4. Do not change individual settings if you are planning to use a logical switch and uplink port profiles. Instead, apply the configuration to the virtual switch on the hosts.

5. Click on **OK** to finish.

See also

▶ _Hyper-V Network Virtualization Overview_:

http://go.microsoft.com/fwlink/p/?LinkId=243484

▶ _Network Virtualization technical details_:

http://technet.microsoft.com/en-us/library/jj134174.aspx

Configuring storage with VMM

VMM 2012 supports **block-level storage devices** and **file storage** solutions:

► **Block-level storage devices**

These expose **logical unit numbers** (**LUNs**) for storage, using fiber channel, iSCSI, and SAS connection mechanisms. You can integrate these arrays with VMM using a storage provider, meaning that you will be able to manage the arrays through the VMM console.

 From Windows 2012 onward, the Windows WMI-based **Windows Storage Management API** (**SMAPI**) replaces the **Virtual Disk Service API** (**VDS**). See `http://blogs.msdn.com/b/san/archive/2012/06/26/an-introduction-to-storage-management-in-windows-server-2012.aspx`.

The supported storage providers in VMM 2012 are as follows:

❏ **SMI-S CIM-XML**: VMM 2012 SP1 uses SMAPI to interconnect with the SMI-S compliant server. This in turn uses the Microsoft Standards-based Storage Management Service to communicate with the SMI-S external storage.

 If your storage is SMI-S compatible, install the SMI-S provider on a server accessible by the VMM management server over the network by an IP address or by a **fully qualified domain name** (**FQDN**). If using FQDN, confirm that the DNS is resolving.

❏ **SMP** (supported only by VMM 2012 SP1): VMM uses SMAPI to directly connect with the SMP storage devices.

 For a complete list of supported storage providers, see `http://social.technet.microsoft.com/wiki/contents/articles/4583.scvmm-2012-storage-and-load-balancer-provider-downloads-en-us.aspx` and `http://go.microsoft.com/fwlink/p/?LinkID=212013`.

► **File storage**

In VMM 2012 SP1, you can use SMB 3.0 network shares for storage, which can reside on a Windows Server 2012 file server or on a vendor **Network Attached Storage** (**NAS**). For more information, refer to *How to Add Windows File Server Shares in VMM*, available at `http://technet.microsoft.com/en-us/library/jj860437.aspx`, and *Assign SMB 3.0 File Shares to Hyper-V Hosts and Clusters in VMM*, available at `http://technet.microsoft.com/en-us/library/jj614620.aspx`.

Getting ready

My first recommendation is to find out whether your storage is compatible with VMM 2012, or better, with VMM 2012 SP1. If your storage is not supported by VMM 2012, don't worry, it still recognizes the local storage and remote storage that is on the storage array. However, you will not be able perform storage management operations such as logical unit creation or removal and assignment of storage through VMM to hosts/clusters. For the unsupported storage, you will need to perform these operations in the vendor storage console.

 The installation of the storage provider on the VMM management server is not supported.

You need to create a Run As account with rights to access the SMI-S provider before configuring it.

In this recipe, I will assume that you have a Dell EqualLogic Storage array iSCSI PS series and that you have installed VMM 2012 SP1. You will also need to have an account to download the Dell EqualLogic Host Integration Tools 4.5.

For our deployment, I will be using the following local server iSCSI network configuration conventions:

Physical NIC	IP address	
Intel(R) 82577LM Gigabit #3	192.168.1.10/24	ISCSI
Intel(R) 82577LM Gigabit #4	192.168.1.11/24	ISCSI

The following table shows the EqualLogic configuration:

Storage	IP	Group name	Log in as	Password
EqualLogic	192.168.1.1	grpAdmin	Administrator	Password1

How to do it...

Carry out the following steps to configure a VMM 2012 SP1 with the Dell EqualLogic Storage Array:

1. Log in to the VMM management server, vmm-mgmt01.

2. Download and install the Dell EqualLogic Host Integration Tools, and then restart the server. To download this, go to http://www.dellstorage.com/WorkArea/ DownloadAsset.aspx?id=1229.

3. Start the VMM command shell with administrative rights (run as the administrator). Import the EqualLogic PowerShell Tools module using the following command:

```
PS C:\> Import-Module -Name "C:\Program Files\EqualLogic\bin\
EQLPSTools.dll"
```

The following steps will help you add/discover the storage:

1. In the VMM console, in the **Fabric** workspace, on the **Fabric** pane to the left, right-click on **Storage** and then click on **Add Storage Devices**.

2. In the **Add Storage Devices Wizard** window, on the **Select Provider Type** page, choose **Add a storage device that is managed by an SMI-S provider** or **Add a storage device that is managed by an SMP provider**.

3. If you chose the SMI-S provider, in the **Specify Discovery Scope** page, on the **Protocol** list, choose between **SMI-S CMXML** and **SMI-S WMI WMI**. Then type the FQDN or IP of the storage provider and then the port number to connect to it, and then select a Run As account by clicking on **Browse**.

4. If you chose the SMP provider, click on **Import** to refresh the list. VMM will then discover and import the storage device information. If you are using SSL, check whether the certificate contains a CN value that matches the value used in VMM or disable CN check by adding a DWORD value of 1 in the HKEY_LOCAL_MACHINE/SOFTWARE/Microsoft/Storage Management/ DisableHttpsCommonNameCheck registry.

5. Click on **Next**, and then on the **Select Storage Devices** page, select the **Classification** column for each storage pool that requires classification and then click on **Next**.

6. On the **Summary** page, click on **Finish**.

How it works...

Storage automation through VMM 2012 is *only supported on Hyper-V*.

In VMM 2012 SP1, there are three possible types of storage management: **SMI-S provider**, **SMP provider**, and **Windows-based file server storage**.

VMM 2012 makes use of the Microsoft Storage Management Service to enable the storage features and communicate with the storages through either SMI-S or SMP providers (VMM 2012 SP1). This is required to be previously installed on a server other than VMM management and Hyper-V hosts.

 Contact your storage vendor to obtain the storage provider and installations steps.

By making use of the storage providers and automating the process, VMM allows you to assign and add storage to Hyper-V hosts and clusters, for example.

The following are the steps to automate the storage in VMM. To install the storage provider, discover and classify the storage, create the logical units (provision), assign the storage to hosts groups, and then as CSV, assign it to Hyper-V hosts/clusters.

Windows-based file server storage makes use of network shares for storage, and it does support SMB 3.0.

Install the **Multipath I/O** (**MPIO**) feature for iSCSI storage and set the **Microsoft iSCSI Initiator** service to start automatically.

For fiber channel storage support, each Hyper-V host must have a HBA zoned correctly.

In addition to that, if the storage pool does support thin provisioning in VMM 2012 SP1 by creating a logical unit, you will be able to select the **Create thin storage logical unit with capacity committed on demand** option.

To view the added/discovered storage, click on **Arrays**, and the following settings will be shown: array name, total and used capacity, managed storage pools, provider name, port, and status.

There's more...

After configuring the storage provider, you will be able to carry out tasks such as bringing storage pools and assigning classifications.

Creating an iSCSI session on a host

Carry out the following steps to create the iSCSI sessions on each Hyper-V server connected to the storage:

1. On each Hyper-V server (for example, **hyperv02**), confirm that **Microsoft iSCSI Initiator Service** is started and set to **Automatic**.

2. In the VMM console, in the **Fabric** workspace, on the **Fabric** pane to the left, expand **Servers**, click on **All Hosts**, right-click on the Hyper-V to configure, and then click on **Properties**.

3. In the **Properties** dialog box, click on the **Storage** tab, and if the storage is not listed, click on **Add** in **iSCSI Arrays** to add it.

4. In the **Create New iSCSI Session** dialog box, select the iSCSI storage in the array list and then click on **Create** if choosing the automatic setup. For manual/customized settings, click on **Use advanced settings** and select the target portal, target name, and the IP address of the initiator, and then click on **Create**.

5. The array will appear under **iSCSI Arrays**.

VMM creates the iSCSI session by matching the host initiator IP address subnets with the iSCSI target portal IP subnets.

Bringing the storage pools under management and assigning classifications

Carry out the following steps:

1. In the VMM console, in the **Fabric** workspace, on the **Fabric** pane to the left, expand **Storage**, click on **Arrays**, right-click on the array, and then click on **Properties**.

2. In the **Array Name Properties** dialog box, in the **Storage Pools** tab, in the **Storage Pools** section, select the storage pool.

3. In the **Classification** section, select a previously created classification. You can create a new one by clicking on **Create classification** and typing the classification name (for example, GOLD). Click on **OK** to confirm.

Configuring the allocation method for a storage array

To configure new logical units that will be allocated while rapidly provisioning VMs through the SAN copy technology, carry out the following steps:

1. In the VMM console, in the **Fabric** workspace, on the **Fabric** pane to the left, expand **Storage**, click on **Arrays**, right-click on the array, and then click on **Properties**.

2. Click on the **Settings** tab, and then in the **Storage array settings** window, choose between **Use snapshots** (default) and **Clone logical units**.

Creating logical units

Carry out the following steps:

1. In VMM 2012 console, in the **Fabric** workspace, on the **Fabric** pane to the left, expand **Storage**, click on **Classifications and Pools**, and then select the storage pool.

2. On the **Home** tab, click on **Create Logical Unit** as shown in the following screenshot:

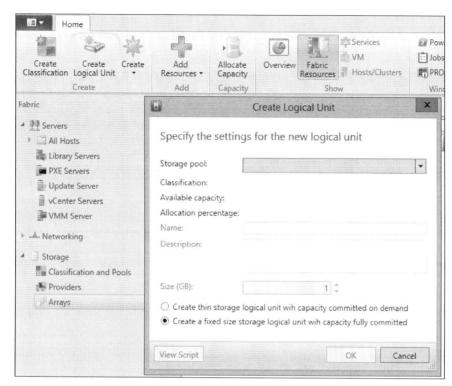

3. In the **Create Logical Unit** dialog box, type the logical name (for example, VMs), an optional description, and the logical unit size.

 If the storage pool supports thin provisioning, you can click on **Create thin storage logical unit with capacity committed on demand**.

4. To format the disk, in **Format new disk**, click on **Format this volume as NTFS volume with the following settings**.

5. In the **Mount point** section, choose **Assign the following drive letter** and select the drive letter (**V**, for example), or choose **Mount in the following empty NTFS folder** and then select an empty folder by clicking on **Browse**; or do not assign a drive letter or path.

6. Click on **OK** to confirm.

Allocating logical units and storage pools to a host group

Carry out the following steps:

1. In the **Fabric** workspace, on the **Fabric** pane, click on **Storage**, and then on the **Home** tab, click on **Allocate Capacity** and select the host group from the **Host groups** list.

> If you are logged as a delegated administrator, right-click on the host group, click on **Properties**, and click on the **Storage** tab.

2. The **Add Storage Devices Wizard** window comes up; on the **Specify Discovery Scope** page, in the **IP address** or **FQDN and port** box, type the IP address or the FQDN of the server where you installed the storage provider, followed by the port number. For example, type `192.168.10.10:40443`.

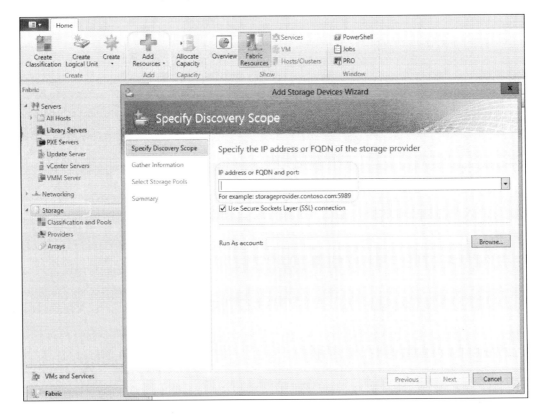

> By default, the **Use Secure Sockets Layer (SSL) connection** option is selected. If you choose not use SSL, clear the checkbox.

3. Click on the **Browse** button next to the **Run As account** box and select the previously created Run As account that can access the storage provider (for example, **vmm-StorageProvider**).

 You can create a Run As account by clicking on **Browse**, and then in the **Select a Run As Account** dialog box, click on **Create Run As Account**.

4. Click on **OK** and then click on **Next**.

5. On the **Gather Information** page, if you selected the option to use an SSL connection, the **Import Certificate** dialog box appears. Review the certificate information for the storage provider, and then click on **Import**.

 To successfully add the storage provider by using SSL, if you receive the error messages **SSL certificate common name is invalid** or **Certificate Authority not recognized**, create the DWORD registry key, HKEY_LOCAL_MACHINE/SOFTWARE/Microsoft/Storage Management/DisableHttpsCommonNameCheck and set the value to 1, to disable the CN verification for the storage provider certificate.

6. If the discovery process is successful, the discovered storage arrays, storage pools, manufacturer, model, and capacity will be listed on the page. When the process is complete, click on **Next**.

7. Information will be presented, on the **Select the storage capacity** window (total and available).

8. For logical units, click on **Allocate Logical Units** and then on the logical units you want to allocate, then click on **Add**.

9. For storage pools, click on **Allocate Storage Pools** and then on the storage pool you want to allocate, then click on **Add**.

10. Click on **OK** to confirm.

See also

- The *How to Allocate Storage Pools to a Host Group in VMM* article at http://go.microsoft.com/fwlink/p/?LinkID=212429
- The *How to Configure Storage on a Hyper-V Host in VMM* article at http://go.microsoft.com/fwlink/p/?LinkID=212536

Provisioning a physical computer as a Hyper-V host – Bare Metal host deployment

In this recipe, we will go through the steps to use VMM 2012 to discover a physical computer, install an operating system, add the Hyper-V role, and then add the machine to a host group with streamline procedures in a highly automated operation.

Getting ready

Before starting a Bare Metal deployment, a one-time configuration of the environment is required, and then when that is completed, you can start provisioning physical servers.

Go through the following steps to prepare the infrastructure for a Bare-Metal deployment:

1. **Deploying a PXE Server**: Install a new server (for example, **w2012-wds01**) with **Windows Deployment Services** (**WDS**) to provide PXE services. Configure both the deployment server and transport server options.

     You can use an existing PXE server if it is provided through Windows Deployment Services.

2. **Configuring the PXE server in VMM 2012**: Configuring is possible by adding the server to VMM 2012 management by using the VMM console. See *How to Add a PXE Server to VMM* (http://technet.microsoft.com/en-au/library/gg610651.aspx).

3. **Adding a base image for the operating system installation**: Using the Windows Server 2012 VHD/VHDX file, you can add a base image for the operating system installation to the VMM library and optional hardware driver files. See *How to Add Driver Files to the VMM Library* (http://technet.microsoft.com/en-au/library/gg610589.aspx).

     Only Windows Server 2012 can boot from a .vhdx file format.

4. **Creating a Run As account**: You need to create a Run As account for the host add operation. We created that before in *Chapter 2, Installing SCVMM 2012* (**vmm-admin**).

5. **Creating a host profile**: We can create a host profile as per the article, *How to Create a Host Profile in VMM*, which is available at `http://go.microsoft.com/fwlink/p/?LinkID=212435` and can use a generalized Windows Server 2012-based VHD/VHDX file.

 If you are using Deep Discovery during the search for the physical computers, VMM will show more detailed information about the computer.

How to do it...

First, we will perform the initial configuration of the physical server:

1. Enable the Virtualization technology and the Execute Disable Bit on the physical server BIOS to support virtualization.

2. Enable booting from a network adapter for access to the **Preboot Execution Environment** (**PXE**).

3. Upgrade the firmware and configure the BMC board by:
   - Enabling the out-of-band management protocol that could be IPMI (Version 1.5 or 2.0), DCMI (Version 1.0), or SMASH (Version 1.0). For example, on a Dell PowerEdge server, enable IPMI over LAN.
   - Configuring the network settings, which include **Host Name**, **Domain Name**, **IP Address**, and **Subnet** (you should be able to ping this IP from the VMM management and console).
   - Enabling system services.
   - Configuring login credentials to allow VMM 2012 remote access.

4. Create DNS entries with the server's name that will be assigned to the hosts when they are deployed.

The next step is to discover the physical server and deploy it as a managed Hyper-V host in VMM 2012 SP1:

1. In the VMM console, in the **Fabric** workspace, click on **Servers**, on the **Fabric** pane to the left.

2. Click on **Add Resources** on the **Home** tab, and then click on **Hyper-V Hosts and Clusters**.

3. On the **Resource location** page, select **Physical computer to be provisioned as virtual machine hosts** and click on **Next**, as shown in the following screenshot:

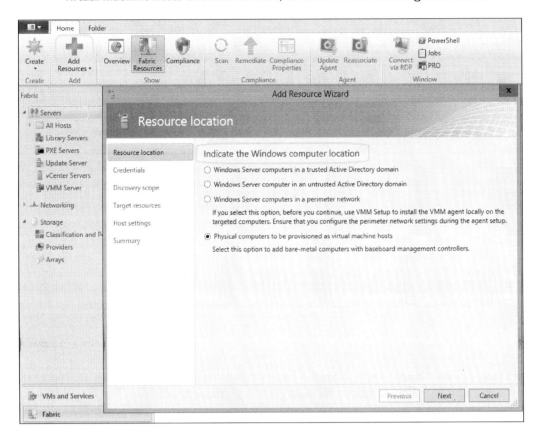

4. On the **Credentials and protocol** page, select the Run As account (with BMC access permissions) by clicking on **Browse** (for example, select **lab\host-admin**), and click on **OK**.

5. In the **Protocol** list, select the out-of-band management protocol previously configured (for example, **Intelligent Platform Management Interface (IPMI)**) and click on **Next**.

> Select **Intelligent Platform Management Interface (IPMI)** to use **Data Center Management Interface (DCMI)**.

6. In the **Discovery scope** page, type the IP scope and click on **Next**.

7. By specifying an IP subnet or an IP address range, select the server(s) to be installed as Hyper-V host in the **Target resources** page, and click on **Next**.

Make sure that you select the correct server(s) and document the IP addresses of the BMCs by creating a spreadsheet to track them.

8. On the **Provisioning options** page, in the **Host group** list, select the target host group for the new Hyper-V host(s), for example, **Sydney\Standalone Hosts\Hyper-V**.

9. Configure the hosts in such a way that they receive the network settings from a DHCP server (**Obtain IP addresses and other network settings through a DHCP service**) or that the hosts will have static IP addresses from a VMM-managed IP address pool (**Specify static IP addresses and customize deployment settings for each host**).

 You need to select a host profile with these predefined settings in the **Host profile** list.

10. Select each server, and then and on the left-hand side, click and amend the settings accordingly if you want it to be different from the host profile for example, specify any missing adapter's information or switches.

As previously mentioned in step 9, the following steps will specify the network settings through DHCP, that is, if you select **Obtain IP addresses and other network settings through a DHCP service**:

1. In the **Host profile** list, select the host profile (for example, **W2012 Host DHCP Profile**) and click on **Next**.

2. In the **Deployment customization** page, select a BMC IP address from the list.

3. Provide a unique computer name for each listed server (for example, `hyperv02.lab.local`), click on **Next**, and then click on **OK**.

 Once these settings are provided, there will be no more warnings: **Missing settings**.

The following steps will specify the network settings through static IP addresses, that is, if you chose **Specify static IP addresses and customize deployment settings for each host**:

1. In the **Host profile** list, select the host profile (for example, **W2012 Host Static Profile**) and click on **Next**.

 Only host profiles with IP settings matching the selected type (`static`), will be displayed.

2. On the **Deployment customization** page, type the server name (for example, `hyperv02.lab.local`).

Although not recommended, you can skip AD validation by clicking on **Skip Active Directory check for this computer name**. By skipping the validation, if the computer already exists, it will be overwritten by the deployment process.

3. Type the **MAC address** of the Hyper-V management network adapter (for example, `10.1.2.10`).

4. Select the logical network (LN) from the **Logical Network** list (**Intranet**).

 The default LN was defined in the host profile. The list of available LNs depends on what is available to the associated host group.

5. Select the correct IP subnet that counterparts the network site location, or else the deployment will fail.

6. You can assign an IP address as follows:

   ❑ To automatically obtain it from a static IP address pool (first available), select **Obtain an IP address corresponding to the selected subnet**

   ❑ To manually specify a specific IP address, select the IP address range and type an available IP address matching the subnet range

When all this is done you can click on **Next** and then click on **OK** to continue. Lastly, on the **Summary** page, click **Finish** to start the deployment.

How it works...

VMM can deploy a physical computer with Windows 2008 R2 or Windows 2012; add a Hyper-V role and then add it to be managed by VMM.

To start, you need a PXE server (it can be an existing one) provided through Windows Deployment Services. Then, you need to add it to VMM management server.

On each physical server, in the BIOS, configure virtualization support and boot from PXE and the BMC.

Then, create the DNS entries for each server; add the required resources to the VMM library. These resources include a generalized Windows Server 2008 R2 or the Windows Server 2012 VHD/VHDX file that will be used as the base image and optional driver files to add to the operating system during installation.

Create host profiles (which include image location, hardware, and OS settings) in the VMM library.

Use VMM to discover (scan) the physical computers, to configure deployment and settings, and to start the deployment of the OS and Hyper-V role configuration. VMM will use BMC commands during this phase to power the servers off/on.

When they restart, the PXE server will respond to the boot request with a customized image (Windows PE). The Windows PE agent will then prepare the server by downloading and applying the OS image and specified driver files from the library and by adding the Hyper-V server role; then, it restarts the server.

On the **Deployment customization** page, a small amount of wait time (in minutes) for the Deep Discovery to complete is normal, and when it is complete, VMM will show a success message.

After the host deployment, if a post-deployment task is required, right-click on the host and click on **Run Script Command** to run a script.

See also

- ▸ *How to Add a PXE Server to VMM*:

  http://technet.microsoft.com/en-US/library/gg610651.aspx

- ▸ *Prepare the Physical Computers in VMM*:

  http://technet.microsoft.com/en-US/library/gg610690.aspx

- ▸ *How to Add Driver Files to the VMM Library*:

  http://technet.microsoft.com/en-US/library/gg610589.aspx

- ▸ *How to Create a Host Profile in VMM*:

  http://technet.microsoft.com/en-US/library/gg610653.aspx

Adding and managing Hyper-V hosts and host clusters with VMM

This recipe will guide you through the steps involved in adding an existing Hyper-V host or a Hyper-V cluster by VMM.

In VMM 2012, you can add Hyper-V hosts/clusters running on the same domain as the VMM, on a trusted domain, or in a disjointed namespace. You can also add Hyper-V hosts (not clusters) running on an untrusted domain and on a perimeter network (for example, DMZ).

In VMM 2012 SP1, you can add Windows Server 2008 R2 and Windows Server 2012 as the OS for managed Hyper-V hosts. Using Bare Metal as we described before, you can add physical computers with no OS as well.

If you want to manage a standalone host that is in a workgroup, use the method to add a host in a perimeter network.

Getting ready

Make sure Virtualization is enabled in the BIOS. If the Hyper-V role is not installed, VMM will install it as part of the setup.

The following steps will guide you through how to add a Hyper-V host or a Hyper-V cluster in a trusted Active Directory domain.

How to do it...

Carry out the following steps to add a trusted Hyper-V host or cluster:

1. In the VMM console, click on the **Fabric** workspace, and then on the **Fabric** pane, click on **Servers**.

2. On the **Home** tab, click on the **Add Resources** button on the ribbon, and then click on **Hyper-V Hosts and Clusters**.

3. On the **Resource location** page, click on **Windows Server computers in a trusted Active Directory domain** and click on **Next**.

4. On the **Credentials** page, specify an existing Run As account, for example, **Hyper-V Host Administration Account** (created in *Chapter 2, Installing SCVMM 2012*) or manually type the user credentials, for example, `lab\vmm-admin`.

> To create a Run As account at this point, click on **Browse**, and in the **Select a Run As Account** dialog box, click on **Create Run As Account** and enter the requested information.

5. Click on **Next**, and in the **Discovery scope** page, select between the following options:

    ❑   **Specify Windows Server computers by names**: Type the IP or server name/ cluster name (one per line). Click on **Next**.

> By typing just part of the name, the wizard will list the servers that match.

❑ **Specify an Active Directory query**: And then type an AD query, or click on **Generate an AD query** to create it. Click on **Next**.

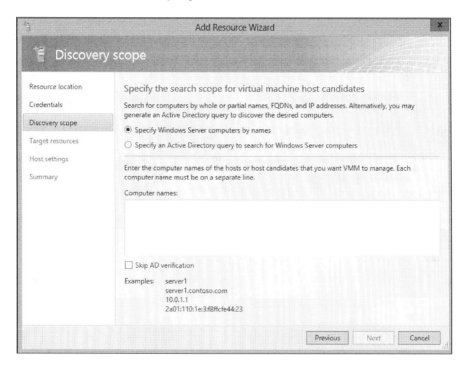

6. On the **Target resources** page, select the computer(s) or cluster name(s).

 If the Hyper-V role is not enabled, a message will be displayed stating that the role will be installed and the server will restart. Click on **OK**.

7. Click on **Next**, and on the **Host settings** page, select the host group from the **Host group** list.

 Click on **Reassociate this host with this VMM environment** if the host was associated with another VMM server.

8. When adding a standalone host, type the local host path to store VM files (for example, D:\VMS), click on **Add**, click on **Next**, and then click on **Finish**.

How it works...

When adding a standalone server or cluster in a trusted domain environment, and the domain is not the same as VMM, make sure that there is a two-way trust factor in place.

Use **Group Policy** (**GPO**) to configure WinRM, which is the only supported method for WinRM Service settings, but consider this:

> ▸ The GPO settings that VMM supports are **Allow automatic configuration of listeners**, **Turn On Compatibility HTTP Listener**, and **Turn on Compatibility HTTPS Listener**, and this is only for hosts that are in a trusted domain

> ▸ WinRM Client settings through GPO are unsupported

> ▸ It may not be possible to install VMM Agent if you enable other WinRM settings by GPO

 The use of the VMM service account to add or remove Hyper-V hosts is not recommended as it could impose security risks.

When installing a standalone server, you will be required to provide a local VM path (if it does not exist, it will be created). If left empty, the default will be used (`%SystemDrive%\ProgramData\Microsoft\Windows\Hyper-V`). When installing a cluster, the path will be located on shared storage.

 Using the OS drive to store VM files is not recommended.

There's more...

You can also add Hyper-V hosts that are not on the same domain or that are on a perimeter network.

Adding Hyper-V hosts in a disjointed namespace

Carry out the same steps to add a trusted Hyper-V host or cluster, considering the following points:

> ▸ On the **Credentials** page, type the domain account credentials (for example, `poc\vmm-admin`)

> ▸ On the **Discovery scope** page, type the FQDN of the host (for example, `hyperv03.poc.local`) and check the **Skip AD verification** checkbox

VMM checks the domain for the SPN. If it does not exist, and if the VMM service account has permission to perform `setspn`, it will be created.

You will be required to add the SPN manually if the account does not have permission.

At the command prompt, with administrator rights, type the following command (of the format *setspn -A HOST/<FQDN> <NetBIOSName>*):

```
setspn –A HOST/hyperv03.poc.local hyperv03
```

Adding Hyper-V hosts in a perimeter network

Carry out the following steps to add a standalone Hyper-V server that is in a perimeter network (for example, DMZ) to be managed by VMM:

1. Create the following spreadsheet for documentation purposes:

Hyper-V server (Hostname)	Encryption key*	Location folder	IP address

 Keep this spreadsheet in a secure place.

Installing the agent on the standalone server

1. Connect to the standalone server, and from there, browse to the VMM setup folder. Right-click on **setup**, and then click on **Run as administrator**.

2. On the **Setup** menu, click on **Local Agent**. Click on **Optional Installation** and click on **Next**. And then, on the **License** page, click on **Next**.

3. On the **Destination Folder** page, enter the installation path and then click on **Next**.

4. On the **Security File Folder** page, check the **This host is on a perimeter network** checkbox and type in and confirm a complex security key.

 Take note of the security key.

5. Specify the location for the storage key by clicking on **Change**, and then copy the security file to a folder on the VMM console.

6. If you require it, select **Use a CA signed certificate for encrypting communications with this host** and type the thumbprint.

To obtain the thumbprint, select **Computer account** in the **Certificates** snap-in. Double-click on the certificate and select and copy the `Thumbprint` field value on the **Details** tab.

7. Click on **Next**, and on the **Host network name** page, choose whether VMM will communicate with the host by using a local computer name or IP address.

8. Click on **Next**, and if you chose **Use IP address**, select an IP address from the list.

9. In the **Configuration settings** page, confirm the port settings (5986 and 443) and click on **Next**; then click on **Install**.

Adding perimeter hosts to VMM

1. In the VMM console, in the **Fabric** workspace, on the **Fabric** pane, click on **Servers**.

2. On the **Home** tab, click on **Add Resources** in the ribbon, and then click on **Hyper-V Hosts and Clusters**.

3. On the **Resource location** page, click on **Windows Server computers in a perimeter network** and click on **Next**.

4. On the **Target resources** page type the hostname or the IP, encryption key, and path for `securityFile.txt`, for each host. Select the target host group and then click on **Add**.

5. Click on **Next**, and in the **Host settings** page, type the local host path to store VM files in (for example, `D:\VMS`), click on **Add**, and then click on **Next**.

6. On the **Summary** page, click on **Finish**.

 For a detailed host status view in VMM, right-click on the host, click on **Properties**, and check the status for overall health, host agent health, and Hyper-V role health. If you find an issue, click on **Repair all**.

See also

▸   *How to Add Untrusted Hyper-V Hosts and Host Clusters in VMM*:

    `technet.microsoft.com/en-us/library/gg610609.aspx`

5
Deploying Virtual Machines and Services

In this chapter, we will cover:

- ▶ Creating private clouds
- ▶ Creating hardware, guest OS, application, and SQL profiles
- ▶ Creating user roles in VMM
- ▶ Creating and deploying virtual machines
- ▶ Creating virtual machine templates
- ▶ Creating and deploying service templates
- ▶ Rapidly provisioning a virtual machine by using SAN Copy

Introduction

In VMM, a private cloud consists of a collection of resources (for example, host groups of servers running common or diverse hypervisors, storage, and networking) and settings that provide virtualization infrastructure for **cloud users** (for example, tenants and self-service users), and it is deployed within your organization boundaries using your own hardware and software.

This chapter guides you through private cloud deployment and management, VMs, and services in VMM 2012 SP1, providing recipes to assist you to get the most out of the deployment.

Creating private clouds

This recipe provides guidance on how to create a private cloud from host groups running diverse hypervisors, such as Hyper-V, Citrix, VMware ESX hosts or from a VMware resource pool in VMM 2012 SP1.

By using VMM 2012 and deploying a private cloud, you will be able to offer a unique experience for creating VMs and services, which will in turn lead towards the consumerization of IT.

A private cloud deployment allows **resource pooling**, where you can present a comprehensive set of fabric resources but limit it by quotas that can be increased or decreased, providing fully optimized elasticity without affecting the private cloud's overall user experience. In addition to this, you can also delegate the management to tenants and self-service users that will have no knowledge of physical infrastructures such as clusters, storage, and networking.

A private cloud can be created using the following resources:

▶ Host groups that contain Hyper-V, VMware ESX to Citrix XenServer hosts

▶ VMware resource pool

Getting ready

First, start by configuring the fabric resources in VMM:

▶ **Network**: Refer to the recipes on networking in *Chapter 4, Configuring Fabric Resources in VMM*

▶ **Storage**: Refer to the *Configuring storage with VMM* recipe in *Chapter 4, Configuring Fabric Resources in VMM*

▶ **Library servers and shares**: Refer to the *Setting up a VMM library* recipe in *Chapter 4, Configuring Fabric Resources in VMM*

▶ **Create the host groups**: Refer to the *Creating host groups* recipe in *Chapter 4, Configuring Fabric Resources in VMM*

▶ **Add the hosts**: Refer to the *Adding and managing Hyper-V hosts and host clusters with VMM* recipe in *Chapter 4, Configuring Fabric Resources in VMM* and the *Adding VMware ESX hosts or host clusters to VMM* recipe in *Chapter 8, Managing VMware ESXi and Citrix XenServer Hosts*

In this recipe, we will create a private cloud that we will name `My Cloud`. It will be created from the resources of previously configured host groups.

How to do it...

Carry out the following steps to create your own private cloud:

1. Connect to the VMM 2012 console by using the VMM admin account that was previously created (for example, `lab\vmm-admin`), and then in the bottom-left pane, click on **VMs and Services** to open on the **VMs and Services** workspace.

2. Under the **Home** tab on the ribbon, click on **Create Cloud**.

3. In the **Create Cloud Wizard** window, type the private cloud's name.

4. Type a description (optional) and then click on **Next**. You can skip the resources page and create them after the private cloud has been created, if you do not have previously configured fabric resources, by clicking on **Next**.

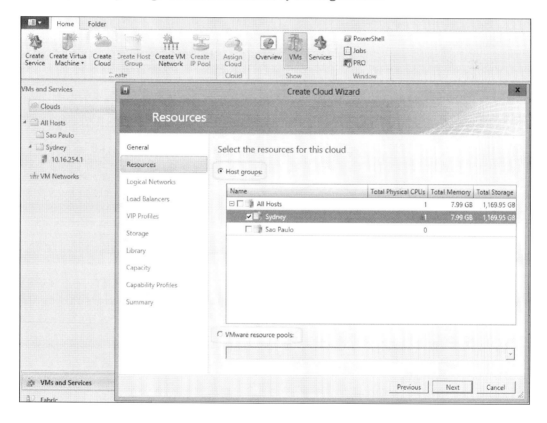

5. On the **Resources** page, select between the following options:

   ❑ Select **Host groups**, then select the host group(s) that will be added to this private cloud (for example, **Sydney**), and then click on **Next**

   ❑ Select **VMware resources pools**, then select a VMware resource pool, and then click on **Next**

6. On the **Logical Networks** page, select the logical network(s) that will be made available to this private cloud (for example, **External Access** that was created in the *Networking – configuring logical networks in VMM* recipe in *Chapter 4, Configuring Fabric Resources in VMM*) and then click on **Next**.

> Only logical networks that are associated with physical network adapters will be listed. Make sure you have configured the logical network and assigned it to the physical network beforehand.

7. On the **Load Balancers** page, if you have a load balancer deployed and integrated with VMM, select it and click on **Next**.

> Only associated load balancers will be displayed.

8. On the **VIP Profiles** page, select the VIP template(s), if any, that will be available to this private cloud (for example, **HTTPS traffic**) and click on **Next**.

9. On the **Storage** page, if you do have a storage managed by VMM and if there are storage classifications for storage pools assigned to selected host groups, select the storage classification that will be available to this private cloud (for example, **GOLD**) and click on **Next**.

> For more information on storage classification, check the *Configuring storage in VMM* recipe in *Chapter 4, Configuring Fabric Resources in VMM*.

10. On the **Library** page, provide the stored VM path by clicking on **Browse**, and in the **Select Destination Folder** dialog box, click on the library server and then select a library or a folder in the share to be used as the location for self-service users to store VMs in (for example, **StoredVMs**); then click on **OK**.

11. In the **Read-only library shares** section, click on **Add**, select the library share(s) for read-only resources, click on **OK** to confirm, and then click on **Next**.

12. On the **Capacity** page, configure the capacity limits and then click on **Next**. You can manually set quotas for the **Virtual CPUs**, **Memory (GB)**, **Storage (GB)**, **Custom quota (points)**, and **Virtual Machines** dimensions, as shown in the following screenshot:

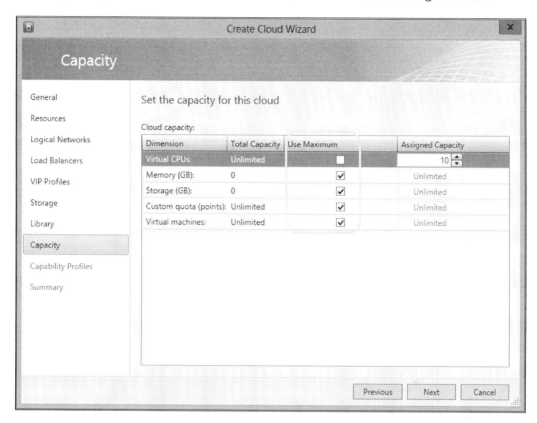

 To set up new quotas, unselect **Use Maximum**. See the *Creating an application administrator (self-service user) role* subsection in the *Creating user roles in VMM* recipe of this chapter.

13. On the **Capability Profiles** page, select the VM capability profile(s), that matches the hypervisor running on the selected host group(s)—for example, **Hyper-V**—and click on **Next**.

 Built-in capability profiles embody the minimum and maximum configured values for a VM, for each hypervisor that is supported.

14. On the **Summary** page, click on **Finish**.

How it works...

Configure the fabric resources, such as storage, network, library, host groups, and hosts, that will be available in the private cloud beforehand. Configure library paths and set the capacity for the private cloud, which can be created from host groups containing a unique mix of hypervisors, such as Microsoft Hyper-V, VMware ESXi, and/or Citrix XenServer hosts, and also from a VMware resource pool (which needs to be under VMM management).

 You cannot use VMM to manage/assign storage classifications for ESX hosts' storage.

In the **Library** workspace, you can create custom capability profiles to limit the resources being used by the private cloud's VMs.

On the **Capacity** page, you can set the capacity limits manually by unselecting the option **Use Maximum**.

To verify if the private cloud library was created, check if it is listed under **Cloud Libraries** in the **Library** workspace. If you configured read-only library shares, they will be listed together with a **Stored Virtual Machines and Services** node.

Self-service users require the store and redeploy permission to save a VM on a library share, which must be located on a different share other than the read-only resource location, that cannot be a child path of the user role data path. The self-service user role data path is configured when creating/modifying the user role.

 In VMM 2012, the self-service user can log in on the VMM console.

When creating the private cloud, VMM creates the read-only library shares and stored VM path.

There's more...

After creating the private cloud, you need to assign users that will have access to manage it.

Assigning the private cloud to a user role

Now that you've created the private cloud, you can assign it to a user role(s). Carry out the following steps to do so:

1. In the VMM console on the bottom-left pane, click on the **VMs and Services** workspace and then expand **Clouds**.

2. Select the created private cloud (for example, **My Cloud**).

3. Under the **Home** tab in the ribbon, click on **Assign Cloud** and select the user role by choosing one of the following options:

   ❑ **Use an existing user role**: This option is enabled only if you had created any user roles previously

   ❑ **Create a user role and assign this cloud**: Click on **OK** to continue and follow the steps to create and assign the user role to the private cloud

See also

▸ *Chapter 4, Configuring Fabric Resources in VMM*

▸ The *Creating an Application Administrator (Self-Service User) role* subsection in the *Creating user roles in VMM* recipe in this chapter

Creating hardware, guest OS, application, and SQL profiles

Profiles are resources that are used to deploy VMs. For example, a SQL profile provides instructions for SQL Server instance deployment and customizations. An application profile provides instructions to install App-V applications.

Getting ready

You can create the following types of profiles in VMM to be used in a VM template:

Profile type	Purpose
Hardware	To configure hardware settings (for example, memory, network adapters, and DVD drives)
Guest OS	To configure common OS settings (for example, computer name, domain name, product key, and time zone)
Application	To provide directives for Server App-V, Web Deploy, and SQL Server data-tier (DACs) applications, and for running scripts when deploying VMs as a service
SQL Server	To provide directives for an SQL customization when deploying a VM as a service

How to do it...

Carry out the following steps to create a hardware profile:

1. In the VMM console on the bottom-left pane, click on the **Library** workspace.

2. Expand **Profiles** on the left pane, click on **Hardware Profiles**, and then right-click and select **Create Hardware Profile**.

3. In the **New Hardware Profile** dialog box on the **General** page, type the hardware profile name, for example, **2 vCPU Server**.

4. Click on **Hardware Profile** on the left pane, configure the hardware settings, and click on **OK** to finish.

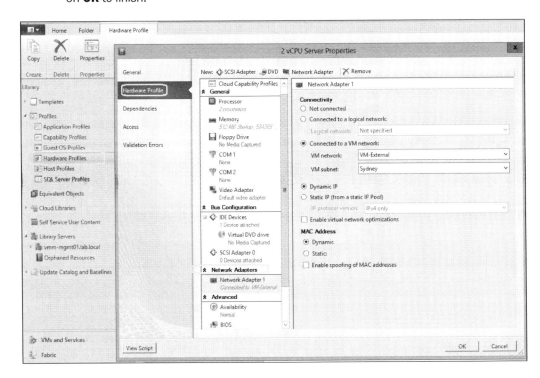

How it works...

Use this recipe to create the profiles that will contain the settings and specifications that VMM will use when deploying a VM.

To start creating a profile, expand **Profiles** in the **Library** workspace; click on **Create**, select the profile you want to create, and provide the settings to be used when deploying a VM.

When deploying the VM to a private cloud, the capability profile must be supported by the private cloud.

When creating an application profile, you can add one or more application scripts, but only after adding and configuring an application with the appropriate settings.

You can also create an application profile to deploy SQL Server DAC packages or scripts to an existing SQL Server in the **Compatibility** list, by selecting **SQL Server Application Host**.

There's more...

The following sections will guide you through creating guest OS, application, and SQL Server profiles.

Creating a guest operating system profile

1. In the **Library** workspace, click on **Guest OS Profiles** by expanding **Profiles** on the left pane, and then right-click on **Guest OS Profiles** and select **Create Guest OS Profile**.

2. In the **New Guest OS Profile** dialog box, type the guest operating system profile name (for example, `W2012 Standard`).

3. Click on **Guest OS Profile** on the left pane and configure the settings, and click on **OK** to finish.

 You can provide a pattern for the computer name. For example, if you type `W2012-SRV###`, the computers will be named `W2012-SRV001`, `W2012-SRV002`, and `W2012-SRV003`.

Creating an application profile

Carry out the following steps to create an application profile:

1. In the **Library** workspace, click on **Guest OS Profiles** by expanding **Profiles** on the left pane, and then right-click on **Application Profiles** and select **Create Application Profile**.

2. In the **Application Profile** dialog box, type the application profile name (for example, `Marketing App`).

3. Click on **Application Configuration** on the left pane and then on **OS Compatibility**, and select the supported OS.

4. If there is an application package, click on **Add**, select the application type, and then provide the application package.

5. If there is a script, click on **Add** and then select the script to add to the application profile.

6. Click on **OK** to finish.

An application package can contain settings that can be used for service deployment. The parameter in the **Value** field is in the format: @<Setting>@.

Creating a SQL Server profile

1. In the **Library** workspace, click on **Guest OS Profiles** by expanding **Profiles** on the left pane, and then right-click on **SQL Server Profiles** and select **Create SQL Server Profile**.

2. In the **New SQL Server Profile** dialog box, type the SQL Server profile name (for example, SQL Production Marketing-Research).

3. Click on **SQL Server Configuration** and then on **Add: SQL Server Deployment**.

4. Select **SQL Server Deployment - Deployment 1**, and type the SQL instance name and the account (Run As account) to be used when installing it.

5. Select **Configuration** and provide information about the configuration (for example, collation or authentication mode).

6. Select **Service Accounts** and provide the SQL Server service Run As accounts.

7. Click on **OK** to finish.

See also

▸ The *VMM 2012 SQL Server Profile* article available at http://blogs.technet. com/b/scvmm/archive/2011/09/27/vmm-2012-sql-server-profile.aspx

▸ The *How to Create a Host Profile* article available at http://technet.microsoft. com/en-us/library/gg610653.aspx

Creating user roles in VMM

User roles in VMM 2012 are used to define the objects and management operations that specified users can create/manage/perform in VMM.

These user roles are as follows:

▸ **Administrator**: The members of this group can perform tasks/actions on all objects managed by VMM. In addition to this, only administrators can add XenServer hosts and clusters, and WSUS servers to VMM.

▸ **Fabric (delegated) administrator**: The members of this group can perform tasks/ actions within their assigned scope (host groups, private clouds, and/or library servers). They can create delegated administrators with a subset of their scope.

> ▶ **Read-only administrator**: The members of this group are able to view the status and properties of objects or jobs within their assigned scope (host groups, private clouds, and/or library servers) and to specify the Run As accounts that they can view.

> ▶ **Tenant administrator**: The members of this group can create/manage self-service users (specifying the tasks/actions they can execute on VMs and/or services), VM networks, and VM services.

> ▶ **Application administrator (self-service user)**: The members of this group can create, deploy, and manage their own VMs and services, such as specifying private clouds to have a VM or service deployed, granting access to logical and physical resources in the VMM library, and configuring quotas and PRO tips settings. Only administrators and delegated administrators (within their scope) have the rights to create application administrator roles, which can only view a simplified placement map (containing only their VMs/services) on a VM or service deployment operation.

Getting ready

If the self-service user role has more than one private cloud within its scope, users select the appropriate cloud before placement runs.

When creating a self-service user role, you will be required to configure quotas, which only apply to the VMs deployed. They do not apply to the VMs in the library.

 The quota is applied individually to each member of the user role.

Quota types supported	Description of what can be consumed
Virtual CPUs	The maximum number of VM CPUs
Memory (MB)	The maximum amount of VM memory
Storage (GB)	The maximum amount of VM storage
Custom quota (points)	For backward compatibility, an arbitrary value that can be assigned to a VM template based on its anticipated "size"
Virtual machines	The number of VMs

How to do it...

Carry out the following steps to add a user to the built-in administrator user role:

1. In the VMM 2012 console to the bottom-left side, click on **Settings** to open the **Settings** workspace and then expand **Security** on the left panel.

2. Click on **User Roles** and then click on the main pane, right-click on the **Administrator** user role, and select **Properties**.

3. In the **Administrator Properties** dialog box, click on **Members** and then on **Add**.

4. In the **Select Users, Computers, or Groups** dialog box, type an AD user account or group (for example, `lab\vmm-admin`).

5. Click on **OK** to continue and then click on **OK** to save and finish.

To delete a user, on the **Members** page select the user or group and click on **Remove**.

The preceding steps can also be used to add users to other user roles.

How it works...

The built-in administrator user role is created when you install VMM, and then the user account that you used to run the VMM setup and all the domain users in the local `Administrators` group are added to the built-in administrator user role.

To add users or groups to, or remove them from roles, you can use this recipe, noting that only administrators can add/remove users to/from the administrator user role.

You can also use this recipe to create the new tenant administrator role if you are an administrator or delegated administrator (with rights). Tenants can have quotas on VMs and resources.

There's more...

There are more user roles that can be created.

Creating a delegated or read-only administrator user role

Carry out the following steps to create an optional delegated or read-only user role:

1. In the VMM 2012 console in the **Settings** workspace, click on **Create User Role** on the ribbon.

2. In the **Create User Role Wizard** window, type the name (for example, `vmm-delegated-admin`) and the optional description, and click on **Next** to continue.

3. To create a delegated or read-only admin, on the **Profile** page select either of the two options:

   ❑ **Fabric Administrator**: Select this to create and add a user as a delegated administrator

❑ **Read-Only Administrator**: Select this to create and add a user as a read-only administrator

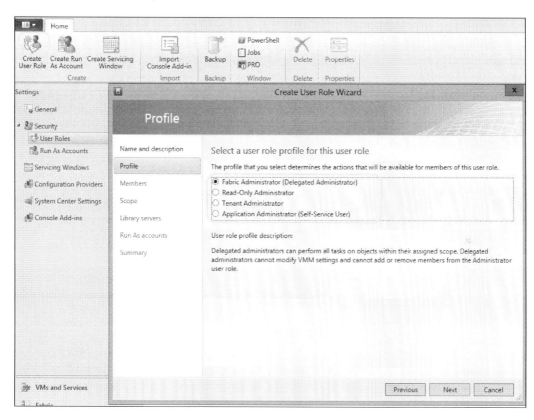

4. Click on **Next** and then on the **Members** page to add the user account(s) or group(s), click on **Add**, and then click on **Next**.

5. On the **Scope** page, select the private cloud(s) or host group(s) (for example, **My Cloud**) that can be managed by this role and then click on **Next**.

6. On the **Library servers** page, to select one or more library servers, click on **Add**, click on **OK** after selecting a server, and then click on **Next**.

7. On the **Run As Accounts** page, click on **Add**, select the Run As account, and then click on **OK** to add the account. When you finish adding the accounts, click on **Next** to continue.

8. Click on **Finish**.

Creating a tenant administrator role

The likely use for this scenario is in hosting environments with multiple customers, or in enterprise environments where you have multiple teams and each one of them wants to have and manage their own environment. Carry out the following steps to create the self-service user:

1. In the VMM 2012 console in the **Settings** workspace, click on **Create User Role** on the ribbon.

2. In the **Create User Role Wizard** window, type the name (for example, `DevTeam-tadmin`) and the optional description (for example, `Development Team Tenant Admin`) and then click on **Next**.

3. On the **Profile** page, click on **Tenant Administrator** and then click on **Next**.

4. On the **Members** page, to add the user account(s) or group(s), click on **Add** and then click on **Next**.

5. On the **Scope** page, select the private cloud(s) (for example, **My Cloud**) that can be managed by this role, select **Show PRO tips** to allow Performance and Resource Optimization management, and then click on **Next** as shown in the following screenshot:

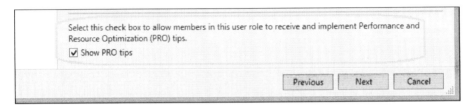

6. On the **Quotas for the DevTeam...** page, check the **Role level quotas** and the **Member level quotas** sections. If you need members of the user role to share quotas, add an AD security group instead of a user account:

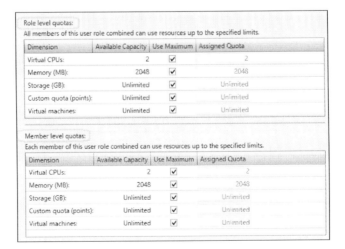

7. On the **Networking** page, select the VM networks that can be used by this role and click on **Next**.

8. On the **Resources** page, click on **Add** to select resources and click on **OK**, and then click on **Browse** and select the library upload data path.

9. Click on **Next**, and on the **Actions** page select the allowed actions and click on **Next** again, as shown in the following screenshot:

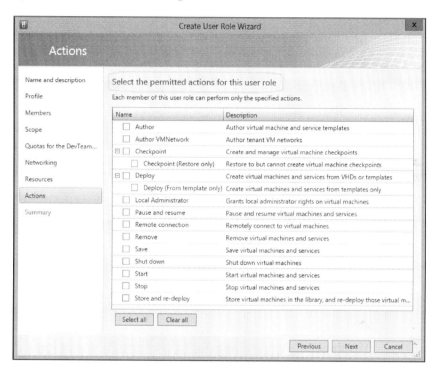

10. On the **Summary** page, click on **Finish**.

 To change **Members**, **Scope**, **Quotas**, **Resource**, and/or **Actions**, select the user role, right-click on it, and then select **Properties**.

Creating an application administrator (self-service user) role

1. In the VMM 2012 console in the **Settings** workspace, click **Create User Role** on the ribbon.

2. In the **Create User Role Wizard** window, type the name (for example, `DevTeam-AppAdmin`) and the optional description (for example, `Development Team Application Admin`) and then click on **Next**.

3. On the **Profile** page, click on **Application Administrator** and then click on **Next**.

4. On the **Members** page, to add the user account(s) or group(s), click on **Add** and then click on **Next**.

 To share a VM's ownership created by other members, use an AD group for the user role or use the **Share** and **Receive** actions.

5. On the **Scope** page, select the private cloud(s) (for example, **My Cloud**) that can be managed by this role, select **Show PRO tips** to allow Performance and Resource Optimization management, and then click on **Next**.

6. On the **Networking** page, select the VM networks that can be used by this role and click on **Next**.

7. On the **Resources** page, click on **Add** to select the resources and click on **OK**; then, click on **Browse** and select the library upload data path.

8. On the **Quotas** page, set quotas for the previously added private cloud(s), and then click on **Next**.

9. On the **Resources** page, click on **Add** to select the resources (for example, hardware, OS, application and/or SQL profiles, VM templates, and/or service templates) and click on **OK**; then click on **Browse** and select the library upload data path.

10. On the **Actions** page, select the action(s) that the self-service users can perform and then click on **Next**, as shown in the following screenshot:

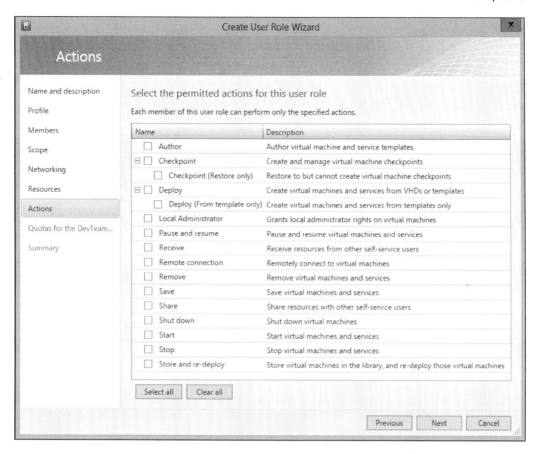

11. On the **Quotas for the DevTeam...** page, check the **Role level quotas** and the **Member level quotas** sections. If you need members of the user role to share quotas, add an AD security group instead of a user account.

> If you select **Author**, click on **Next** and select the Run As account that will be used to create the VMs and services, and click on **Next**.

12. On the **Summary** page, click on **Finish**.

Configuring self-service user roles to share and receive resources

Carry out the following steps to enable sharing and receiving resources between role members:

1. In the VMM 2012 console in the **Settings** workspace, expand **Security** and click on **User Roles** on the left pane.

2. In the **User Roles** pane, select user role, right-click on it, and then select **Properties**.

3. Click on the **Actions** page, select **Share** and **Receive**, and then click on **OK**.

See also

▶ Refer to the *Configuring the Library to Support Self-Service Users* article available at `http://technet.microsoft.com/en-us/library/gg610608`

▶ Refer to the *Available actions to Self-Service User Roles in VMM 2012* article available at `http://social.technet.microsoft.com/wiki/contents/articles/12554.actions-available-to-self-service-user-roles-in-vmm-2012.aspx`

Creating and deploying virtual machines

In this recipe, we will create a virtual machine that will later be used as a template.

Getting ready

Creating a VM is straightforward. You can create a new virtual machine using an existing virtual hard disk, or you can create a machine with a blank virtual hard disk and then install the OS.

If you are creating a new VM from a blank VHD/VHDX disk, be prepared to link an ISO hosted in the VMM library or a CD/DVD drive with the OS media that is to be installed.

How to do it...

Carry out the following steps to create a virtual machine:

1. In the VMM 2012 console in the bottom-left corner, click on the **VMs and Services** workspace.

2. On the ribbon, click on **Create Virtual Machine** and then select **Create Virtual Machine**.

3. On the **Select Source** page, choose between the **Create the new virtual machine with a blank virtual hard disk** (the OS will have to be installed after the VM's creation) and **Use an existing virtual machine, VM template or virtual hard disk** options and then click on **Next**.

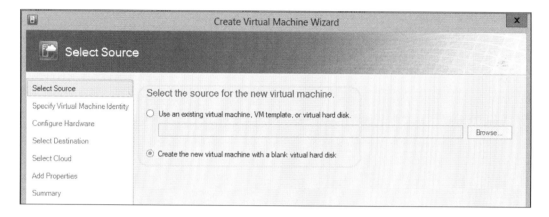

4. On the **Specify Virtual Machine Identity** page, type the virtual machine name (for example, W2012-FS02) and a description (optional), and then click on **Next**.

5. On the **Configure Hardware** page, provide the hardware settings or select a previously created hardware profile, and then click on **Next** as shown in the following screenshot.

For the VM to boot from the network (PXE Boot), in order to install an OS in the **Network Adapters** section, add a legacy network adapter type.

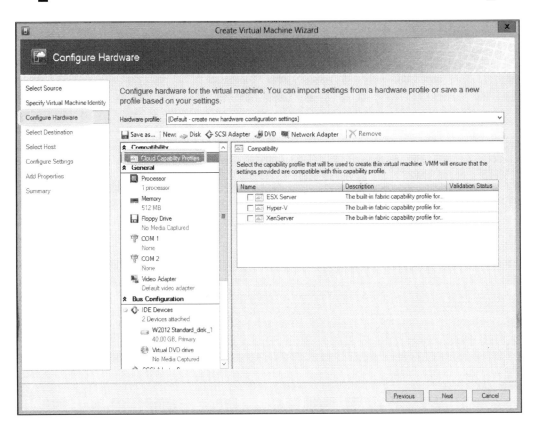

6. If you are creating a new VM from a blank VHD/VHDX disk, click on the **Bus Configuration** section; then click on **IDE Devices** and on the **Virtual DVD Drive** map within it, and select the ISO hosted in the VMM library or a CD/DVD drive with the OS media to be installed.

 To make the VM highly available, select **Make this virtual machine highly available** in the **Availability** section under the **Advanced** section.

7. On the **Select Destination** page, choose whether to deploy or store the VM (shown in the following screenshot) and click on **Next**.

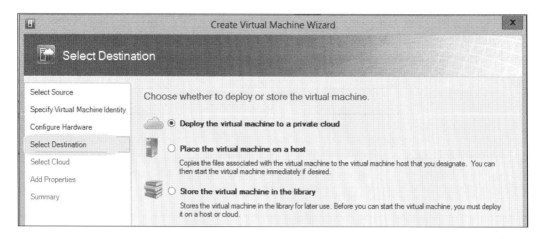

8. If you choose **Deploy the virtual machine to a private cloud**, select the cloud and click on **Next**.

9. If you choose **Place the virtual machine on a host**, select the host and click on **Next**. Then on the **Configuration settings** page, review/update the VM settings and click on **Next**. In the **Select Networks** section, select the VM network, virtual switch, and/or the VLAN to be used by this VM and then click on **Next**.

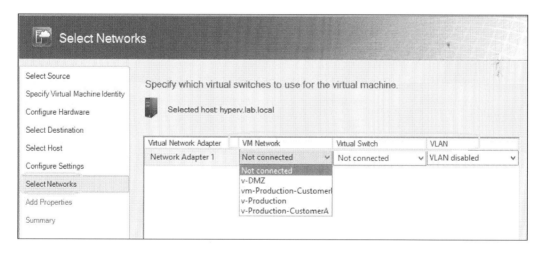

10. If you choose **Store the virtual machine in the library**, select the library server and click on **Next**. Then, click on **Browse** to select the share location path to deploy the VM and click on **Next**.

11. If you selected a cloud or a host, on the **Add properties** page, select the automatic actions that need to be taken.

12. On the **Summary** page, click on **Create**.

 Check the rating explanation for a better place to deploy.

How it works...

This recipe guided you to create and deploy VMs to a private cloud, to a specific host, or to store it in a VMM library. When **Create Virtual Machine Wizard** starts, select if VMM will deploy the new VM either to the private cloud, directly to a host, or to a library. Once VMM knows that the VM is to be deployed to a cloud or to a host, a list will be provided and each one will be rated (check the **Rate Explanation** tab) for how well it will be able to handle the VM.

 If a private cloud is configured, the options will differ depending on the user role and rights you are connected to.

VMM uses intelligent placement by analyzing hosts performance and rating them on a scale of one to five stars in order to weigh the better host/cloud available for deployment. The following table indicates how the ratings are calculated:

Rating	Formula
CPU	[1 – (CPU utilization / (100 – CPU reserve))] x CPU weight
Memory (RAM)	[1 – (RAM used / (Total RAM – RAM reserve))] x RAM weight
Disk I/O capacity	[1 – (Disk IOPS / Max disk IOPS] x Disk weight
Network	[1 – (Network utilization / (100 – Network reserve))] x Network weight

In **Configure Hardware**, take into account that the VMM adds a **legacy network adapter** by default. You should delete it and then add a **synthetic network adapter** to make use of it, and then connect it to a VM network or virtual switch.

 If you have standalone hosts running different processor versions in the same family (Intel to Intel, AMD to AMD), to allow live migration between the hosts, select **Allow migration to a virtual machine host with a different processor version** in the **Processor** section.

For private cloud support, click on the **Cloud Compatibility Profile** menu option and select the capability profile (Hyper-V, VMware ESX, or Citrix XenServer). VMM uses capability profiles to define the virtual machine's limits. By specifying the capability profile, VMM will determine how much maximum RAM, disk, and other resources can be assigned to a virtual machine.

You can use the **Save as...** option to save the hardware profile configuration.

If you are storing the VM in the VMM library before deploying it to a host, you need to use one of the default VMM library blank virtual hard disks on the **Select Source** page.

You can also use this recipe to create a VM template by running through the **Create a New Virtual Machine** wizard and selecting **Store the virtual machine in the library**. Name the file appropriately, for example, `W2012 Datacenter`.

 VMM will generalize the VM while running the **Create Virtual Machine Template** wizard from a deployed VM, but if you are creating a VM from an existing VHD file, make sure it has been generalized using **Sysprep** (`http://technet.microsoft.com/en-us/library/hh824816.aspx`), or the VM will have the same ID as the source.

There's more...

If you are creating a VM from an existing VHD file, you need to generalize the guest OS.

Generalizing the guest OS using Sysprep

1. Start the virtual machine.

2. Go through the steps to install the OS.

3. Once the OS has been installed, configure the server roles and features if necessary.

4. Run the Sysprep process (for Windows 2008 R2 it is found at `C:\Windows\System32\sysprep`).

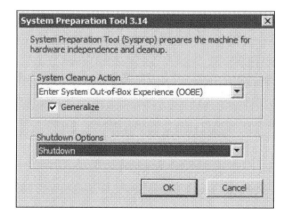

5. After the VM has shut down, copy the `SYSPREP VHD/CHDX` file to the library share.

6. The VM is now ready to be used as a template.

See also

▸ The *Creating virtual machine templates* recipe

▸ Refer to the *How to Create and Deploy a Virtual Machine from an Existing Virtual Machine* article available at `http://technet.microsoft.com/en-us/library/hh882400.aspx`

▸ Refer to the *How to Create and Deploy a Virtual Machine from an Existing Virtual Hard Disk* article available at `http://technet.microsoft.com/en-us/library/hh882391.aspx`

Creating virtual machine templates

In this recipe, we will create virtual machine templates that use a generalized image as the source.

VMM virtual machine templates are used to perform the automated installation and configuration of servers, dramatically reducing the time to release a server, and automate all these processes in a simple and uncomplicated deployment method.

Getting ready

Before you can create the virtual machine template, you need to create a new VM and install a Vanilla OS into it that will be used as the basis for the template. See the *Creating and deploying virtual machines* recipe of this chapter.

To create a VM template, you can select the source for which the template will be created from an existing template, a virtual disk (VHD) with a preinstalled operating system, or even a virtual machine that is being used in any host managed by VMM.

How to do it...

Carry out the following steps to create a VM template that is based on either an existing virtual hard disk or on a virtual machine template:

1. In the VMM 2012 console, click on the **Library** workspace, then on the ribbon, and then click on **Create VM Template**.

2. On the **Select Source** page, select **Use an existing VM template or a virtual hard disk stored in the library**.

3. Click on **Browse**, select a generalized Windows Server `.vhdx` file, then click on **OK**, and then click on **Next**.

4. Type the VM template name (for example, `W2012 Standalone Template`) and click on **Next**.

5. On the **Configure Hardware** page, provide the hardware settings or select a hardware profile and then click on **Next**.

> To make the template highly available, in the **Availability** section, which is present under the **Advanced** section, select **Make this virtual machine highly available**.
>
> If the network adapter is configured to use static IP addresses, the MAC address also needs to be configured as static.

6. On the **Configure Operating System** page, select a guest OS profile or provide the settings for the same, and then click on **Next** as shown in the following screenshot.

> The **Roles and Features** settings can only be installed if the VM template is used in a service template and the source virtual hard disk has Windows Server 2008 R2 or higher installed.

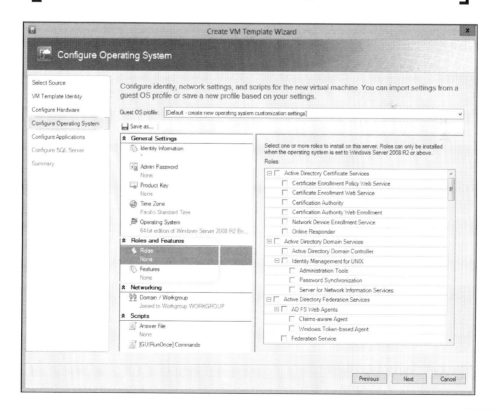

7. On the **Configure Applications** page, configure the settings or select an application profile, if any, and then click on **Next**.

8. On the **Configure SQL Server** page, configure the settings or select a SQL Server profile, if any, and then click on **Next**.

Application and SQL Server deployment settings do not apply if the template is designated for standalone VMs that are not part of a service.

9. On the **Summary** page, click on **Create**.

To verify if the template has been created, in the **Library** workspace expand **Templates** on the left-hand side pane and then click on **VM Templates**.

How it works...

Start by selecting the source for which the template will be created. You can use an existing template, a virtual disk (VHD/VHDX) with a preinstalled operating system, or even a virtual machine that is being used in any host managed by VMM.

On the **Configure Hardware** pane, specify the hardware configuration, such as a disk, network, memory, processor, or select an existing hardware profile. VMM adds a legacy network adapter by default. You should delete it and then add a synthetic network adapter to make use of it, and then connect it to a logical network or to a virtual network. Click on the **Cloud Compatibility Profile** menu option to select the capability profile to validate against the hardware profile for private cloud support. You can also use the **Save as...** option to save the hardware profile configuration.

On the **Configure Operating System** pane, specify the information for the Windows automated installation, such as computer name, product key, local administrator password, and operating system. By using the **#** symbol, the virtual machine will be named based on a numeric sequence. To create random names use the ***** symbol. If the template used has Windows 2008 R2 or the new Windows 2012 operating system, you can use the new **Roles and Features** option, which makes it possible to select the server roles and/or features that will automatically be installed.

In the **Configure Applications** option, you can add and configure applications and scripts to automatically be installed after the OS installation:

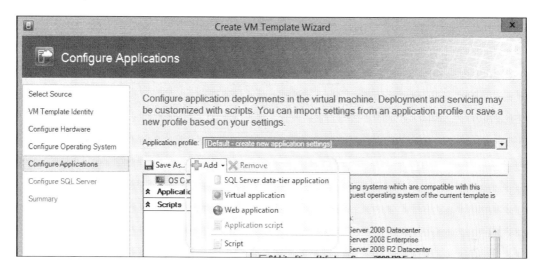

On the last screen in **Configure SQL Server**, you can also specify the SQL installation information and configuration.

To use the same options provided for automating the creation of templates through PowerShell, click on **View Script**.

There's more...

Now that the VM template has been created, let's see how we can deploy it.

Enabling MAC spoofing

The **Enable spoofing of MAC address** setting is required when planning to host the VM on a Windows 2008 R2 Hyper-V host with **Network Load Balancing** enabled.

There is a known issue when selecting the **Enable spoofing of MAC addresses** checkbox that it does not change the setting on the GUI.

The only way to enable MAC spoofing is by using the VMM command shell to configure this setting after you create the template. This is done in the following manner:

```
PS C:\> $VMTemp = Get-SCVMTemplate -Name "W2008R2 Enterprise"

PS C:\> $vNetAdapter = Get-SCVirtualNetworkAdapter -VMTemplate $VMTemp

PS C:\> Set-SCVirtualNetworkAdapter -VirtualNetworkAdapter $vNetAdapter
-EnableMACAddressSpoofing $True
```

Deploying virtual machines from virtual machine templates

Carry out the following steps to create virtual machines from the virtual machine templates:

1. In the VMM 2012 console at the bottom-left corner, click on the **VMs and Services** workspace.

2. On the ribbon, click on **Create VM Template**, then select **VM Template**.

3. On the **Select Source** page, select **Use an existing virtual machine, VM template, or virtual hard disk** and click on **Browse**.

4. Select the template (for example, `W2012 Standalone`), click on **OK**, and then click on **Next**.

5. In the **Specify Virtual Machine Identity** section, type the VM name (for example, `W2012-web01`) and click on **Next**.

6. On the **Configure Hardware** page, adjust any settings for the new VM and click on **Next**.

7. On the **Configure Operating System** page, provide the identity, network settings, and scripts (if any) for the new VM as shown in the following screenshot:

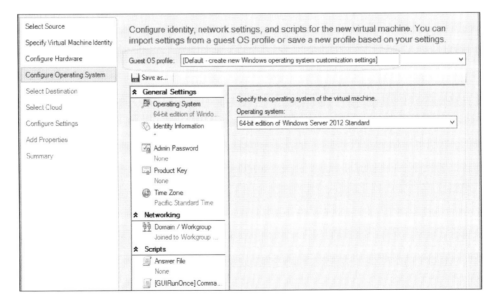

8. On the **Select Destination** page, choose whether to deploy the VM to a host or to a private cloud and click on **Next**.

9. If you choose **Deploy the virtual machine to private cloud**, select the cloud, and on the **Configuration settings** page, review/update the VM settings and click on **Next**.

10. If you choose **Place the virtual machine on a host**, select the host, click on **Next**, and on the **Configuration settings** page, review/update the VM settings and click on **Next**. On the **Select Networks** page, select the VM network, virtual switch, and/or VLAN to be used by this VM, and then click on **Next** as shown in the following screenshot:

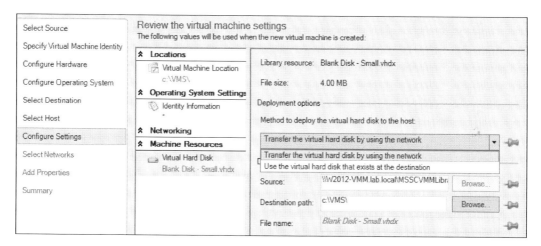

11. If you selected a cloud or a host, on the **Add properties** page select the automatic actions that are to be undertaken.

12. On the **Summary** page, click on **Create**.

 If you are placing the virtual machine on a host cluster, if you click on **Browse** in the **Select Destination Folder** dialog box, the file shares will be listed under the **File Shares** node.

See also

▸ Refer to the *How to Configure NLB for a Service Tier* article available at http://technet.microsoft.com/en-us/library/hh335098

Creating and deploying service templates

In VMM 2012, a **service** is a set of VMs configured and deployed together and managed as a single entity. For example, like the deployment of a three-tier business application or a frontend web application with SQL Server running in the background.

A service template provides the capability to separate the OS configuration from the application installation, leaving you with fewer OS images.

By using service templates, you will be able to leverage variations in capacity, easily adding or removing VMs needed to support the application.

[It is the best practice to wrap even a single VM template into a service template as you, for example, scale it out.]

Getting ready

Ensure that the resources that you need in order to create the service are available. Review and document all the elements that the service needs to be up and running before starting. For example:

▶ **What servers need to be deployed to support the service?**

▶ Which existing VM template will be used?

▶ What roles/features should be installed? What applications or scripts need to be deployed?

▶ Have the needed VMM resources been created and configured?

▶ Which networking components are to be connected to?

▶ Who will use the service?

[
 Take a look at a few important things you need to know:

▶ To install applications beforehand, have the installation files, scripts, and configuration made available

▶ To use Server App-V, make sure to have sequenced the applications

▶ To deploy a SQL Server instance on to a VM, make sure to have a VHD/VHDX file with a generalized SQL Server installation
]

How to do it...

Carry out the following steps to create the service template:

1. In the VMM 2012 console at the bottom-left corner, click on the **Library** workspace.

2. In the **Home** tab on the ribbon, click on **Create Service**, select **Create a service template**, and click on **OK**.

3. In the **New Service Template** dialog box, type the name for the service template (for example, `Marketing WebApp`).

4. Type the service template's release value for the version (for example, `1.0` or `CTP`) in replacement for the value **new**.

> The release value is important for when you need to update the service. It helps identify the version of the service template.

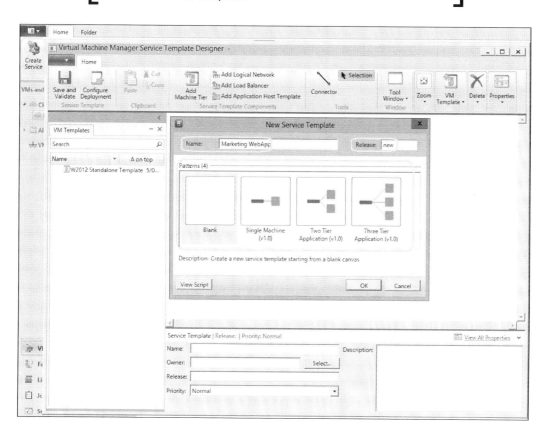

5. Select the number of tiers to create in the service template (for example, **Two Tier Application**, which creates blocks to be configured as VMs) and click on **OK**. Wait for the service to be created.

6. Depending on the option selected, the design area could be empty or could contain some default tiers.

You can add a tier to a service template by dragging a VM template on to the canvas area or by using the **Create Machine Tier Template** wizard.

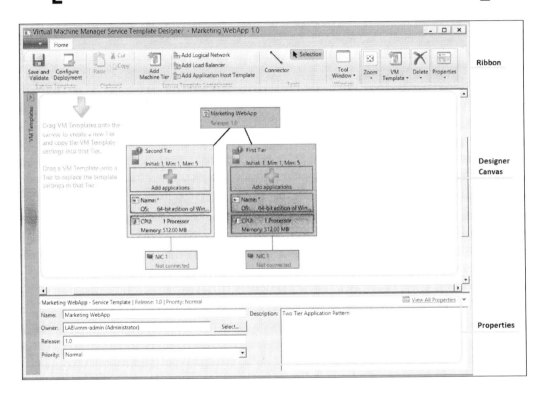

7. In the **Virtual Machine Manager Service Template Designer** window, perform the following steps for each of the networking components:

   ❏ On the ribbon, click on **Add Logical Network** (to add a box representing the logical network) and select the logical network box (for example, **NIC 1**)

   ❏ In the properties pane (bottom), select the network to be associated from the **Network** list

   ❏ On the ribbon, click on **Connector** and then drag the connector from the logical network box to the network adapter box

> A connecting line linking both boxes will appear, indicating that the logical network is connected to the network adapter.

8. On the ribbon, click on **Save and Validate** and then click on **Configure Deployment**.

   Type the name of the service template to be published and click on **OK**.

   A configuration issues warning icon will be displayed if there is a validation error, and an error icon indicating which tier/element is causing the error will be displayed as shown in the following screenshot:

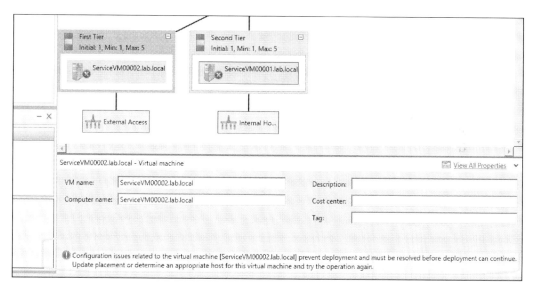

How it works...

A **service template** is a set of elements (for example, VMs, apps, network) bonded to define the services' configuration.

To create a service template in the VMM console, click on **Create a Service** to open the **Virtual Machine Manager Service Template Designer** window.

You can use an existing VM template on a service template, which includes the VMs (deployed as a service), applications to be installed, and network settings.

After the service template is created, you can add/remove elements (for example, VMs, network, apps), deploy it to a private cloud/host, and/or deploy the updated service template to a deployed service to update it as well.

After the service template has been saved, it will be located in the **Library** workspace on the service templates node. To open an existing one, click on the **Library** workspace, then in the designer select the service template. On the ribbon in the **Service Template** tab, click on **Open Designer**.

 If you are changing a service template that is in use by a deployed service, a new release value will be required before saving.

There's more...

Now that we have created the service template, let's deploy it.

Deploying a service from the VMs and Services workspace

The **Deploy Service** window contains three panes. The left pane contains two tabs, namely **Services Components**, which lists the service tiers that will be deployed, and **Settings**, which shows the configuration that will be used for application deployment.

The center pane shows the service design with all instances that will be deployed as part of the service.

The right pane is a **Minimap**, which contains a map of the service. This is illustrated in the following screenshot:

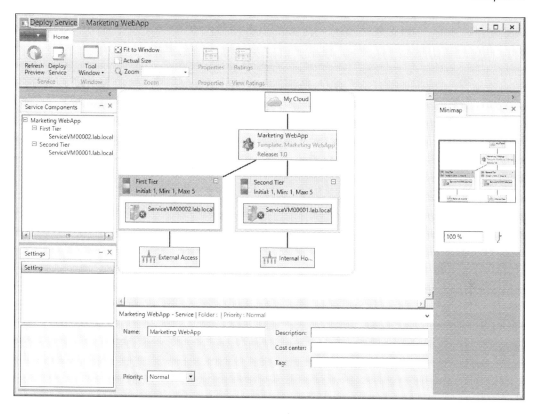

Carry out the following steps to deploy a service:

1. In the VMM 2012 console at the bottom-left corner, click on the **VMs and Services** workspace.

2. Select the private cloud or host group to deploy the service.

3. Under the **Home** tab on the ribbon, click on **Create Service**.

4. In the **Create Service** dialog box, click on **Use an existing service template**, then click on **Browse** and select the service template (for example, **Marketing WebApp**), and click on **OK**.

5. Type the service name and enter the location in the **Destination** list.

6. Click on **OK**.

VMM performs a placement check to determine the best location on which to deploy the service and then opens the **Deploy Service** window. Follow the steps described to resolve any errors and warnings, and then deploy the service. For information about making changes, refer to *How to Configure Deployment Settings for a Service* available at `http://technet.microsoft.com/en-us/library/hh411278`.

Scaling out a service in VMM

The **scale out** feature in VMM is useful if you are required to set up additional VMs on any tier of a deployed service. For example, during Australian Boxing Day, due to the increase in online sales and hence an increase in web traffic, your website may require additional servers (IIS, app, or SQL Server, for example) to handle the increase in traffic. The scale out process creates a new VM identically configured to the other VMs in the tier, deploying OS roles and features and required applications.

It requires a load balancer and a VIP template in the service definition. See *Configuring Load Balancing in VMM Overview* available at `http://technet.microsoft.com/en-us/library/jj721573.aspx`.

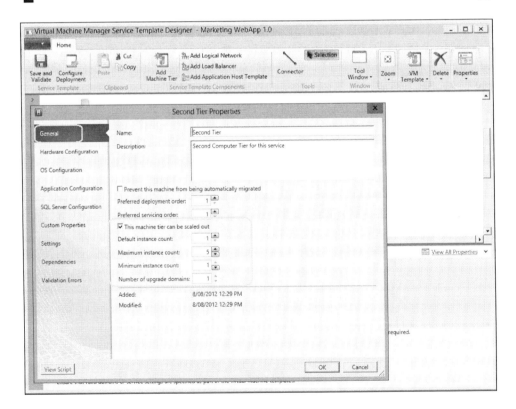

Updating a service in VMM

To allow an update on a deployed service based on a service template, VMM retains the trail of which service template was used to deploy that service (that is why you are required to increase the release version before saving the new version). To update a deployed service, you can use the following two methods:

▶ **Apply updates to existing virtual machines in-place**

▶ **Deploy new virtual machines with updated settings**

The following screenshot illustrates the use of these methods:

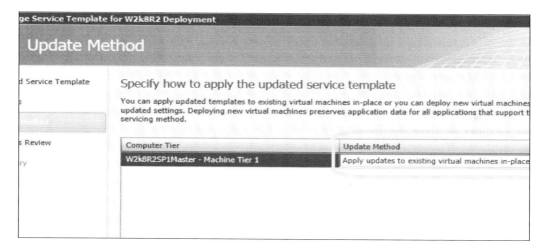

See also

▶ The *How to Configure the Properties of a Service Template* article available at
http://technet.microsoft.com/en-us/library/hh410346

▶ The *How to Add a Tier to a Service Template* article available at
http://technet.microsoft.com/en-us/library/hh410345

▶ The *How to Deploy a Service in VMM* article available at
http://technet.microsoft.com/en-us/library/gg650471

▶ The *How to scale out a service in VMM* article available at
http://technet.microsoft.com/en-us/library/gg675080.aspx

▶ The *How to Create an Updated Service Template in VMM* article available at
http://technet.microsoft.com/en-us/library/gg675120

▶ The *How to Apply Updates to a Deployed Service in VMM* article available at
http://technet.microsoft.com/en-us/library/gg675106

Rapidly provisioning a virtual machine by using SAN Copy

This recipe will guide you through the steps to rapidly provision a virtual machine by using the **Storage Area Network** (**SAN**) Copy technology (for example, snapshots and cloning).

Rapid provisioning can quickly create and deploy VMs, but to use a SAN Copy-capable template, the storage must support SAN Copy through cloning or snapshots.

The SAN Copy-capable template allows VMM, when deploying a new VM, to create a read/write copy of the LUN containing the VHD/VHDX file, which then places the VM files on the new LUN assigned to a destination host/cluster. For this operation, storage transfer is used instead of a network transfer.

Getting ready

Make sure that the following prerequisites are met if you want to use the SAN Copy capability:

▶ Storage support for VMM storage management using SMI-S or SMP provider.

▶ Storage support for cloning or snapshots.

▶ Storage providers installed, configured, and accessible from the Hyper-V servers and **VMM management server**.

▶ If you are planning rapid provisioning, **VMM** should be managing the storage pool and it should be allocated to a host group. Also included are the following prerequisites:

  ❑ The target Hyper-V hosts should be members of a host group and should use the same type of storage connectivity

  ❑ The library server should be a member of the same host group and a Hyper-V host, if you are planning to create a SAN Copy-capable template from an existing VM and want to create and assign the LUN from a library server

▶ The **Multipath I/O** (**MPIO**) feature should be added to each host that needs a fiber channel or iSCSI storage array.

> Making use of the **Microsoft Device Specific Module** (**DSM**), VMM automatically enables MPIO for supported storages.
>
> If you have already installed vendor-specific DSMs, they will be used to communicate with the storage instead.
>
> If before adding the MPIO feature you add a Hyper-V host to a VMM management server, you will be required to configure the MPIO or install vendor-specific DSMs manually outside VMM.

▸ If you are using fiber channel storage, each host that will access the storage array must have a **host bus adapter** (**HBA**) installed and should be zoned accordingly so that it can access the storage array.

▸ If you are using an iSCSI SAN, make sure that iSCSI portals have been added, the iSCSI initiator is logged into the array, and the **Microsoft iSCSI Initiator Service** on each host has been started and is set to **Automatic**.

You need to create an NTFS-formatted LUN beforehand and assign a drive letter from the managed storage pool. You can use one of the following steps to carry out this process:

▸ Using the VMM console in the Hyper-V host properties window, click on the **Storage** tab. See `http://go.microsoft.com/fwlink/p/?LinkID=212536`.

▸ Using the VMM console in the **Fabric** workspace, click on **Storage**. See `http://go.microsoft.com/fwlink/p/?LinkID=213750`.

▸ Use the storage vendor management tool.

How to do it...

Carry out the following steps to create a SAN Copy-capable VHD/VHDX on a host:

1. In the VMM console at the bottom-left corner, click on the **VMs and Services** workspace.

2. Under the **Home** tab on the ribbon, click on and select **Create Virtual Machine**.

3. On the **Select Source** page, click on **Create the new virtual machine with a blank virtual hard disk** and then click on **Next**.

4. On the **Specify Virtual Machine Identity** page, type the VM name (for example, `W2012-Datacenter`), an optional description, and click on **Next**.

5. On the **Configure Hardware** page, confirm/change the hardware settings and click on **Next**.

6. On the **Select Destination** page, select **Place the virtual machine on a host** and click on **Next**.

7. On the **Select Host** page, select a host with the assigned LUN and click on **Next**.

8. On the **Configure Settings** page, click on **Virtual Machine Location**.

9. On the results pane, click on **Browse**, verify the text that the **SAN (Migration Capable)** field displays after the drive information, and select the drive (for example, **(S:\) [199.2 GB free of 200 GB, SAN (Migration Capable)]**).

10. Click on **OK**, and in **Machine Resources** click on **Virtual Hard Disk**.

11. In the results pane, click on **Browse**, select the same drive selected in step 9 (that is, **S**), and click on **OK**.

12. Click on **Next** to continue.

13. On the **Select Networks** page, select the VM network, virtual switch, and/or VLAN setting.

14. On the **Add properties** page, select the automatic actions to be undertaken.

15. On the **Summary** page, click on **Create**.

 Once the new virtual machine is deployed, install and configure the guest OS, server roles, features, and applications. Generalize the image. See the *Generalizing the guest OS using Sysprep* subsection in the *Creating and deploying virtual machines* recipe of this chapter.

How it works...

To use the SAN Copy capability, you must create and assign an empty storage LUN from a storage pool to the target host beforehand. You can either use VMM or the storage vendor management tools for this purpose.

The next step is to create a VM with a blank virtual hard disk (VHD/VHDX) file on that LUN.

Then, install and customize the guest OS and applications and generalize the image by using Sysprep.

To finalize, using **New VM Template** create a SAN Copy-capable template from the created VM. VMM will then transfer the files in the LUN from the host to the VMM library, through a SAN transfer.

 The library will index the new VHD/VHDX file during the next refresh.

There's more...

Now let's create a SAN Copy-capable template and then deploy it.

Creating a SAN Copy-capable template

Carry out the following steps to create a SAN Copy-capable template:

1. In the VMM 2012 console at the bottom-left corner, click on the **Library** workspace.

2. On the ribbon, click on **Create VM Template**.

3. On the **Select Source** page, click on **From an existing virtual machine that is deployed on a host**.

4. Click on **Browse**, select the VM (for example, **W2012-Datacenter**), click on **OK**, and then click on **Next**.

5. Then, click on **Yes**.

6. On the **VM Template Identity** page, type the VM template name (for example, W2012 Datacenter Template - SAN Provision) and click on **Next**.

7. On the **Configure Hardware** and **Configure Operating System** pages, click on **Next**.

8. On the **Select Library Server** page, select the VMM library after verifying if the **Transfer Type** column indicates **SAN**, and click on **Next**.

9. On the **Select Path** page, click on **Browse**. Select the path to store the VM files, click on **OK**, and then click on **Next**.

10. On the **Summary** page, click on **Create**.

Deploying a virtual machine through rapid provisioning

Carry out the following steps to deploy a VM using rapid provisioning:

1. In the VMM console at the bottom-left corner, click on the **VMs and Services** workspace.

2. In the **Home** tab on the ribbon, click on and select **Create Virtual Machine**.

3. On the **Select Source** page, click on **Use an existing virtual machine, VM template or virtual hard disk** and then click on **Browse**.

4. In **Type: VM Template**, select the previously created template (for example, **W2012 Datacenter Template – SAN Provision**) and click on **OK**.

 Make sure **SAN Copy Capable** shows **Yes**.

5. On the **Select Source** page, click on **Next**.

6. Complete the steps featured in the wizard to create and deploy the VM by taking the following points into consideration:

   ❑ On the **Configure Hardware** page in the **Bus Configuration** section, select the storage classification that ties the LUN classification (or do not use classification at all—leave it empty)

   ❑ On the **Select Host** page or the **Select Cloud** page, verify that the **Transfer Type** field indicates **SAN**

See also

▶ The *How to Create a SAN Copy-Capable Template from an Existing Virtual Machine* article available at `http://technet.microsoft.com/en-us/library/gg610597.aspx`

▶ The *How to Deploy a New Virtual Machine from the SAN Copy-Capable Template* article available at `http://technet.microsoft.com/en-us/library/gg610618`

▶ The *Storage Automation in VMM 2012* article available at `http://blogs.technet.com/b/scvmm/archive/2011/03/29/storage-automation-in-vmm-2012.aspx`

6
Upgrading from SCVMM 2008 R2 SP1

In this chapter, we will cover the following topics:

- ▶ Reviewing the upgrade options
- ▶ Checking the VMM system requirements and preparing for the upgrade
- ▶ Upgrading to VMM 2012 SP1
- ▶ Reassociating hosts after upgrading
- ▶ Updating the VMM agents
- ▶ Performing other post-upgrade tasks

Introduction

This chapter is about guiding you through the requirements and steps necessary to upgrade your VMM 2008 R2 SP1 to VMM 2012 or VMM 2012 SP1.

 There is no direct upgrade path from VMM 2008 R2 to VMM 2012 SP1. You must first upgrade to VMM 2012, and then to VMM 2012 SP1. SCVMM 2008 R2 SP1-> SCVMM 2012-> SCVMM 2012 SP1 is the correct upgrade path.

As discussed in *Chapter 1, VMM 2012 Architecture*, VMM 2012 is a huge product upgrade and there are many improvements. With VMM 2012, you will have the ability to:

 ▶ Deliver a flexible and cost-effective private cloud fabric by pooling and dynamically allocating virtualized resources (computer, network, and storage), and also enabling a self-service infrastructure experience

 ▶ Provision applications by using service modeling, service configuration, and image-based management

 ▶ Create and manage a Private Cloud across multiple hypervisors (Microsoft Hyper-V, VMware ESXi, and Citrix XenDesktop)

 ▶ Optimize the usage of resources based on workload demands

For more details on the new improvements, go through *Chapter 1, VMM 2012 Architecture.*

 Before we start, I would recommend you to go through *Chapter 1, VMM 2012 Architecture*, paying special attention to the recipe *Specifying the correct system requirements for a real-world scenario.*

Reviewing the upgrade options

This recipe will guide you through the upgrade options for VMM 2012 SP1. Keep in mind that there is no direct upgrade path from VMM 2008 R2 to VMM 2012 SP1.

How to do it...

Read through the following recommendations in order to upgrade your current VMM installation.

In-place upgrade from VMM 2008 R2 SP1 to VMM 2012

Use this method if your system meets the requirements for a VMM 2012 upgrade and you want to deploy it on the same server. The supported VMM version to upgrade from is VMM 2008 R2 SP1. If you need to upgrade VMM 2008 R2 to VMM 2008 R2 SP1, see `http://go.microsoft.com/fwlink/?LinkID=197099`.

Also keep in mind that if you are running the SQL Server Express version, you will need to upgrade SQL Server to a fully supported version beforehand as the Express version is not supported in VMM 2012.

Once the system requirements are met and all of the prerequisites are installed, the upgrade process is straightforward. To follow the detailed recipe, see the *Upgrading to VMM 2012 SP1* section.

Upgrading to VMM 2012 or to VMM 2012 SP1 on a different computer

Sometimes, you may not be able to do an in-place upgrade to VMM 2012, or even to VMM 2012 SP1. In this case, it is recommended that you use the following instructions:

1. Uninstall the current VMM *retaining the database*, and then restore the database on a supported version of SQL Server.

2. Next, on a new server (or on the same server, as long it meets the hardware and OS requirements), install the VMM 2012 or VMM 2012 SP1 prerequisites.

3. Finally, install VMM 2012, providing the retained database information on the **Database configuration** dialog and the VMM setup will upgrade the database. When the install process finishes, upgrade the Hyper-V hosts with the latest VMM agents.

The following figure illustrates the upgrade process for VMM 2008 R2 SP1 to VMM 2012:

When performing an upgrade from VMM 2008 R2 SP1 with a local VMM database to a different server, the encrypted data will not be preserved as the encryption keys are stored locally. The same rule applies when upgrading from VMM 2012 to VMM 2012 SP1 and not using **Distributed Key Management** (**DKM**) in VMM 2012.

Upgrading to VMM 2012 SP1

To upgrade to VMM 2012 SP1, you should already be running VMM 2012. VMM 2012 SP1 requires Windows Server 2012. If planning an in-place upgrade, back up the VMM database, uninstall VMM 2012 and App Controller (if applicable) *retaining the database*, perform an OS upgrade, and then install VMM 2012 SP1 and App Controller.

More planning considerations

- ▸ **Virtual Server 2005 R2**: VMM 2012 does not support Microsoft Virtual Server 2005 R2 anymore.

 If you have Virtual Server 2005 R2 or an unsupported ESXi version running, and you do not remove these hosts before the upgrade, they will be removed automatically during the upgrade process.

- ▸ **VMware ESX and vCenter**: For VMM 2012, the supported versions of VMware are from ESXi 3.5 to ESXi 4.1, and vCenter 4.1. For VMM 2012 SP1, the supported VMware versions are from ESXi 4.1 to ESXi 5.1, and vCenter 4.1 and 5.0.

- ▸ **SQL Server Express**: It is not supported by VMM 2012. A full version is required. For more details, go through *Chapter 1, VMM 2012 Architecture*.

- ▸ **Performance and Resource Optimization (PRO)**: The PRO configurations are not kept during an upgrade to VMM 2012. If you have an Operations Manager (**SCOM**) integration configured, it will be removed during the upgrade process. Once the upgrade process is finished, you can integrate SCOM with VMM.

- ▸ **Library server**: VMM 2012 does not support a library server on Windows Server 2003. If you have it running and you continue with the upgrade, you will not be able to use it. To use the same library server in VMM 2012, move it to a server running a supported OS before starting the upgrade.

- ▸ **Choosing a service account and Distributed Key Management (DKM) settings during an upgrade**: During an upgrade to VMM 2012, on the **Configure service account and distributed key management** page of the setup, you are required to create a VMM service account (preferably a domain account) and choose whether you want to use DKM to store encryption keys in **Active Directory** (**AD**).

   Make sure to log on with the same account that was used during the VMM 2008 R2 installation. This needs to be done because, in some situations after the upgrade, depending on the selected VMM service account, the encrypted data (for example, passwords in templates) will not be available and you will be required to re-enter them manually.

   For the service account, you can use either the Local System account or a domain account (*recommended*). However, when deploying a highly available VMM management server, the only option available is a domain account.

 Note that DKM is not available in versions prior to VMM 2012.

▶ **Upgrading to a highly available VMM 2012**: If you're thinking of upgrading to a High Available (HA) VMM, consider the following:

  ❑ **Failover Cluster**: You must deploy the failover cluster before starting the upgrade.

  ❑ **VMM database**: You cannot deploy the SQL server for the VMM database on the highly available VMM management servers. If you're planning on upgrading the current VMM server to an HA VMM, you need to first move the database to another server. For best practice, it is recommended to have the SQL Server cluster separated from the VMM cluster.

  ❑ **Library server**: On a production or High Available environment, you need to consider all of the VMM components to be High Available as well, and not only the VMM management server. After upgrading to an HA VMM management server, it is recommended, for best practice, to relocate the VMM library to a clustered file server. In order to keep the custom fields and properties of the saved VMs, deploy those VMs to a host and save them to a new VMM 2012 library.

  ❑ **VMM Self-Service Portal**: It is not supported in VMM 2012 SP1. I would recommend you to install System Center App Controller instead.

How it works...

There are two methods to upgrade to VMM 2012 from VMM 2008 R2 SP1, in-place upgrade and upgrading to another server. Before starting, review the initial steps and the VMM 2012 prerequisites, and perform a full backup of the VMM database.

Uninstall VMM 2008 R2 SP1 (retaining the data), and restore the VMM database to another SQL server running a supported version. During the installation, point to that database in order to have it upgraded. After the upgrade is finished, upgrade the host agents.

 VMM will be rolled back automatically in the event of a failure during the upgrade process, reverting to its original installation/configuration.

There's more...

The names of the VMM services have been changed in VMM 2012. If you have any applications or scripts referring to these service names, update them accordingly:

VMM version	VMM service display name	Service name
2008 R2 SP1	Virtual Machine Manager	vmmservice
	Virtual Machine Manager Agent	vmmagent
2012 / 2012 SP1	System Center Virtual Machine Manager	scvmmservice
	System Center Virtual Machine Manager Agent	scvmmagent

See also

▶ The *Release notes for Virtual Machine Manager in System Center 2012 SP1* page at `http://technet.microsoft.com/en-us/library/jj656801.aspx`.

▶ The *Software requirements* section in the *Specifying the correct system requirements for a real-world scenario* recipe in *Chapter 1, VMM 2012 Architecture*.

▶ To move the file-based resources (for example, ISO images, scripts, and VHD/VHDX), refer to `http://technet.microsoft.com/en-us/library/hh406929`.

▶ To move virtual machine templates, refer to `http://go.microsoft.com/fwlink/p/?LinkID=212431`.

Checking the VMM system requirements and preparing for the upgrade

This recipe will guide you through the steps required to check if your current VMM 2008 R2 SP1 installation meets the requirements for an upgrade to VMM 2012. The recipe will also help you with the initial steps that need to be carried out in order to prepare the environment for a VMM 2012 in-place upgrade.

Getting ready

First, you need to know that upgrading from the Beta versions and versions prior to VMM 2008 R2 SP1 is not supported.

Confirm that your system meets the requirements. See the *Supported OS and Servers* section of the *Specifying the correct system requirements for a real-world scenario* recipe in *Chapter 1, VMM 2012 Architecture*.

A direct upgrade from VMM 2008 R2 SP1 to VMM 2012 SP1 is not supported. You need to first upgrade to VMM 2012.

How to do it...

Carry out the following steps to check if your environment meets the system requirements, and to perform the initial steps for an in-place upgrade to VMM 2012:

1. Remove the integration of SCOM with SCVMM.

2. Remove the integration of SCVMM with VMware vCenter.

3. Wait for the completion of all jobs running in VMM.

4. Close the VMM console, the VMM command shell, and the VMM Self-Service Portal.

5. Perform a full backup of the VMM database (see `http://go.microsoft.com/fwlink/?LinkID=162661`).

6. If your VMM library is running on another machine, make sure that the OS version meets the minimum requirements. Upgrade the OS if necessary.

7. Update the server by running Windows Update.

8. Verify that there are no pending restarts on the server. Restart the server if necessary.

 The job history will be deleted during the upgrade.

Uninstalling previous versions of Windows Automated Installation Kit (WAIK)

VMM 2012 requires WAIK for Windows 7. In VMM 2012 SP1, Windows ADK replaced WAIK as a VMM prerequisite. To uninstall WAIK, follow these instructions:

1. In **Control Panel | Programs | Programs and Features**, select **Windows Automated Installation Kit**.

2. Click on **Uninstall** and then follow the wizard to uninstall the program.

3. Click on **Yes** to confirm, click on **Finish**, and then restart the server.

Checking whether Windows Remote Management (WinRM) is started

It is a prerequisite to have the WinRM service running and set to **Automatic**. The following steps will help you with this:

1. In the **Services** console (services.msc), locate and select the **Windows Remote Management (WS-Management)** service. If the **Status** is not showing **Started** and/ or the **Startup Type** is showing **Manual**, change the settings by right-clicking on the service and then clicking on **Properties**. This is shown in the following screenshot:

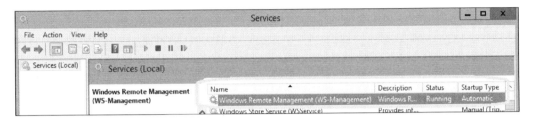

2. On the **Properties** dialog box, change the **Startup Type** to **Automatic**, click on **Start** to initiate the service, and then click on **OK**.

How it works...

If your VMM 2008 R2 does not have the SP1 update applied to it, start by applying it in order for it to be supported for the upgrade to VMM 2012. If you are planning to do an in-place upgrade to VMM 2012 SP1, and if you are running Windows Server 2008 R2, you need to carry it out in two phases:

1. **Upgrade from VMM 2008 R2 SP1 to VMM 2012**: Carry out a VMM database backup, remove VMM 2008 R2 SP1 (choosing to retain data), and then during the VMM 2012 installation, provide the previously saved database. VMM 2012 will upgrade the database during the installation.

2. **Upgrade from VMM 2012 to VMM 2012 SP1**: As VMM 2012 SP1 requires Windows Server 2012, you first need to run an in-place upgrade of the OS to Windows Server 2012 (see *Installing Windows 2012*, `http://technet.microsoft.com/en-us/library/jj134246.aspx`), install the prerequisites, and then carry out the upgrade from VMM 2012 to VMM 2012 SP1.

During the upgrade process, if you did not install the **Command Line Utilities** for SQL Server beforehand, a warning will be shown in the prerequisites check phase. Although you can proceed without installing these utilities, it is not recommended as they are required to perform some management tasks (see the *SQL Server Connectivity Feature Pack Components* section under the *Installing VMM dependencies* recipe in *Chapter 2, Installing SCVMM 2012*).

The Windows Remote Management (WS-Management) service must be started and set to automatic before starting the upgrade, otherwise an error will appear during the prerequisites check.

There's more...

Review the software requirements for VMM Management as given in *Chapter 1, VMM 2012 Architecture* under the recipe *Specifying the correct system requirements for a real-world scenario*.

Install these prerequisites as well:

- Windows Assessment and Deployment Kit (Windows ADK)
- SQL Server Command Line Utilities (for the supported and installed version of SQL)
- Microsoft SQL Server Native Client

Upgrading to VMM 2012 SP1

This recipe will guide you through the tasks required to upgrade VMM 2008 R2 SP1 to VMM 2012, showcasing the possible options and actions. It will then highlight the upgrade path to VMM 2012 SP1.

 A direct upgrade from VMM 2008 R2 SP1 to VMM 2012 SP1 is not supported. You need first to upgrade to VMM 2012. See the *Upgrading to VMM 2012 SP1* section in this recipe to upgrade VMM 2012 to VMM 2012 SP1.

Getting ready

Go through the recipe *Checking the VMM system requirements and preparing for the upgrade* after deciding the upgrade method (in-place upgrade or upgrade to another server), and make sure you've installed all of the prerequisites.

If you're planning an in-place upgrade of VMM 2008 R2 SP1 running on a server with an OS other than the supported version, first upgrade the OS, and then carry out the steps to upgrade to VMM 2012, as described in this recipe.

How to do it...

To upgrade to VMM 2012 SP1 from VMM 2008 R2, you first need to carry out the following steps in order to upgrade your VMM 2008 R2 SP1 to VMM 2012:

1. On the VMM 2008 R2 SP1 console, click on **General** in the **Administration** view. Next, click on **Back up Virtual Machine Manager** in the **Actions** pane. All of these are depicted in the following screenshot:

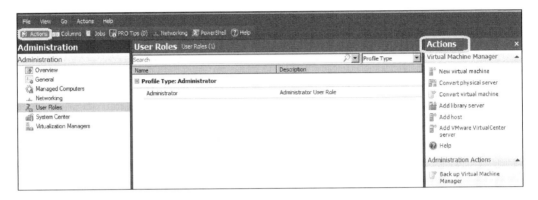

2. In the **Virtual Machine Manager Backup** dialog box, type in the path for the destination folder for the backup file. The folder must not be a root directory and it must be accessible to the SQL Server database.

3. Take note of the backup location as we will need it later during the VMM 2012 upgrade.

4. If you're doing an in-place upgrade and running a full version of SQL Server, go to step 7.

5. If you're upgrading to another server or running SQL Server Express, uninstall SCVMM 2008 R2 SP1, remove all of the components, and choose **Retain Database** during the removal of the SCVMM 2008 R2 SP1 Server service.

6. If you're running SQL Server 2005 Express Edition:

   i. Click on **Start** and in the **Search programs and files** box, or in the **Run** window, type in `services.msc` and press *Enter*. Stop the **SQL Server (MICROSOFTVMM)** service.

   ii. Copy **VirtualManagerDB** and **VirtualManagerDB_log** from `C:\Program Files(x86)\Microsoft SQL Server\MSSQL.1\MSSQL\Data` to a backup folder (for example, `C:\backup`).

iii. In **Control Panel\Programs\Programs and Features**, select **Microsoft SQL Server 2005** and click on **Uninstall**, as shown in the following screenshot:

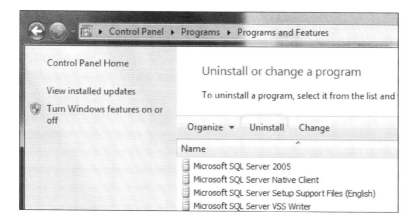

iv. On the **Component Selection** page, select the **Remove SQL Server 2005 instance components** checkbox, and also select the **Workstation Components** checkbox.

v. On the confirmation page, click on **Finish** to complete the uninstall process.

vi. In **Add or Remove Programs**, select **Microsoft SQL Native Client**, and then click on **Remove**.

vii. In the confirmation dialog box, click on **Yes**. Install a full version of SQL Server (it is recommended to install it on another server). See the *Deploying a Microsoft SQL Server for VMM implementation* recipe in *Chapter 2, Installing SCVMM 2012*.

viii. Restore the VMM database backup to SQL Server. For doing this, open SQL Server Management Studio and select **Restore Database**. On the **Specify Backup** window, click on **Add** and navigate to C:\backup. Enter VirtualManagerDB as the new name. Select **Restore** and click on **OK**. On successful restoration, a pop-up will be displayed. Click on **OK** and close SQL Server Management Studio.

7. Browse to the installation media and double-click on setup.exe.

8. On the main setup page, click on **Install**.

9. Click on **Yes** to confirm the upgrade to VMM 2012, as shown in the following screenshot:

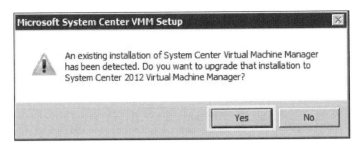

10. On the **Features to be upgraded** page, confirm that **VMM management** and **VMM console** are selected and click on **Next**.

11. On the **Product registration information** page, enter the VMM product key, and then click on **Next** (if you don't provide a product key, VMM 2012 will be installed as a trial version).

12. On the **Please read this license agreement** page, tick the **I have read, understood, and agree with the terms of the license agreement** checkbox, and click on **Next**.

13. On the Join the Customer Experience Improvement Program (CEIP)... page, choose either one of the options, **Yes** or **No**, and click on **Next**.

14. On the **Microsoft Update** page, select **On (recommended)** to use Microsoft Update and click on **Next**.

15. On the **Installation location** page, provide the path for the installation and then click on **Next**.

 My recommendation is to use the OS partition (C:) only for the operating system. It is recommended to place the VMM program files on a separate drive.

16. In the **Database Configuration** page, specify the **Server name** of the SQL Server and the **Instance name**; for example, **MSSQLSERVER**.

17. Select **Existing database** and choose **VirtualManagerDB** (or whichever name the restored database has) from the drop-down menu, as shown in the following screenshot:

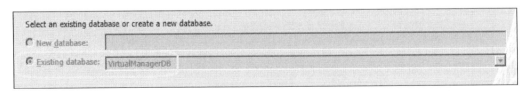

18. Click on **Next**, and click on **Yes** when you get the "The selected database...Do you want to upgrade it?" message, as shown in the following screenshot:

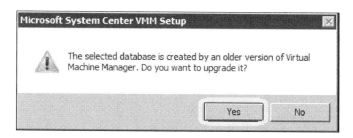

19. On the **Configure service account and distributed key management** page (shown in the next screenshot), select the account for Virtual Machine Manager Service.

20. If your selection is **Domain Account**, type in the username and domain in the format `domain\user`, enter the password, and click on **Next**.

 You will not be able to change the account after the VMM installation is complete, as this is not supported.

21. In the **Distributed Key Management** section, select **Store my keys in Active Directory** if you decide to use DKM (recommended approach).

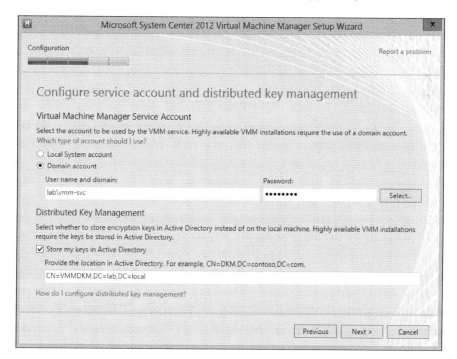

22. On the **Port configuration** page, leave the default port numbers unchanged or provide a unique value for each feature, and then click on **Next**.

 Plan and document the ports before choosing them as you cannot change them again; it would require reinstalling VMM.

23. You might find certain issues listed on the page that says **Upgrade compatibility report**. In this case, you can either click on **Next** to proceed with the upgrade, or click on **Cancel** to cancel the upgrade and resolve the issues.

24. On the **Installation summary** page, click on **Install**, and then click on **Close** to finish.

How it works...

Just like all upgrade processes, the VMM upgrade process requires planning. Start by confirming that the current server/VM meets the system requirements for VMM 2012.

Decide the upgrade method among an in-place upgrade and upgrading to another server. An in-place upgrade will not be successful if the database version is not supported.

Back up the current VMM database. If you're running SQL Express Edition, you will need to uninstall VMM 2008 R2 SP1, retaining the data. You will then need to install a fully supported SQL version, restore the VMM database, and then start the VMM 2012 upgrade process.

 If you are running a small VMM 2012 installation, you can install SQL on the same server, as long it is not an HA VMM, as discussed in *Chapter 1, VMM 2012 Architecture*.

Start the VMM 2012 installer and carry out the upgrade steps, reviewing and paying special attention to the database and DKM configuration, and confirming your options in all of the upgrade dialogs. At the end of the process, open the VMM console to confirm the upgrade and update the agent hosts to VMM 2012.

During the migration process, if the database is not compatible, the following pop-up dialog (showing an error) will appear:

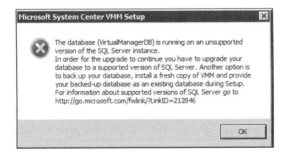

There's more...

Now let's talk about the VMM 2012 SP1 upgrade and the upgradation of the other VMM components.

Upgrading to VMM 2012 SP1

If you are running VMM 2012, you can upgrade to VMM 2012 SP1. As VMM 2012 SP1 requires Windows Server 2012, you will need to upgrade the OS beforehand.

Make sure you take a backup of the VMM database. Next, I would recommend that you uninstall VMM 2012, *retaining the database*, followed by the installation of the VMM 2012 SP1 prerequisites.

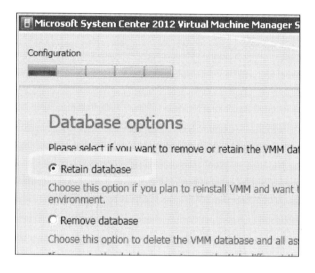

Proceed with the VMM 2012 SP1 installation using the same database. For more details on installing VMM 2012 SP1, see the *Installing a VMM management server* recipe in *Chapter 2, Installing SCVMM 2012*.

Upgrading a VMM console

Close the VMM Administrator Console and the Virtual Machine Manager command shell (if open), and then pick one of the following options:

▶ **Option 1**: In-place upgrade

▶ **Option 2**: Uninstallation of the VMM 2008 R2 SP1 console

If you picked option 1, you will need to carry out the following steps:

1. Browse to the installation media and run the setup file.
2. On the main setup page, click on **Install**.
3. Go through the installation steps.

If you picked option 2, you will need to carry out the following steps:

1. In **Control Panel\Programs\Programs and Features**, click on **Microsoft System Center Virtual Machine Manager 2008 Administrator Console**, and then click on **Uninstall**.
2. On the confirmation page, click on **Uninstall**.
3. Browse to the VMM 2012 media and double-click on the setup file to run it.
4. On the main setup page, click on **Install**.
5. Go through the installation steps.

Upgrading the VMM Self-Service Portal

As VMM 2012 SP1 does not support the Self-Service Portal anymore, I strongly recommend the removal of the Self-Service Portal and the installation of the System Center App Controller instead. See the *Deploying SC App Controller 2012 SP1 for hybrid cloud management* recipe in *Chapter 9, Managing Hybrid Clouds, Fabric Updates, Creating Clusters, and New Features of SP1*.

Uninstalling the VMM Self-Service Portal

To uninstall the VMM Self-Service Portal, carry out the following steps:

1. In **Control Panel\Programs\Programs and Features**, click on **Microsoft System Center Virtual Machine Manager 2008 Self-Service Portal** and then click on **Uninstall**.
2. On the confirmation page, click on **Uninstall**.

See also

▶ The *Deploying a Microsoft SQL Server for VMM implementation* recipe in *Chapter 2, Installing SCVMM 2012*.
▶ The following recipes in this chapter:
   ❑ *Reassociating hosts after upgrading*
   ❑ *Updating the VMM agents*
   ❑ *Performing other post-upgrade tasks*

Reassociating hosts after upgrading

After upgrading to a new version of VMM, you will need to reassociate the Hyper-V hosts. This recipe will guide you through the steps required to do so.

How to do it...

To reassociate hosts and library servers, carry out the following steps after upgrading VMM:

1. In the **Fabric** workspace on the VMM console, expand **Servers**. Under **Servers**, expand **All Hosts**. In the **Hosts** pane, right-click on the column header and select **Agent Status**.

    If a host needs to be reassociated, the **Host Status** column will display **Needs Attention** and the **Agent Status** column will display **Access Denied**.

   Select the host(s) to reassociate (use the *Shift* or the *Ctrl* key if you need to select multiple hosts), then right-click on the host(s) and click on **Reassociate**.

2. In the **Reassociate Agent** dialog box, type in the account name and password.

3. Click on **OK**. The **Agent Status** column will display **Reassociating**.

4. After the host has been reassociated successfully, it will display **Responding**.

5. On the **Hosts** tab in the ribbon, click on **Refresh**. The **Host Status** will display **OK**.

How it works...

After upgrading to VMM 2012, you will need to reassociate the Hyper-V servers and VMM library servers with VMM. If a host needs to be reassociated, the **Host Status** column will exhibit **Needs Attention** and the **Agent Status** column will exhibit **Access Denied**.

Library agents are treated in the same way as host agents, and therefore, the same procedure needs to be followed for them. Reassociate the VMM library server using the same steps. To view a list of the VMM library servers, in the **Fabric** workspace, expand **Servers**, then click on **Library Servers**.

 After reassociation, all the agents will display the status **Update Needed**.

There's more...

DMZ and other untrusted domain hosts will display an **Access Denied** state. They can't be reassociated; they will need to be removed and re-added to the VMM 2012 management.

See also

▸ *Updating the VMM agents*

▸ *Performing other post-upgrade tasks*

Updating the VMM agents

After upgrading to a new version of VMM, you will also need to update the VMM agents running on the Hyper-V server hosts. This recipe will guide you through the steps.

How to do it...

To update the VMM agent of a host, carry out the following steps after upgrading:

1. In the **Fabric** workspace on the VMM console, expand **Servers** and then go to **All Hosts**. In the **Hosts** pane, right-click on the column header and select **Agent Status**.

2. On the **Hosts** tab in the ribbon, click on **Refresh**.

 If a host requires the VMM agent to be updated, it will display **Needs Attention** in the **Host Status** column and **Upgrade Available** in the **Agent Version Status** column.

3. To update the VMM agent, select and right-click on the host, and then click on **Update Agent**.

4. In the **Update Agent** dialog, type in the user credentials, and click on **OK**.

5. The **Agent Version Status** column will exhibit **Upgrading**, which will then change to **Up-to-date** once the update process is completed successfully.

6. On the **Hosts** tab in the ribbon, click on **Refresh**. The **Host Status** for the host will display **OK**.

 Use the same steps as the ones used before to update the VMM agent on a VMM library server. To view a list of the VMM library servers, in the **Fabric** workspace, expand **Servers**, and then click on **Library Servers**.

How it works...

After upgrading to VMM 2012, you are required to update the VMM agent on the Hyper-V hosts and VMM library servers. Although this process does not require immediate action after the upgrade (as the previous VMM agent versions are supported by VMM 2012) take into account that the previous versions do not provide the functionalities that the new VMM agent does. The following is a list of the older versions of the VMM agent supported by VMM 2012:

- ▸ VMM 2008 R2 SP1 (2.0.4521.0)
- ▸ VMM 2008 R2 QFE4 (2.0.4275.0)
- ▸ VMM 2008 R2 QFE3 (2.0.4273.0)
- ▸ VMM 2008 R2 (2.0.4271.0)

See also

- ▸ *Reassociating hosts after upgrading*
- ▸ *Performing other post-upgrade tasks*

Performing other post-upgrade tasks

There are some others tasks that need to be performed after upgrading to VMM 2012. This recipe will guide you through them.

How to do it...

To update a VM template, carry out the following steps after upgrading VMM:

1. On the VMM console, in the **Library** workspace, expand **Templates** and click on **VM Templates**.

2. In the **Templates** pane, right-click on the VM template that is to be updated and select **Properties**.

3. On the **Hardware Configuration** page, configure the following:

   ❑ **VLAN ID**: If previously configured in a hardware profile.

 In VMM 2012, the VLAN ID will be resolved automatically based on the logical network specified when deploying a VM from a template.

   ❑ **Logical Network/VM Network**: Ensure that the correct network is specified in the hardware profile.

How it works...

The VM template settings specifying the VHD file that contains the OS are not preserved during the VMM upgrade. After upgrading to VMM 2012 SP1, you will have to update the upgraded VM templates to specify which VHD file contains the OS.

There's more...

There are a couple of other tasks that you need to perform if you had driver packages in the previous version.

Updating driver packages

After upgrading to VMM 2012, remove any previously added driver packages and then add them again so that they are correctly discovered. Use the following steps to add the driver packages to the library:

1. Locate a driver package and create a folder in the VMM library share to store the drivers (for example, you could create a folder named **Drivers**).

 Do not include other library resources (for example, ISO images, VHD/VHDX files, or scripts with a `.inf` extension) in this folder or else it will not be discovered by the VMM library for indexing.

2. Copy the driver package to a folder within this folder, that is, create a separate subfolder for every driver package.

3. In the **Library** workspace on the VMM console, expand **Library Servers** in the **Library** pane. Select and right-click on the new folder (for example, **Drivers**), and then click on **Refresh** to update the display and show the newly created folder.

 Be careful when you delete an INF driver package from a VMM library folder as the entire folder will be deleted.

Relocating the VMM Library

If you're upgrading to an HA VMM management server, the best practice is to relocate the VMM library to a cluster file server, create a new VMM library, and move the resources. Carry out the following steps to import physical resources:

1. On the VMM console, in the **Library** workspace, on the **Home** tab, click on **Import Physical Resource** and choose one of the following:

   ❑ **Add custom resource** to import a folder and its contents. If you select a folder with a `.cr` extension, it will be imported as a custom resource package. Without a `.cr` extension, only the supported file types will show up in the VMM library.

 You can use Windows Explorer to access the VMM library share in order to access all the files in the folder (if your account has the requisite access rights).

   ❑ **Add resource** to import file(s) of a supported type from another library location.

2. Under **Select library server and destination for the imported resources**, click on **Browse**.

3. Select the library server, library share, and folder location (optional), click on **OK**, and then click on **Import**.

See also

▸ The *How to Export a Service Template in VMM* page at
  `http://technet.microsoft.com/en-US/library/gg675114.aspx`

▸ The *How to Import a Service Template in VMM* page at
  `http://technet.microsoft.com/en-US/library/gg675092.aspx`

▸ The *How to Add File-Based Resources to the VMM Library* page at
  `http://technet.microsoft.com/library/gg610607.aspx`

7
Scripting in Virtual Machine Manager

In this chapter, we will cover:

- ▸ VMM PowerShell overview
- ▸ Finding the command to automate tasks in VMM
- ▸ Creating a script from VMM wizards
- ▸ Storing and running scripts in VMM
- ▸ VMM sample scripts

Introduction

In this chapter, you will get an insight into the useful VMM command shell, which allows administrators to perform all the VMM administrative functions using commands or scripts (configuration and management of the virtualization host, networking, and storage resources in order to create and deploy VMs and services).

The VMM command shell includes all the standard Windows PowerShell **cmdlets** and a comprehensive set of cmdlets that are designed specifically for VMM, which can be used to create scripts to automate complex tasks.

 Each cmdlet noun is now preceded with SC, including cmdlets that were included in the previous versions of VMM; for example, Get-SCVMHost.

VMM PowerShell overview

Windows PowerShell is based on object-oriented programming and the Microsoft .NET Framework Class Library. An object contains the following types of data:

- Object type
- Methods
- Properties

VMM objects can be used to manipulate data and take specific actions. Properties contain information about the state of an object. Methods are actions that you can perform on the item that an object represents. Methods can return data.

How to do it...

To be able to use the VMM PowerShell module, you must first ensure that it is already installed.

Installing the VMM PowerShell module

In order to install VMM Windows PowerShell, you need to install the VMM console. If you have already installed the VMM console, you don't need to install it again. For more information on installing the VMM console, see the *Installing the VMM console* recipe in *Chapter 2, Installing SCVMM 2012*.

Starting VMM PowerShell

When you start the VMM command shell, a Windows PowerShell session opens, automatically imports the VMM module, and establishes a connection to a VMM management server.

To open the VMM command shell window, carry out the following steps:

1. On the VMM console, click on **PowerShell** on the **Home** tab in the ribbon.

2. On a Windows 8 or a Windows Server 2012-based computer (with the VMM console installed), do the following:

    i. Press the Windows Key (⊞).

    ii. Right-click on **Virtual Machine Manager Command Shell**.

iii. On the taskbar, click on **Run as administrator**.

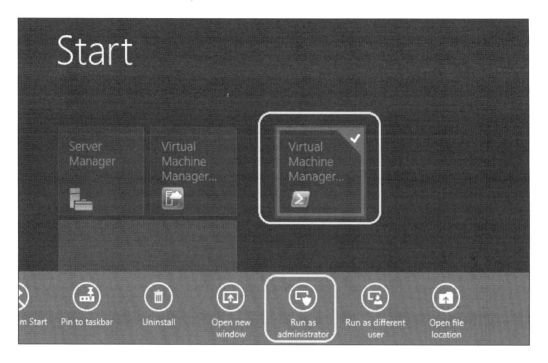

3. On a Windows 7 or a Windows 2008 R2 Server-based computer (with the VMM console installed), do the following:

    i. Click on **Microsoft System Center 2012**.

    ii. Click on **Virtual Machine Manager**.

    iii. Click on **Virtual Machine Manager Command Shell**.

4. Import the VMM PowerShell module into an existing Windows PowerShell session on a computer with the VMM console installed:

    i. Run the PowerShell command prompt with administrator rights.

    ii. Set the Windows PowerShell execution policy to allow you to run scripts using SET-ExecutionPolicy. For example, to allow scripts to run without restrictions, type in the following line:

    PS C:>Set-ExecutionPolicy Unrestricted

  iii. For help on setting the execution policy, type in `Get-Help Set-ExecutionPolicy`, as shown in the next line:

```
PS C:>Get-Help Set-ExecutionPolicy
```

  iv. To import the VMM module, type in the following line in the command prompt window:

```
PS C:\>Import-Module -Name virtualmachinemanager
```

How it works...

The default security settings built into Windows PowerShell prevent the execution of PowerShell scripts. The execution policy determines how (or if) PowerShell runs scripts. By default, PowerShell's execution policy is set to `Restricted`, which means that scripts will not be executed.

You can verify the execution policy settings on the server by typing in `Get-ExecutionPolicy` in the PowerShell prompt.

The `Set-ExecutionPolicy` cmdlet enables you to determine which Windows PowerShell scripts (if any) will be allowed to run; you can use one of the following execution policies for this purpose:

 ▶ `Restricted`: No scripts can be run. PowerShell can be used only in interactive mode.

 ▶ `AllSigned`: Only scripts signed by a trusted publisher can run.

 ▶ `RemoteSigned`: Downloaded scripts must be signed by a trusted publisher before they can run.

 ▶ `Unrestricted`: No restrictions; all Windows PowerShell scripts can run. For example, the following command sets the execution policy to `Unrestricted`:

```
PS C:\> Set-ExecutionPolicy Unrestricted
```

There's more...

Let's learn more about the PowerShell cmdlets.

Properties

To get the available properties of an object, use the `Get-Member` cmdlet and set the `MemberType` parameter to `property`.

For example, to get the properties for a logical network, get the logical network object and then use the pipeline operator (|) to send the object to `Get-Member`.

```
PS C:\> Get-SCLogicalNetwork -Name "Intranet" | Get-Member -MemberType
property
```

The result of the previous command line will be:

```
Intranet
```

To get the value of a property, use the dot (.) method. Do the following two steps to use the dot method:

1. Get a reference to the object (for example, a variable that contains the object) or type in a command that gets the object.
2. Then, type in a dot (.) followed by the property name.

The following example stores the value of the `Name` property of a logical network object in a variable called `$LogicalNet`:

```
PS C:\> $LogicalNet = Get-SCLogicalNetwork -Name "Intranet"
```

You can check the value stored in this variable by typing in the following line in the command shell:

```
PS C:\> $LogicalNet.Name
```

The result is:

```
Intranet
```

Methods

You can get the available methods for an object by using the `Get-Member` cmdlet and setting the `MemberType` parameter to `method`.

The following example shows how to get the methods for a logical network:

```
PS C:\> Get-SCLogicalNetwork -Name "Intranet" | Get-Member -MemberType
method
```

The result is:

```
Intranet
```

To invoke a method, type in a reference to the object and then specify the method name, separating the object reference and the method with a dot (.).

> To pass arguments to the method, enclose the arguments in parentheses, followed by the method name.
>
> An empty set of parentheses indicates that the method requires no arguments.

The following example shows how to use the `GetType` method to return the base type of a logical network (using our previously created `$LogicalNet` variable).

```
PS C:\> $LogicalNet.GetType()
```

The result is:

```
Intranet
```

Object synchronization

VMM synchronizes its objects, which means that if you create two or more variables and then change a property of an object that is stored in either variable, VMM will synchronize the object property in both the variables.

The following example demonstrates how two variables get synchronized:

1. We first use `Get-SCLogicalNetwork` to get a value, and store it in the variable `$LogicalNet`.

   ```
   PS C:\> $LogicalNet = Get-SCLogicalNetwork -Name "Intranet"
   ```

2. Then we use `Get-SCLogicalNetwork` to get a value and store it in a second variable called `$Intranet`.

   ```
   PS C:\> $Intranet = Get-SCLogicalNetwork -Name "Intranet"
   ```

3. We then change the name of the logical network object using `$Intranet`.

   ```
   PS C:\> Set-SCLogicalNetwork -LogicalNetwork $Intranet -Name
   "VMInternalTraffic"
   ```

4. When we look at the name of the logical network stored in both the variables, `$Intranet` and `$LogicalNet`, the results are identical. When we type in the command `$Intranet.Name`, the result is:

   ```
   VMInternalTraffic
   ```

5. On typing in the following line, the result is the same, that is, `VMInternalTraffic`:

   ```
   PS C:\> $LogicalNet.Name
   ```

See also

▸ The *Windows PowerShell Basics* page at `http://go.microsoft.com/fwlink/?LinkId=242715`

▸ The *Getting Started Windows PowerShell* guide at `http://go.microsoft.com/fwlink/?LinkId=242708`

- To learn more about signing scripts, type the command `Get-Help About_Signing` in the PowerShell prompt

- Information on VMM 2012's backward compatibility for cmdlets at `http://technet.microsoft.com/library/hh801915.aspx`

Finding the command to automate tasks in VMM

This recipe will show you how to find the VMM PowerShell command to automate tasks in VMM. The `Get-Help` cmdlet not only displays information about the cmdlet, but it also displays references, examples of usage, and notes.

Getting ready

Start the VMM PowerShell command with administrator rights. For more information, see the *VMM PowerShell overview* recipe.

How to do it...

Help topics are provided for each VMM PowerShell cmdlet, including general examples.

To display a list of all of the VMM cmdlets, start the VMM PowerShell and use the `Get-Command` cmdlet:

```
PS C:\>Get-Command -CommandType Cmdlet
```

You can also use `Get-Command` to view all VMM cmdlets that contain specific nouns or verbs; for example, all related `SCCloud` commands:

```
PS C:\>Get-Command -Noun SCCloud
```

The result of this command is shown in the following screenshot:

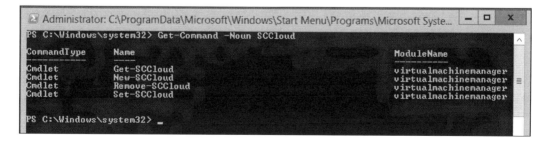

Using the Get-Help cmdlet

To get more specific help, you can use the `Get-Help` cmdlet. For example, to view a help topic for the `New-SCCloud` cmdlet, type in the following line in the command prompt window:

```
PS C:\>Get-help New-SCCloud
```

After running the preceding command, the results will be displayed as follows:

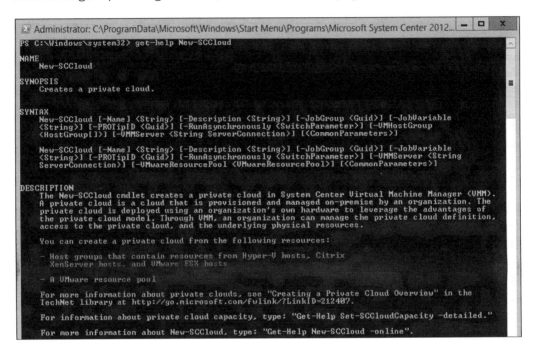

How it works...

The `Get-Help` command displays a help topic about a cmdlet. The default output that is returned contains basic information about the cmdlet.

To change what information is shown when using the `Get-Help` cmdlet, you can use some of the parameters associated with `Get-Help`:

- ► `-full`: Shows all available help for the cmdlet
- ► `-detailed`: Shows the synopsis, syntax, detailed description, parameter descriptions, and examples
- ► `-examples`: Shows only the synopsis and examples
- ► `-Online`: Opens the online version of the help topic in your default browser

The following screenshot shows the result of the `Get-Help` command for the `Get-SCCloud` cmdlet, using the `-examples` parameter:

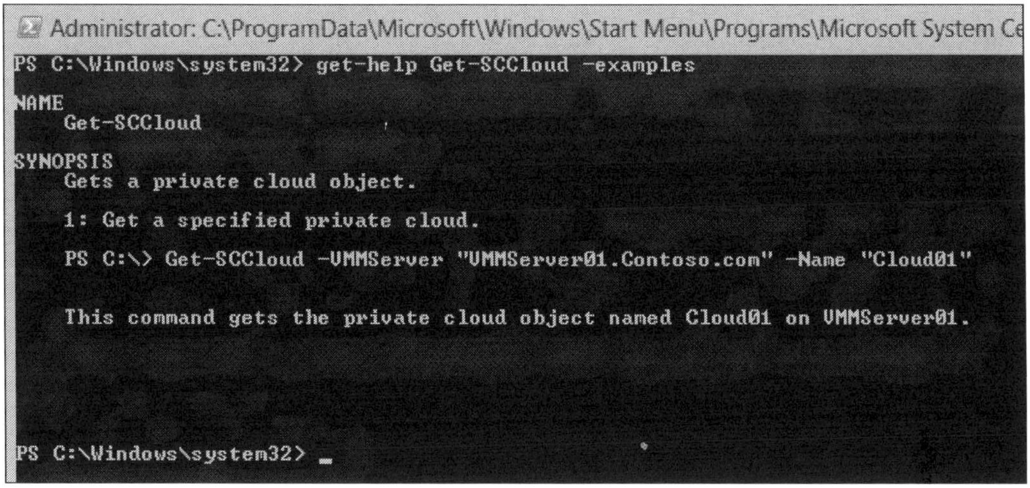

```
Administrator: C:\ProgramData\Microsoft\Windows\Start Menu\Programs\Microsoft System Ce
PS C:\Windows\system32> get-help Get-SCCloud -examples

NAME
    Get-SCCloud

SYNOPSIS
    Gets a private cloud object.

    1: Get a specified private cloud.

    PS C:\> Get-SCCloud -VMMServer "VMMServer01.Contoso.com" -Name "Cloud01"

    This command gets the private cloud object named Cloud01 on VMMServer01.


PS C:\Windows\system32> _
```

There's more...

This section is about getting more help on PowerShell cmdlets.

About topics

To display the available about help topics for VMM, use the following command line:

```
PS C:\>Get-Help about_VMM*
```

To display an individual about help topic, type in the following line in the command prompt:

```
PS C:>Get-Help about_VMM_2012_Virtual_Networking
```

See also

Help topics and about topics for VMM PowerShell cmdlets are available online in the TechNet Library.

  ▸ The VMM cmdlet online reference at `http://go.microsoft.com/fwlink/?LinkID=241986`

  ▸ VMM about topics at `http://go.microsoft.com/fwlink/?LinkId=242616`

Creating a script from VMM wizards

You can use the VMM console to help you with the PowerShell script to automate tasks.

Getting the script from a previous task that had been executed in the VMM console will save you time when working with scripts. Save it, and then personalize it to make it generic. Every task that is created in VMM can be scripted.

How to do it...

You can create a script from one of the VMM wizards. In this recipe, we will create a script based on the creation of a hardware profile. Carry out the following steps in order to do so:

1. Connect to the VMM 2012 console using the VMM admin account that has been created previously (`lab\vmm-admin`).
2. On the left-bottom pane, click on the **Library** workspace, expand **Profiles** on the left-hand side pane, and then click on **Hardware Profiles**.
3. Select and right-click on **Create Hardware Profile**.
4. In the **New Hardware Profile** dialog box, on the **General** page, type in the hardware profile name; for example, `1 vCPU Server`.
5. Click on **Hardware Profile** on the left-hand side pane and configure the hardware settings.
6. On the left-bottom pane, click on **View Script**.
7. A window will open, displaying the script (as shown in the following screenshot). Copy and paste this to Notepad or any PowerShell editor and save it with a `.ps1` extension.

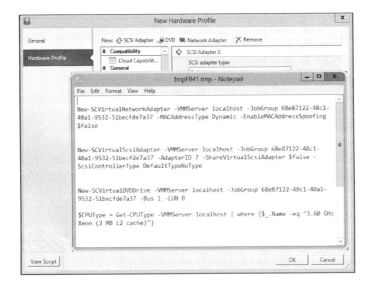

8. Click on **OK** to finish and save the hardware profile, or click on **Cancel** if you wish to abort the operation.

> You can also click on **Cancel** and then execute it after saving the script in order to see the hardware profile that was created using the command shell.

How it works...

To help get you started with writing scripts, you can try generating a script by running any wizard or updating properties in the VMM console.

Use the **View Script** button on the **Summary** page of a wizard in the VMM console or the **Properties** page to view the set of cmdlets that will run. Save the script as a file with the `.ps1` extension and then modify the commands as necessary.

There's more...

After creating a script, you can modify it according to your requirements.

Modifying a generated script

Most generated scripts have an ID parameter to identify specific objects on which they will take actions.

As we want to allow the script to take parameters, we can use a `Get` cmdlet to get an object that will make our script available for use with other objects.

The following is a generated script, created after changing the private cloud's name. By changing a property value, the generated script uses the ID parameter to get the object to change:

```
$cloud = Get-SCCloud -ID "1f6a5a0a-83ed-46fd-a369-d45ee4ec6492"


Set-SCCloud -Cloud $cloud -Name "My Cloud-Renamed" -Description ""
-RunAsynchronously
```

As we want to start building a script library for future use, we replace the ID parameter with something that we can use as a standard. The following sample shows how to retrieve all those private clouds that have names beginning with `My Cloud` and place them in an array:

```
$Clouds = @( Get-SCCloud | where { $_.Name -like "My Cloud-Renamed*" })
```

We place the first private cloud in the array, and then update its name to **New Private Cloud**.

```
Set-SCCloud -Cloud $clouds[0] -Name "MyCompany Private Cloud"
-RunAsynchronously
```

Adding parameters to a generated script

Another way to make a generated script more accessible is by defining parameters in the script. Script parameters work like function parameters. The parameter values are available to all the commands in the script. While running the script, script users type in the parameters after the script name.

To add parameters to a script, use the `Param` statement. So let's modify our previous script to accept parameters. Save the script as `ChangeCloudName.ps1`:

```
Param(
    [parameter(Mandatory=$true)]
    [String] $OldName = $(throw "Provide an existing Cloud."),

    [parameter(Mandatory=$true)]
    [String] $NewName = $(throw "Provide a new name.")


Set-SCCloud -Cloud $OldName -Name $NewName -RunAsynchronously
```

When we run the script, we need to provide the name of an existing logical network and a new name for it:

```
.\ChangeCloudName.ps1 -OldName "MyCompany Private Cloud " -NewName "My
Cloud"
```

 If you do not provide values for `OldName` and `NewName`, you will be prompted for them.

See also

▶   The *Creating a Script from VMM Wizards and Property Pages* page at
    `http://technet.microsoft.com/en-us/library/hh875023.aspx`

Storing and running scripts in VMM

A script is a text file that contains one or more Windows PowerShell commands. You can save PowerShell scripts to a folder that will be executed from the VMM command shell, or you can save them to the VMM library and run them using the VMM console.

For the script to be recognized as a Windows PowerShell script, it has to be saved with a `.ps1` extension.

Getting ready

Before you can run a script, check the Windows PowerShell execution policy. The default execution policy (`Restricted`) prevents all scripts from running.

How to do it...

After writing a script, you can save it in the VMM library for using later.

Storing a script in the VMM library

Carry out the following steps to save a particular script to the VMM library:

1. Connect to the VMM 2012 console using the VMM admin account that has been created previously (`lab\vmm-admin`).

2. On the left-bottom pane, click on the **Library** workspace; expand **Library Servers** in the left pane and then select the library share in which the script is to be stored.

3. On the **Home** tab in the ribbon, click on **Import Physical Resource**.

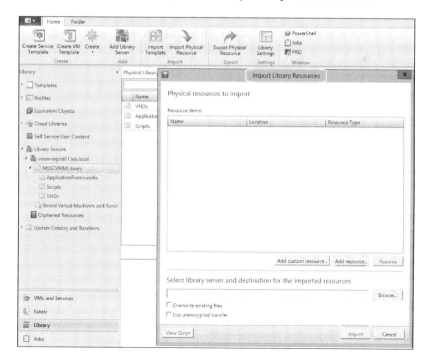

4. On the **Import Library Resources** dialog box, click on **Add resource...**, select a particular library by clicking on **Browse**, and then click on **Import**.

 Alternatively, you can select a script in that share, and then click on **Open File Location** on the **PowerShell** tab in the **Window** group. This opens a Windows Explorer window showing the location of the library share. Copy your script to the share and then close the Explorer window.

Viewing and updating a script in the VMM library

Carry out the following steps to update a script in the VMM library:

1. On the VMM console that is on the **Library** workspace, select the script and click on **View File** on the **PowerShell** tab.

2. Update the script and then click on **Save**. Close the file.

Running a script from the VMM library

Carry out the following two steps to run a script from the VMM library:

1. On the VMM console that is on the **Library** workspace, select the script, and then click on **Run** on the **PowerShell** tab.

2. The VMM command shell opens and the script runs.

Running a script from the command prompt

Carry out the following steps to run a script from the command prompt:

1. On a computer on which the VMM console has been installed and the Windows PowerShell execution policy has been set to allow you to run (if you have not done the latter, type in Get-Help Set-ExecutionPolicy in the command prompt) scripts, click on **Windows PowerShell** and type in the following line in the command prompt:

   ```
   PS C:\>Import-Module -Name virtualmachinemanager
   ```

2. Then type the command or script. For example:

   ```
   $vHost = Get-SCVMHost -ComputerName "HyperV02"
   ```

How it works...

Store the scripts in a centralized location, such as a VMM library share, to make them easier to manage, share, and document. You can store, view, update, and run the scripts directly from the VMM library.

If a script is stored on a local server, you can only run it from the VMM command shell (PowerShell). For example, to run a script called `ChangeCloudName.ps1`, run PowerShell and import the VMM module, or open the VMM command shell and type in the script name as follows:

```
PS C:\Scripts> .\ChangeCloudName.ps1 -OldName "My Cloud" -NewName "My New Clould"
```

 If the script is not in the current directory, type in the path to the script.

There's more...

This section covers the topic of working with credentials in PowerShell.

Credentials

When performing certain actions in the VMM command shell, such as adding Hyper-V hosts, you will need to provide credentials.

To accomplish this, you can create a Windows PowerShell `PSCredential` object, and store that object in a variable that you can use within a script. To create a `PSCredential` object, use the `Get-Credential` cmdlet.

```
PS C:\>$Credential = Get-Credential
```

```
PS C:\>$$Add-SCVMHost "Hyperv02.lab.local" -RemoteConnectEnabled $True -RemoteConnectPort 5900 -Credential $Credential
```

 You can create a `PSCredential` object programmatically, without requiring any user interaction. However, this method requires that the username and password appear as plain text within the script, which is not recommended for security reasons.

Using VMM Run As accounts

In VMM 2012, it is possible to use Run As accounts to provide credentials for the PowerShell scripts or cmdlets that support the `VMMCredential` parameter type.

Use the `Get-SCRunAsAccount` cmdlet to get a Run As account within a script, which provides credentials without the need for user interaction.

This gets a Run As account object named `vmm-admin` and stores the object in the `$RunAsAccount` variable.

```
PS C:\> $RunAsAccount = Get-SCRunAsAccount -Name "vmm-admin"
```

Add the SMI-S storage provider, with the name `DellStorageProvider`:

```
PS C:\> Add-SCStorageProvider -SmisWmi -Name "DellStorageProvider"
-RunAsAccount $RunAsAccount -ComputerName "StorageMGMTHost.lab.local"
```

Using the JobGroup parameter

To work with a `JobGroup` parameter, you need to provide a globally unique identifier (GUID). The following command shows how to create a GUID and store it in the `$JobGroupGUID` variable:

```
$JobGroupGUID = [Guid]::NewGuid().ToString()
```

After creating the GUID, you can add other commands, always specifying the job group GUID. The command will not run by just carrying out these steps; a final command is required, which will also include `-JobGroup $JobGroupGUID`.

The tasks carried out by the following sample script are queued and do not run until the `New-SCVirtualMachine` cmdlet is executed. The `New-SCVirtualMachine` cmdlet is the last command that includes `JobGroup` and initiates work.

```
$VMMServer="vmm-mgmt01.lab.local"

$Owner="lab\vmm-admin"

$NewVMname="W2012-Web02"

$HyperVHost="Hyperv02.lab.local"


#Generate a GUID for the JobGroupGUID variable.

$JobGroupGUID = [Guid]::NewGuid().ToString()


$VirtualHardDisk = Get-SCVirtualHardDisk -VMMServer $VMMServer | where
{$_.Location -eq "\\vmm-mgmt01.lab.local\MSSCVMMLibrary\VHDs\Blank Disk -
Large.vhdx"}


# This is the first cmdlet that uses the JobGroup variable.
```

```
New-SCVirtualDiskDrive -VMMServer $VMMServer -IDE -Bus 0 -LUN 0 -JobGroup
$JobGroupGUID -VirtualHardDisk $VirtualHardDisk -VolumeType BootAndSystem


$HardwareProfile = Get-SCHardwareProfile -VMMServer localhost | where
{$_.Name -eq "2 vCPU Server"}


$vHost = Get-SCVMHost -ComputerName $HyperVHost

$operatingSystem = Get-SCOperatingSystem | where { $_.Name -eq "64-bit
edition of Windows 8" }


# As this is the last cmdlet, use the JobGroup variable

New-SCVirtualMachine -Name $NewVMname  -JobGroup $JobGroupGUID -VMMServer
$VMMServer  -Owner $Owner -VMHost $vHost -Path "G:\VMS\" -HardwareProfile
$HardwareProfile -OperatingSystem $operatingSystem -RunAsynchronously
-StartAction TurnOnVMIfRunningWhenVSStopped -StopAction SaveVM
-DelayStartSeconds 0
```

Cmdlets with which you can use JobGroup

Refer to the following Microsoft TechNet page for the PowerShell cmdlets that can use the JobGroup parameter:

```
http://technet.microsoft.com/ru-ru/library/hh875035.aspx
```

VMM sample scripts

The sample scripts in this recipe illustrate how to use Windows PowerShell for centralized management.

You can use VMM PowerShell cmdlets to automate VMM tasks by executing them from a machine with the VMM console installed.

The following section contains some samples to add storage and convert the VHD disk format to the VHDX disk format.

How to do it...

You can use PowerShell scripts to automate various tasks. The following sample script counts the number of VMs per OS.

Counting the number of virtual machines per operating system

```
Import-Module virtualmachinemanager

$vHosts = Get-SCVMHost

foreach ($vHost in $vHosts){

    Get-SCVirtualMachine -VmHost $vHost | Group-Object OperatingSystem |
Sort Count -Descending | Select Name, Count

}
```

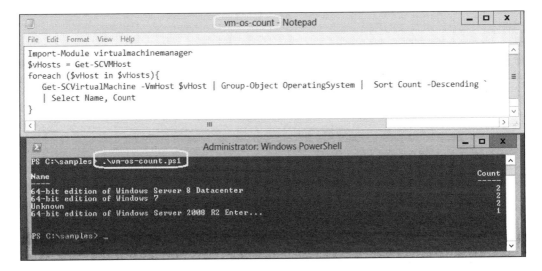

How it works...

The script starts by importing the `virtualmachinemanager` module. It then creates a variable that will store all hosts.

For each host, it gets all the virtual machines and groups them by the operational system (OS) property. Finally, it lists the OS and the number of VMs associated with it.

You can change this script to accommodate your needs; for example, you can use it to check only the number of running machines.

There's more...

Let's have a look at more PowerShell sample scripts.

Adding a storage provider by its IP address

This step will add (integrate) an already installed SMI-S storage provider to VMM. Carry out the following steps to add a storage provider by its IP address:

1. Get the Run As account and store it in the `$RunAsAcount` variable.

```
PS C:\> $RunAsAccount = Get-SCRunAsAccount -Name "vmm-admin"
```

2. Add the storage provider with an IP address of `192.168.10.10`.

```
PS C:\> Add-SCStorageProvider -NetworkDeviceName "http://
192.168.10.10" -TCPPort 5988 -Name "SampleStorageProvidere"
-RunAsAccount $RunAsAccount
```

[Make sure to type in the correct `TCPPort` for your storage provider. Consult the storage provider's manual for help.]

Converting a dynamic VHD to a fixed VHDX

You can customize this example by adding a parameter that queries for a VM name and searches for all hard disks to convert to the VHDX format. Carry out the following steps to convert a dynamic VHD to a fixed VHDX:

1. Get the virtual disk drive object that is attached to the virtual machine and store the object in the `$VirtDiskDrive` variable.

```
PS C:\> $VirtDiskDrive = Get-VirtualDiskDrive -VM (Get-
SCVirtualMachine -Name "VM-W2012")
```

2. Convert the virtual hard disk stored in `$VirtDiskDrive` to a VHDX disk.

```
PS C:\> Convert-VirtualDiskDrive -VirtualDiskDrive $VirtDiskDrive
-VHDX
```

[For this example, it is assumed that the virtual machine has only one virtual hard disk attached, and the VM is stopped.]

Creating a new virtual disk drive and adding it to an existing virtual machine

You can customize this example by querying the VM to find out which slot is free to add to. Carry out the following steps to create a new virtual disk drive and add it to an existing VM:

1. Get the virtual machine object and store the object in the `$VM` variable.

```
PS C:\> $VM = Get-SCVirtualMachine -Name "VM-W2012"
```

2. Create a new dynamic virtual disk drive on the first IDE channel in the second slot of the virtual machine and specify its size as 40 GB.

```
PS C:\> New-SCVirtualDiskDrive -VM $VM -Dynamic -Filename "VM-
W2012" -IDE -Size 40000 -Bus 0 -LUN 1
```

 For this example, it is assumed that the virtual machine already has an attached virtual hard disk on the first slot.

Testing a dynamic VHD attached to a fixed-format virtual disk drive on a virtual machine

For this example, it is assumed that the virtual machine has only one virtual disk drive. You can customize the script for your needs, for example, by adding a parameter to get the VM name.

1. Get the virtual machine object and store the object in the $VM variable.

```
PS C:\> $VM = Get-SCVirtualMachine -Name "VM-W2012"
```

2. Get the attached virtual disk drive and store it in the $VirtDiskDrive variable.

```
PS C:\> $VirtDiskDrive = Get-SCVirtualDiskDrive -VM $VM
```

3. If the VM is running, then shut down the VM.

```
PS C:\> If ($VM.Status -eq "Running") {Stop-SCVirtualMachine -VM
$VM -Shutdown}
```

4. Test the virtual hard disk stored in $VirtDiskDrive.

```
PS C:\> Test-SCVirtualDiskDrive -VirtualDiskDrive $VirtDiskDrive
```

See also

▶ The *Creating a Script from VMM Wizards and Property Pages* page at
http://technet.microsoft.com/en-us/library/hh875023.aspx

▶ VMM cmdlet online help topics at
http://go.microsoft.com/fwlink/?LinkID=241986

▶ The System Center Virtual Machine Manager 2012 cmdlet reference at
http://technet.microsoft.com/en-us/library/hh875037.aspx

8
Managing VMware ESXi and Citrix XenServer Hosts

In this chapter, we will cover:

- ▸ Adding a VMware vCenter Server to VMM
- ▸ Adding VMware ESX hosts or host clusters to VMM
- ▸ Configuring network settings on a VMware ESX host
- ▸ Configuring host BMC settings
- ▸ Importing VMware templates
- ▸ Converting VMware virtual machines to Hyper-V
- ▸ Managing Citrix XenServer hosts and pools
- ▸ Converting Citrix XenServer virtual machines to Hyper-V

Introduction

This chapter has recipes that will help administrators manage the daily operations of VMware ESX and Citrix hosts and host clusters, such as the identification and management of hosts. In addition, it will provide the ability to create, manage, save, and deploy VMs on VMware ESX and Citrix hosts, all from the VMM console.

System Center 2012 has the concept of a fabric, which is made up of hosts, host groups and library servers, as well as networking and storage configurations. This architecture abstracts the underlying infrastructure from the users, but lets them deploy VMs, applications, and services irrespective of whether the infrastructure is running on Microsoft hypervisor technology or hypervisors from VMware or Citrix.

As multiple hypervisors can be managed through a common console, we can deploy VMs and applications in a consistent manner and get the same capabilities from different hypervisors. We can choose to utilize a mix of hypervisors, aggregating one or more hypervisors' host groups into a private cloud without worrying about underlying hypervisor capabilities and limitations. Abstracting the hypervisor layer reduces complexity and makes it easier to perform common actions on heterogeneous environments.

Note that in order to fully monitor and manage VMware and Citrix environments, you will need the following System Center 2012 family components:

- **VMM**: This enables you to deploy and manage virtual machines and services across multiple hypervisor platforms, including Citrix, VMware ESX, and ESXi hosts.

- **Orchestrator**: At the time of writing, this included over 41 built-in workflow activities to perform a wide variety of tasks; you can expand its functionality by installing integration packs; for example, the integration pack for VMware vSphere helps you automate actions by enabling full management. For more information about Orchestrator Integration packs, see `http://technet.microsoft.com/en-us/library/hh295851.aspx`.

- **Operations Manager**: This helps in monitoring VMware environments by using third-party management packs like those from Veeam (see the *Monitoring VMware vSphere infrastructure from Operations Manager using management packs* recipe in *Chapter 10, Integration with Systems Center Operations Manager 2012 SP1*), which will enable all Operations Manager functionalities, such as alerts on performance and events, integrated notifications, responses and automation, and detailed reporting and auditing for all VMware components (ESXi hosts, vCenter, and so on).

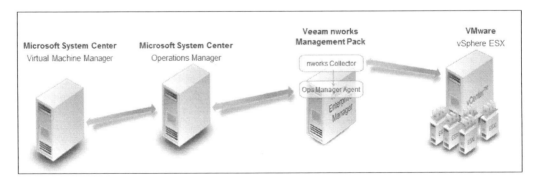

Adding a VMware vCenter Server to VMM

In order to manage VMware hosts, you need to integrate VMM with any existing VMware vCenter Server. VMM supports the VMware vCenter Server virtualization management software for managing hosts.

The features that are supported when VMM manages ESX/ESXi hosts are as follows:

Functionality Supported by VMM	Notes
Private clouds	The ESX/ESXi host resources are available to a VMM private cloud when creating the private cloud from host groups with ESX/ESXi hosts, or from a VMware resource pool.
Dynamic Optimization	The new VMM Dynamic Optimization features can be used with ESX hosts.
Power Optimization	For this functionality, the Dynamic Optimization feature in VMM or the VMware Distributed Resource Scheduler can be used.
Live migration	Live migration between hosts within the cluster is supported by VMM 2012.
Live storage migration	Supported by VMM 2012.
Networking	VMM identifies and uses the existing VMware vSwitches and port groups for VM deployment.
Storage	VMM supports and identifies VMware Paravirtual SCSI (PVSCSI) storage adapters and thin-provisioned virtual hard disks.
Library	You can organize and store VMware VMs, **VMware Virtual Machine Disk (VMDK) files**, and templates in the VMM library. You can create new VMs from templates or by converting stored VMware VMs to Hyper-V VMs.
VMM command shell	VMM PowerShell commands are common across the supported hypervisors.

Getting ready

There are some prerequisites that need to be taken into account when integrating VMware vCenter with VMM 2012 SP1. The following are the requirements:

- One of the following supported versions of VMware vCenter is running:
    - VMware vCenter Server 4.1
    - VMware vCenter Server 5.x

> ▶ An SSL certificate is required for communication between the VMM management server and the VMware vCenter Server if encryption is being used, to verify the identity of the vCenter Server.

> ▶ You must create a Run As account that has administrative permissions on the vCenter Server. It is possible to use a local account or a recommended domain account (for example, **lab\VMwareAdmin**). Either way, the account needs local admin rights on the vCenter Server.

How to do it...

Carry out the following steps to integrate the vCenter Server with VMM.

Importing the VMware self-signed SSL certificate

For this integration to work, SCVMM needs to communicate with the vSphere infrastructure via vCenter over SSL. Carry out the following steps to import the self-signed SSL certificate:

1. Make sure you log on to the VMM server as a local administrator, or with a domain account with local administrator rights (for example, **lab\vmm-admin**).

2. Open Internet Explorer and navigate to `https://vCenter.lab.local/`.

 If you have logged in using an account that doesn't have local administrator rights, hold down the *Shift* key and right-click on the Internet Explorer icon, and then click on **Run as administrator**.

3. Click on **Continue to this web site (not recommended)** when you get a warning saying that the SSL certificate is not trusted.

4. Click on **Certificate Error** in the Security Status bar, select **View Certificate**, and click on **Install Certificate**.

5. On the **Certificate Import Wizard** window, click on **Place all certificates in the following store** and then click on **Browse**.

6. On the **Select Certificate Store** window, select the checkbox for **Show physical stores**.

7. Expand **Trusted People**, select **Local Computer**, and click on **OK**.

 If you don't see the **Local Computer** option under **Trusted People**, it means that you are logged in with an account that does not have sufficient permissions.

8. Click on **Finish** to complete the process of importing the certificate.

9. Click on **OK** when a window is displayed saying that the import was successful.

10. To verify the process, close Internet Explorer and then reopen it. Next, browse to the location of the vCenter Server (for example, `https://vCenter.lab.local/`); if you do not receive a certificate error, the certificate was correctly imported and you can proceed to the next step.

Adding vCenter to VMM

1. Open the VMM console and in the **Fabric** workspace in the **Fabric** pane, click on **Servers**, and click on **vCenter Servers**, as shown in the following figure:

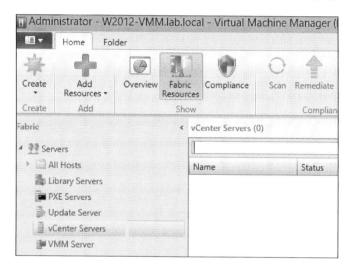

2. On the **Home** tab in the ribbon, click on **Add Resources** and select **VMware vCenter Server**.

> You can also select **vCenter Servers** in the left-hand side pane, and then right-click on it and select **Add VMware vCenter Server**.

3. On the **Add VMware vCenter Server** dialog, in the **Computer name** field, type in the name of the vCenter Server (for example, **vcenter.lab.local**), that is, you can enter the NetBIOS name, FQDN, or the IP address.

4. On the **TCP/IP port** field, type in the port number that is required to connect to the vCenter Server (the default is `443`) or use the drop-down arrows.

5. For the **Run As account** field, click on **Browse** and select a Run As account that has administrative rights on the vCenter Server; then click on **OK**.

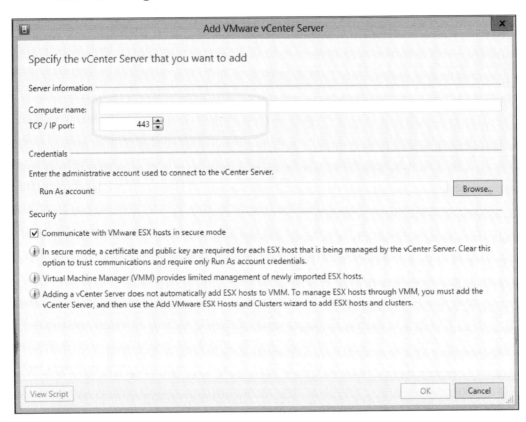

6. In **Security**, select **Communicate with VMware ESX hosts in secure mode** to use SSL encryption.

When **Communicate with VMware ESX hosts in secure mode** is selected (recommended approach), a certificate and a public key will be required for each vCenter host.

If this option is not selected, you will only need the Run As account credentials for communication between VMM and vCenter.

7. Click on **OK** to finish and then verify that the vCenter Server has the status of **Completed** in the **Jobs** dialog box.

8. If you are making use of a self-signed certificate for vCenter, make sure you have copied it first into the **Trusted People certificate store** on the VMM management server. Otherwise, click on **Import** in the **Import Certificate** dialog to have the certificate added to the Trusted People certificate store.

How it works...

VMM has an abstraction layer that lets you manage multiple hypervisor platforms: Hyper-V, Citrix XenServers, and VMware vSphere, making resources from these platforms available for data center and private cloud deployments by using a common user interface (VMM console and PowerShell).

In order to manage VMware hosts, VMM requires integration with the VMware vCenter Server. You can then use the VMM console to manage VMware ESX/ESXi hosts and host clusters, such as the discovery of these hosts and the ability to create, manage, save, and deploy VMs on them.

Before integrating VMware vCenter with VMM, it is highly recommended that you create a Run As account with local administrative access rights on the vCenter Server.

In VMM 2012, on adding/integrating a VMware vCenter Server, VMM no longer imports, merges, or synchronizes the VMware tree structure. You will need to manually select and add ESX servers and hosts to a VMM host group. Therefore, you will come across fewer issues during synchronization.

For best practices, it is recommended to use secure mode communication to integrate VMM and VMware vCenter. To do that, you can import the self-signed SSL certificate from vCenter or you can use a third-party certificate. You can choose to use the self-signed certificate in addition to the vCenter certificate; in this case, you will be required to resolve the ESX hosts' SSL certificates so that they are trusted or you can choose to simply rely on the Run As account.

 If you choose to use a public third-party certificate, you are not required to import the SSL certificate into the Trusted People certificate store.

See also

▶ The *System Requirements: VMware ESX Hosts* page at
  http://technet.microsoft.com/library/gg697603.aspx

Adding VMware ESX hosts or host clusters to VMM

Now that you've integrated vCenter with VMM, you can start adding the ESX hosts that are to be managed by VMM.

Getting ready

The following is a list of some prerequisites and recommendations that need to be taken into account when adding VMware hosts to VMM 2012 SP1:

> ▶ The VMware vCenter Server that manages the ESX hosts must already be configured and integrated into VMM.

> ▶ The host must be running a supported version of VMware vSphere. For more information, see *Chapter 1, VMM 2012 Architecture*.

> ▶ If encryption is required for communication between VMM and the vSphere hosts, a certificate and public key for each managed ESX/ESXi host will be needed.

> ▶ Although it is not a requirement, you can create a host group to organize the hosts (for example, **VMware Hosts**).

> ▶ As per best practices, create a Run As account with root credentials on the VMware **ESX hosts**.

 Although it is possible to create the Run As account when adding the ESX hosts, as per VMM best practices, it is recommended to create it before the addition of hosts.

How to do it...

Carry out the following steps to add VMware ESX hosts or clusters to VMM:

1. On the **Fabric** workspace in the VMM console, click on **Add Resources** on the **Home tab**; then click on **VMware ESX Hosts and Clusters**.

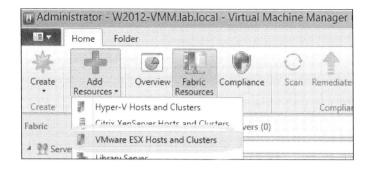

2. On the **Run As account** box in the **Credentials** page in the **Add Resource Wizard** window, click on **Browse** and select a Run As account with root credentials on the VMware ESX/ESXi host.

3. Click on **OK** and then click on **Next**.

4. On the **VMware vCenter Server** list in the **Target resources** page, select the vCenter Server (for example, **vCenter**).

 The available ESX hosts and clusters will be listed for the selected vCenter Server.

5. Select the VMware ESX host(s) or host cluster to be added.

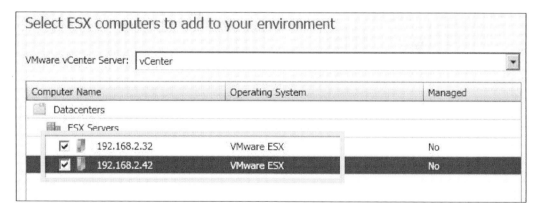

6. Click on **Next**.

7. On the **Location** list in the **Host settings** page, select the host group to assign the hosts to, and click on **Next**.

You can change the placement path for these hosts if you want to.

8. On the **Summary** page, click on **Finish**.

9. After verifying that the **Job Status** column displays **Completed**, close the dialog box.

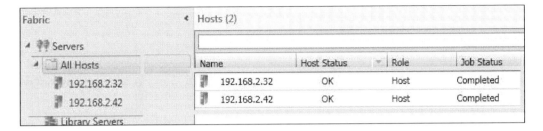

How it works...

The steps that need to be carried out to add VMware hosts or clusters are pretty straightforward. After integrating vCenter, on the **Add Resources** wizard, select **VMware ESX Hosts and Clusters**, making sure you have created a Run As account that has root credentials on the ESXi hosts.

You can add one or more hosts as well as VMware clusters.

If you require encryption, you can either use the self-signed certificate that was created when you installed the VMware ESX/ESXi hosts, or a public, trusted certificate. Note that if you decide to use the self-signed certificate, you are required to import it from each ESX host to the VMM management server. You don't need to carry out this task if you are using an SSL certificate from a trusted certification authority.

There's more...

Carry out the following steps to verify that the ESX host or host cluster was added correctly:

1. On the **Fabric** workspace in the VMM console, expand **Servers**; go to **All Hosts**, and then expand and select the host group where you had previously added the ESX host/ cluster (for example, **VMware Hosts**).

2. Verify that each host in the **Hosts** pane has a status of either **OK** or **OK (Limited)**.

 If the status of the host shows **OK (Limited)**, it could indicate that the specified Run As account does not have the correct credentials (that is, it does not have the root credentials or the account does not have the requisite permissions) or that you have enabled the secure mode but did not import an SSL certificate and public key.

3. If the host status is **OK (Limited)**, you should correct the credentials or remove the secure mode for that host to enable management through VMM.

Updating the host status to OK

To update the host status to **OK**, follow these steps:

1. On the **Fabric** pane in the VMM console, expand **Servers** and then expand **vCenter Servers**.

2. On the **vCenter Servers** pane, select and right-click on the vCenter Server; click on **Properties**, confirm the secure mode setting, and click on **OK** to close.

3. For each VMware host that has the status **OK (Limited)**, right-click and click on **Properties**.

4. Select the **Management** tab and confirm the Run As account.

5. Click on **Retrieve** to claim the host SSL certificate and public key, and then click on **View Details** to see the certificate.

6. Click on **Accept the certificate for this host** to confirm, and then click on **OK**.

7. If the credentials of the secure mode are correctly configured, the host status will display **OK** in the **Hosts** pane.

8. Repeat these tasks for each host with the status **OK (Limited)**.

See also

▸ The *Adding a VMware vCenter Server to VMM* recipe.

Configuring network settings on a VMware ESX host

This recipe will guide you through the configuration of a logical network on the VMware host and to view compliance data for the physical network adapters on that host.

To make the host physical network adapters visible to the VMs that need external network access, you will need to assign them to logical networks.

Compliance data specifies whether or not IP subnets and/or VLANs allotted to a logical network are assigned to a host physical network adapter.

How to do it...

Carry out the following steps to associate logical networks with a physical network adapter:

1. On the **Fabric** pane in the VMM console, expand **Servers**; expand **All Hosts**, and then select the host group where the VMware ESX host resides (for example, **VMware Hosts**).

2. On the **Hosts** pane, select the VMware ESX host and then click on **Properties** on the **Host** tab in the ribbon.

3. Select the **Hardware** tab, and select the physical network adapter to configure in **Network Adapters**.

4. On the **Logical network connectivity** list, select the logical network(s) that are to be associated with the physical network adapter.

 Be careful when selecting the logical network, as all the logical networks for this host group will be listed, not just the available ones.

5. Click on **Advanced**, and then select a logical network from the **Logical network** list.

 In the **Advanced Network Adapter Properties** dialog box, for an ESX host you can view the IP subnets and VLANs available for a specified logical network, on the physical network adapter.

6. In the **Logical network** list, when the **Unassigned** option is available, the VLANs connected to a physical network adapter but not included in a network site will be displayed. You can then define them in a network site, if you want to.

How it works...

To assign VMM logical networks with a physical network adapter, in the **Fabric** workspace, select the VMware ESXi host and then the physical network adapter under **Hardware**. Note that when selecting the logical network, *all logical networks* are listed.

By default, for each selected logical network, the IPs and VLANs defined for a host group or inherited through the parent host group will be assigned to a physical network adapter.

If no IPs or VLANs show up in the **Available** or **Assigned** columns, no network site exists for the selected logical network that is defined on or inherited by the host group.

If you're using VLANs, you will need to make use of VMware vCenter to configure the port groups with the VLAN for the corresponding network site.

There's more...

You can verify a VMware ESX host's network settings and the compliance information in VMM. We'll see how to do this in the upcoming sections.

Verifying the settings for a virtual network

Carry out the following steps to check the network settings for a virtual network:

1. On the **Fabric** pane in the VMM console, expand **Servers**; under **Servers**, expand **All Hosts** and select the host group where the VMware ESX host resides (for example, **VMware Hosts**).

2. On the **Hosts** pane, select the ESX host; then, on the **Host** tab in the ribbon, click on **Properties** and click on the **Virtual Networks** tab.

3. On the **Virtual Networking** list, select the virtual network whose properties you'd like to view.

4. In the **Logical network** list, check if the logical network is assigned to a physical network adapter.

Viewing compliance information for a physical network adapter

Carry out the following steps to see the compliance information for a physical network adapter:

1. On the **Fabric** workspace in the VMM console, on the **Fabric** pane, expand **Networking**; then click on **Logical Networks**.

2. On the **Home** tab in the ribbon, click on **Hosts**.

3. On the **Logical Network Information for Hosts** pane, expand the host and select a physical network adapter. For this network adapter, the assigned IP subnets and VLANs will be displayed in the details pane.

4. On the **Compliance** column, the compliance status will show one of the following values:

    ❑ **Fully compliant**: This status confirms that all the IPs and VLANs that are included in the network site are allotted to a physical network adapter.

    ❑ **Partially compliant**: Indicates incomplete information. The IPs and/or VLANs that are in the network list and those assigned to a network adapter do not match.

[Check the reason for partial compliance in the **Compliance errors** section.]

    ❑ **Non-compliant**: Indicates that there are no IPs and/or VLANs defined for the logical networks that are associated with a physical network adapter.

See also

▸ The *Adding a VMware vCenter Server to VMM* recipe

Configuring host BMC settings

VMM 2012 supports Dynamic Optimization and Power Optimization on Hyper-V host clusters and on managed VMware ESX and Citrix XenServer host clusters that support live migration.

Power Optimization, an optional feature of Dynamic Optimization, is enabled only if a host group is configured for live migration of VMs through Dynamic Optimization. For meeting resource requirements and saving energy, it shuts down hosts not needed by the cluster and turns them on only when they are needed.

There is a requirement that the servers must have a **baseboard management controller (BMC)** that supports out-of-band management.

In order to configure the host BMC, the installed BMC controller must support one of the following BMC protocols:

▸ **System Management Architecture for Server Hardware (SMASH)** Version 1.0 over WS-Management (WS-Man)

▸ **Intelligent Platform Management Interface (IPMI)** Version 1.5 or 2.0

▸ **Data Center Management Interface (DCMI)** Version 1.0

How to do it...

Carry out the following steps to configure the BMC settings:

1. On the **Fabric** pane in the VMM console, expand **Servers**; under **Servers**, expand **All Hosts**; then, in the **Host** pane, select the host you want to configure.

2. On the **Host** tab in the ribbon, click on **Properties**.

3. Select the **Hardware** tab and click on **BMC Setting**; then select **This physical machine is configured for OOB management with the following settings**.

4. In the **This computer supports the specified OOB power management configuration** list, select the BMC protocol.

5. In the **BMC address** field, type the IP address of the BMC.

[VMM will automatically fill in the port number for the selected BMC protocol.]

6. For the Run As account field, click on **Browse** and select the Run As account with BMC access rights, and click on **OK**.

How it works...

For Power Optimization to work, the servers must have a supported BMC controller. It is important to verify that your server has a supported BMC and that you have installed one of the supported protocols before carrying out the process to configure the BMC on each host, in order to benefit from Power Optimization.

By using a BMC, VMM can power the host on or off.

There's more...

Now that the BMC is configured, you can use it to turn the servers on or off.

Powering a computer on or off through VMM

Carry out the following steps to turn servers on or off through VMM:

1. On the **Fabric** pane in the VMM console, expand **Servers**; then expand **All Hosts** and select the host that is to be configured in the **Host** pane.

2. On the **Host** tab, select one of the following available options: **Power On**, **Power Off**, **Shutdown**, or **Reset**.

> To view the BMC log information, select the **Hardware** tab in the host properties, and in the **Advanced** section click on **BMC Logs**.

See also

▶ The *Configuring Dynamic and Power Optimization in VMM* page at
  `http://technet.microsoft.com/en-us/library/gg675109.aspx`

Importing VMware templates

This recipe focuses on importing VMware templates to VMM.

In VMM 2012, the VMware virtual machine disk (.vmdk) file is not copied/moved to the VMM library while importing a VMware template. Now, VMM copies the metadata associated with the VMware template and the VMDK file remains in the VMware datastore.

By employing this approach, when using templates VMM allows you to deploy VMs more efficiently and quickly. Moreover, VMM 2012 does not delete the source template.

> VMM 2012 is highly dependent on the VMware template that resides on the vCenter Server.

How to do it...

Carry out the following steps to configure the BMC settings:

1. On the **Library** workspace in the VMM console, on the **Home** tab in the ribbon, click on **Import VMware Template**.

2. Select the VMware template(s) to import and click on **OK**.

3. To confirm that the template was added, expand **Templates** and click on **VM Templates** in the **Library** pane.

How it works...

In VMM, only the metadata associated with a VMware template is copied to the VMM library. The virtual machine disk (`.vmdk`) file remains in the VMware datastore.

If the template is removed from vCenter Server, it will go into a missing state in VMM. On the other hand, if you convert it into a VM, make some changes, and then convert it back to a template, the ID will remain the same and VMM will set its state as `OK` instead of `missing`.

When the VMware template is removed from the VMM library, it is not deleted from the VMware datastore.

See also

► The *Adding VMware ESX host clusters or cluster to VMM* recipe

Converting VMware virtual machines to Hyper-V

You can convert any virtual machine running on a VMware ESX host or stored in the VMM library, but VMM does not support virtual-to-virtual (V2V) conversion of a VMware VM that has an Integrated Drive Electronics (IDE) bus.

The following versions of VMware ESX are supported for V2V conversions by VMM 2012 SP1:

► ESX/ESXi 3.5 Update 5
► ESX/ESXi 4.0
► ESX/ESXi 4.1
► ESX/ESXi 5.0
► ESXi 5.1

Before you convert a VMware VM to a Hyper-V VM, you must uninstall VMware Tools on the source VM.

This recipe will guide you on how to convert a VMware VM to a Hyper-V VM through the V2V conversion process.

How to do it...

Carry out the following steps to convert VMs:

1. On the **VMs and Services** workspace in the VMM console, on the **Home** tab in the ribbon, click on **Create Virtual Machine** and then on **Convert Virtual Machine**.

2. On the **Select Source** page in **Convert Virtual Machine Wizard**, click on **Browse** and select the VMware VM that is to be converted.

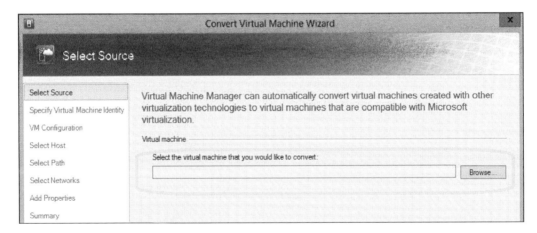

3. Click on **OK**; then, in the **Select Source** page, click on **Next**.

4. On the **Specify Virtual Machine Identity** page, confirm the VM name (you can change it if you want to), type in a description (optional), and click on **Next**.

 The VM name does not have to match the computer name (the NetBIOS name), but as a best practice it is recommended that you keep both names the same.

5. On the **Virtual Machine Configuration** page, set the the number of processor(s) and the memory, and click on **Next**.

6. On the **Select Host** page, select the target Hyper-V host and click on **Next**.

7. On the **Select Path** page, specify the VM file's storage location.

 The default VM paths on the target host will be displayed now. You can select a different path. Click on **Browse**, select the path/folder, and click on **OK**. Then, you can click on **Add this path to the list of default storage locations on the host** if you want this path to be a part of the default VM's path.

8. On the **Select Networks** page, select the VM network, logical network, and VLAN (if applicable) and click on **Next**.

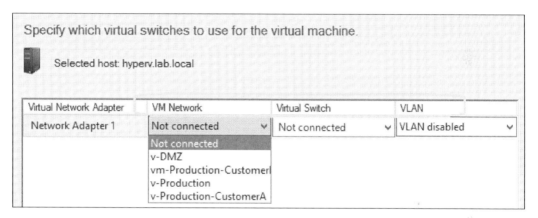

9. On the **Add properties** page, select your preferred actions from the **Automatic actions** list.

10. On the **Summary** page, click on **Start the virtual machine after deploying it**; then click on **Create**.

11. Verify that the job status shows **Completed** and then close the dialog box.

12. To verify that the virtual machine was converted, in the **VMs and Services** workspace, select the Hyper-V host that you had chosen earlier in this task.

13. On the **Home** tab, click on **VMs**; then, in the **VMs** pane verify that the VM appears.

How it works...

If you are running a supported version of a VMware VM, start by confirming that the source VM does not have an Integrated Drive Electronics (IDE) bus, as VMM does not support it.

Then, open the VMM console and click on **Convert Virtual Machine** on the ribbon. Carry out the steps given in the previous section, by first selecting the VM that you want to convert.

You can change the VM name when prompted for the VM identity, and optionally you can type in a description for it. The VM name does not necessarily have to match the computer name (NetBIOS name), but as a best practice it is recommended that you keep them the same.

On the VM's configuration page, you can change the number of allocated processors and the memory assigned while keeping the source configuration or changing it for the target VM.

By default, the VM paths on the target host will be displayed when selecting the path for the VM, but you can specify a different one (if required) and make it the default path as well.

Select the network you want the VM to be assigned to, and configure the desired settings on the **Add Properties** page. Confirm all the settings on the summary page and click on **Create** to start the virtual-to-virtual machine conversion process.

See also

▸ The *Adding VMware ESX hosts or host clusters to VMM* recipe

Managing Citrix XenServer hosts and pools

Using VMM, you can deploy and manage Citrix XenServer hosts and pools (clusters). VMM manages XenServer hosts directly.

You can perform functions like discovery, creation, management, storage, and deployment of VMs and services on XenServer hosts and pools.

You can also make XenServer resources available to private cloud deployments using the VMM console or PowerShell.

The following Xen features are supported by VMM:

- ▸ Standalone XenServer hosts and pools (clusters).

- ▸ VM placement based on host ratings when creating, deploying, and migrating XenServer VMs.

- ▸ Deployment of VMM services to XenServer hosts.

- ▸ XenServer resources, which can be made available to a private cloud when creating it from host groups that have XenServer hosts.

- ▸ You can configure quotas for private clouds and application (self-service) roles assigned to private clouds.

- ▸ The VMM Dynamic Optimization feature for XenServer hosts and clusters.

- ▸ Live migration between XenServer hosts in a cluster (pool); it is only supported through Citrix XenMotion.

- ▸ LAN migration between a host and the library through BITS.

- ▸ A XenServer host can be placed in the maintenance mode using the VMM console, if it is managed by VMM.

- ▸ You can store XenServer VMs, VHD files, and VMM templates in the VMM library. VMM supports the creation of new VMs from those templates.

- ▸ Although you cannot use XenServer templates with VMM, you can use XenCenter to create a VM and then create a VMM template from this VM.

- ▸ VMM networking management features are supported on XenServer hosts, but you are required to create external virtual switches through XenCenter. VMM will recognize and use existing external networks for VM deployment.

- ▸ All virtual disk storage repositories that XenServer supports.

- ▸ Converting a XenServer VM running a supported guest OS to a Hyper-V VM is supported, using (physical-to-virtual) P2V machine conversion.

It is not required to remove Citrix Tools before the P2V process.

- ▸ VMM can also support Paravirtual (PV) and hardware-assisted virtualization (HVM) VMs, but with restrictions.

- ▸ Monitoring and alerting for XenServer hosts through VMM, when it is integrated with SC Operations Manager and PRO.

The following Xen features are not supported by VMM:

- ▸ LAN migration (host-to-host migration of VMs that have been stopped) between XenServer and other hosts

- ▸ Updating management through VMM (you cannot use WSUS to update XenServer hosts)

- ▸ Conversion of a bare-metal computer to a XenServer host, and cluster creation

This recipe will take you through the process of integrating Citrix XenServer with VMM.

Getting ready

Make sure you install and configure XenServer before adding the hosts to VMM management.

 If you want to add a XenServer pool (multiple XenServer host installations that are bound together as a single managed entity), you will first need to create and configure it in Citrix XenCenter.

Also, you must have a DHCP server to assign the IP addresses automatically; it needs to be accessible from the management network for Citrix Transfer VMs; these are templates for virtual machines supporting Paravirtualization, created and deleted on the XenServer host during operations in XenServer.

Also check whether the following conditions are met:

- ▸ Whether the Citrix Host(s) meets the requirements. See the *System Requirements: Citrix XenServer Hosts* page at `http://go.microsoft.com/fwlink/p/?LinkID=217487`.

- ▸ Whether you've already created a Run As account with root credentials on the Citrix hosts that you want to add.

How to do it...

We have to carry out the procedures discussed in the upcoming sections to integrate Citrix with VMM.

Creating a pool on Citrix XenCenter

1. Open XenCenter, and on the toolbar click on the **New Pool** button.

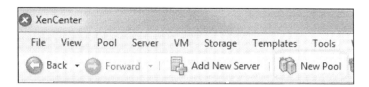

2. Type in a name and optional description for the new pool (for example, **XS Pool1**).

3. Nominate the pool master by selecting a host from the **Master** list; then select the second host to place in the new pool from the **Additional members** list.

4. Click on **Create Pool** and confirm that the new pool is showing in the **Resources** pane.

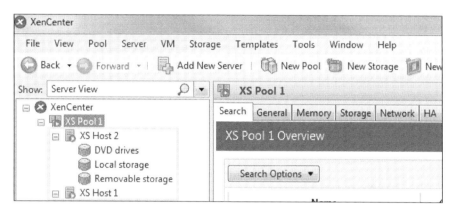

Adding Citrix XenServer Hosts to VMM

1. On the **Fabric** pane in the VMM console, expand **Servers**; on the **Home** tab in the ribbon, click on **Add Resources**.

2. Click on **Citrix XenServer Hosts and Cluster**; in the **Add Resource Wizard** window, go to the **Server Settings** page and type in the name of the XenServer host in the **Computer name** field.

 You can type in the FQDN, the NetBIOS, or the IP address. To add a XenServer pool, you can type in the IP address or the name of any XenServer host in the pool.

3. On **TCP port**, specify the XenServer host port.

The default XenServer host port is TCP 5989.

4. Select **Use certificates to communicate with this host**.

5. Click on **Browse** to select the Run As account with root credentials (or equivalent) on the XenServer host(s), click on **OK**, and then click on **Next**.

6. On the **Host group** list, select the target host group (for example, **Citrix Servers**) and click on **Add**.

7. Each XenServer host that is listed should match the name of the issued certificate. Confirm that the certificate for each host is valid, select **These certificates have been reviewed and can be imported to the trusted certificate store**, and click on **Next**.

8. On the **Summary** page, click on **Finish**.

9. Verify that the job has the status of **Completed**, and then close the dialog box.

How it works...

You can add Citrix XenServer hosts and clusters (pools) using **Add Resources** in the **Fabric** pane, on the VMM console. When adding a Xen pool (cluster), you don't need to specify the master host as you can select it during the operation.

You can specify an IP address or name, but it needs to be resolved by your DNS servers.

VMM discovers the XenServer(s) and lists them in the lower pane. When you add a pool, it will be listed along with each XenServer host in the pool.

During the addition process, you need to verify whether each XenServer listed matches the name of the issued certificate by clicking on a host and then clicking on **View certificate**. If you find a XenServer with a certificate that is not valid, click on **Remove** to delete it from the list.

If all XenServer hosts have a valid certificate, you can select **These certificates have been reviewed and can be imported to the trusted certificate store**.

Confirm the settings and click on **Finish** to add the XenServer(s) to the VMM management.

There's more...

If you have issues adding a XenServer host, check whether the DNS name is getting resolved and whether you can ping the host.

Troubleshooting a failed job when adding XenServer hosts

Carry out the following steps to troubleshoot a failed job when adding XenServer hosts:

1. Check whether it is possible to ping the host by the name or IP address.

   ```
   C:\> ping 192.168.4.21
   ```

2. Check whether the server/computer name is getting resolved by the DNS server.

   ```
   C:\>nslookup  xen-host1
   C:\>ping   -a xen-host1
   ```

3. Verify that the supplemental pack is correctly installed on each XenServer host.

   ```
   C:\>winrm enum http://schemas.citrix.com/wbem/wscim/1/cim-
   schema/2/Xen_HostComputerSystem -r:https://<XenHost>:5989
   -encoding:utf-8 -a:basic -u:<USER> -p:<PASSWD> -skipcacheck -
   skipcncheck
   ```

   Here, `<XenHost>` is the XenServer host, `<USER>` is the XenServer root user, and `<PASSWD>` is the password of the root user.

    If the command does not return information about the host computer, it could indicate that the supplemental pack is not installed or is malfunctioning. In such a case, reinstall it.

4. Verify whether the host was added successfully; in the **Fabric** pane on the VMM console, expand **Servers**; then expand the host group (for example, **Citrix Hosts**) and select the XenServer host. In the **Hosts** pane, confirm that the XenServer host status is showing **OK**.

See also

* The *System Requirements: Citrix XenServer Hosts* page at `http://go.microsoft.com/fwlink/p/?LinkID=217487`

* The *How to Configure Network Settings on a Citrix XenServer Host* page at `http://technet.microsoft.com/en-us/library/gg610697.aspx`

* The *Citrix Quick Start Guide* PDF document at `http://support.citrix.com/servlet/KbServlet/download/25588-102-666369/QuickStartGuide_BasicVersion.pdf`

Converting Citrix virtual machines to Hyper-V

Converting a Citrix XenServer VM to a Hyper-V VM is supported, and it is done using the P2V process. The procedure described in this recipe is exactly the same as the one used for converting physical servers to Hyper-V VMs.

You are not required to remove Citrix Tools from the source VM to start the P2V conversion.

However, note that only running VMs are supported for the conversion in VMM 2012. The source VM must also be running a supported Windows guest OS. You can check the supported operating systems at `http://technet.microsoft.com/en-us/library/hh427293.aspx`.

Additionally, the source machine needs to meet the following requirements:

- ▶ A minimum RAM of 512 MB
- ▶ Cannot have a volume larger than 2 TB
- ▶ Must have an Advanced Configuration and Power Interface (ACPI) BIOS
- ▶ Must be accessible to the VMM management server and the host
- ▶ Should not have encrypted volumes

How to do it...

Carry out the following steps to convert a Citrix VM to a Hyper-V VM:

1. In the **VMs and Services** workspace on the VMM console, on the **Home** tab in the ribbon, click on **Create Virtual Machine** and then select **Convert Physical Machine**.

2. In the **Convert Physical Server (P2V) Wizard** window, in the **Computer name or IP address** field in the **Select Source** section, type in the name or IP address of the XenServer virtual machine to be converted.

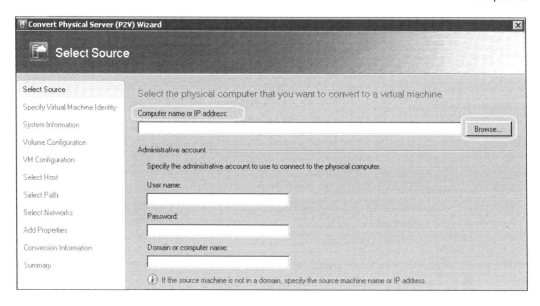

3. On the **Administrative account** section, specify the administrator credentials: **User name**, **Password**, and **Domain or computer name** (if applicable) to connect to the VM; then click on **Next**.

4. On the **Specify Virtual Machine Identity** page, type in the VM's name and description (optional) and click on **Next**.

5. On the **System Information** page, click on **Scan System** to collect information about the VM; then click on **Next** to continue.

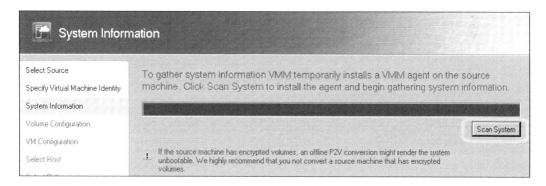

VMM will install a VMM agent on the XenServer virtual machine to gather system information.

6. In the **Volume Configuration** section, select the volumes to convert or clear the checkbox next to a particular volume if you don't want to convert it.

 You cannot deselect the system or system reserve volume.

7. Confirm or modify the **VHD Size (MB)**, **VHD Type**, and **Channel** settings.

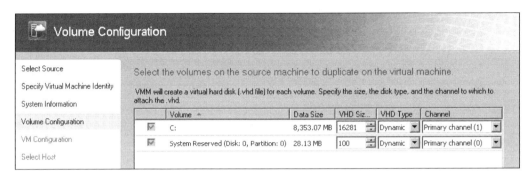

8. Click on **Conversion Options**; in the **Conversion Options** section, select **Online conversion** or **Offline conversion** and click on **Next**.

 Optionally, click on **Turn off source computer after conversion**.

9. If you select **Offline conversion**, in the **Offline Conversion Options** section you can either choose to use DHCP to automatically obtain an IP address or you can choose a specific IP address. In the latter case, you will need to provide the IP address manually and click on **Next** to continue.

10. On the **VM Configuration** page, set the number of processors and the amount of memory for the new VM; then click on **Next**.

11. On the **Select Host** page, review the host placement ratings, select a host (for example, **Hyperv01**), and click on **Next**.

12. On the **Select Path** page, specify the host storage location for the VM files and then click on **Next**.

13. On the **Select Networks** page, configure the **VM Network**, **Logical Network**, and **VLAN** (if applicable) settings for each virtual network adapter; then click on **Next**.

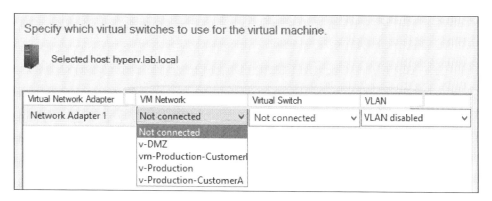

14. On the **Add properties** page, select your preferred actions from the **Automatic actions** list.

15. If issues (for example, the guest OS not supported, encrypted volumes) show up on the **Conversion Information** page, select the issue to view the error and see the suggested resolution. You should resolve the issues before continuing to the next step.

16. If no issues are detected, click on **Next**.

17. On the **Summary** page, click on **Start the virtual machine after deploying it** and then click on **Create**.

18. Check the job status and then close the dialog box.

How it works...

To start, open the VMM console and go to the **Home** tab in the **VMs and Services** workspace; then click on **Convert Physical Machine** under the **Create Virtual Machine** button on the ribbon.

Specify the IP address or machine name, followed by the domain and login credentials. Keep in mind that you need administrative rights on the physical server that should be accessible from the VMM server.

It is possible to select which volume(s) will be included in the conversion, but you cannot remove the system volume or system reserve volume. By default, VMM creates a VHD file for each volume.

If you choose to manually enter an IP address, after typing the address you can select the network adapter that the IP address will be bound to.

After you click on the **Create** button to start the P2V process, it will take some time to process the VM conversion as it depends on network speed and data size.

Make sure to turn off the XenServer VM if not selected in the steps, otherwise there will be a conflict between the two servers because the newly converted VM is a clone of the XenServer VM.

See also

- ▶ The list of supported operating systems on the *P2V Prerequisites* page at `http://technet.microsoft.com/en-us/library/hh427293.aspx`
- ▶ The *How to Convert Physical Computers to Virtual Machines* page at `http://technet.microsoft.com/en-us/library/hh427286.aspx`

9

Managing Hybrid Clouds, Fabric Updates, Creating Clusters, and New Features of SP1

In this chapter, we will cover:

- ▶ Creating Hyper-V clusters with VMM
- ▶ Managing fabric updates in VMM
- ▶ Configuring Dynamic Optimization and Power Optimization in VMM
- ▶ Live-migrating virtual machines with VMM 2012 SP1
- ▶ Linux virtual machines in VMM 2012 SP1
- ▶ Configuring availability options and Virtual NUMA for VMs in VMM 2012 SP1
- ▶ Configuring resource throttling in VMM SP1
- ▶ Deploying SC App Controller 2012 SP1 for hybrid cloud management

Introduction

In this chapter, we take a closer look at the additional improvements provided by VMM 2012. The chapter also explores some of the key features of System Center Service Pack 1.

There are many new features and improvements in SC 2012 SP1. In this chapter, we will continue to learn more about them: live migration, availability options, resource throttling, and virtual NUMA (Non-Uniform Memory Access). We will also see the SC App Controller (which is the replacement of the VMM Self-Service Portal) that will allow you to integrate with Windows Azure and manage your hybrid cloud.

Creating Hyper-V clusters with VMM

This recipe will guide you to create a Hyper-V cluster using VMM. By using the steps provided here, you will be able to select the Hyper-V servers and join them to a cluster, configuring networking and storage resources in the process.

Prerequisites for cluster creation using VMM 2012

Make sure that the following prerequisites are met:

- You need at least two standalone Hyper-V servers and they need to be under VMM management already (see the *Adding and managing Hyper-V hosts and host clusters in VMM* recipe in *Chapter 4, Configuring Fabric Resources in VMM*).

- The hosts should meet the requirements for Failover Clustering and should be running one of the following operating systems:

    1. **For VMM 2012**: Windows Server 2008 R2 Enterprise Edition (SP1 or earlier) or Windows Server 2008 R2 Datacenter Edition (SP1 or earlier).

    2. **For VMM 2012 SP1**: Windows Server 2008 R2 (Enterprise or Datacenter Edition) or Windows Server 2012 (any edition).

 The roles and features are the same for all Windows 2012 editions (Standard or Datacenter).

- The OS is updated and the required hotfixes have been applied.

 For clusters with three or more nodes running Windows Server 2008 R2 SP1, check the following Microsoft Knowledge Base (KB) article: `http://go.microsoft.com/fwlink/p?LinkId=225883`

- The Hyper-V hosts must all be part of the same domain to be added as cluster nodes.

- The VMM management server must either be in the same domain as the hosts or on a trusted domain.

- If the Hyper-V hosts are configured with static IP addresses, make sure those IP addresses are in the same subnet.

- The Hyper-V hosts that are going to be added as cluster nodes need to be in the same host group.

- Each Hyper-V host must have access to the storage array.

- The Multipath I/O (MPIO) driver must be installed on each host that will access the Fibre Channel or iSCSI storage array.

> If the MPIO driver is already installed (before the host is added to VMM), VMM will enable it for supported storage arrays by using the Microsoft-provided **Device Specific Module (DSM)**.
>
> If you installed vendor-specific DSMs for your supported storage arrays and then added the host to VMM, the vendor-specific MPIO settings will be used to connect with the storage arrays.
>
> If you added a host to VMM before installing the MPIO feature, you will need to manually install and configure the MPIO driver or vendor-specific DSMs to have the device hardware IDs added.

Prerequisites for fabric configuration

Make sure that the fabric configuration meets the following prerequisites:

- For VMM-managed shared storage:
    1. It is essential that the storage be added, configured, and classified in the **Fabric** workspace.
    2. The logical units need to be created and allocated to the target host group or parent host group and should not be provisioned to any host.

- For unmanaged shared storage:
    1. Disks must be made available to all the nodes in the new cluster.
    2. Provision one or more of the logical units to the hosts.
    3. Mount the cluster disk on one of the hosts and format it.

> When working with asymmetric storage in VMM, you must configure each node of the cluster as a possible owner of the cluster disk. *VMM is agnostic regarding the use of asymmetric storage.*

When using a Fibre Channel storage area network (SAN), each node must have a host bus adapter (HBA) installed with its ports correctly zoned.

When using an iSCSI SAN, make sure the iSCSI portals have been added and the iSCSI initiator logged into the storage array. Likewise, make sure the **Microsoft iSCSI Initiator** service on each host is configured to start automatically, and is started.

Network

Make sure the following prerequisites are met:

▸ The Hyper-V hosts should be configured in the **Fabric** workspace, with at least one common logical network; if it has associated network sites, a network site should be defined for the target host group.

▸ In addition, on each Hyper-V host, the logical networks should be linked with physical network adapters.

▸ External virtual switches don't need to be created beforehand; if you do create them, make sure the names of the external switches and associated logical networks are exactly the same on all Hyper-V hosts.

[After creating the cluster in VMM, you can create and configure the external switches (virtual networks) on all the nodes of the cluster. You can also configure the virtual network settings for the cluster after it is created.]

Getting ready

Check whether you have configured the fabric resources and deployed the Hyper-V servers (see *Chapter 4, Configuring Fabric Resources in VMM*), and whether the prerequisites are met.

How to do it...

Carry out the following steps to deploy a cluster in VMM:

1. Go to the **Fabric** pane in the **Fabric** workspace on the VMM console, and click on **Servers**.

2. On the **Home** tab in the ribbon, click on **Create**; then click on **Hyper-V Cluster**.

3. On the **Create Cluster Wizard** window, in the **Cluster name** box on the **General** tab, type in a cluster name (for example, `ProdHyperClust.lab.local`).

4. Specify a Run As account (recommended) or type in credentials for an account with local admin rights on all the servers that will be added to the cluster, in the format `domain\username` (for example, `lab\host-admin`).

> The domain for the account must be the same for the servers being added. Additionally, the account needs the permissions **Create Computer objects** and **Read All Properties** in the container that is used for the server computer accounts in AD.

5. Click on **Next**.

6. In the **Host group** list on the **Nodes** page, click to select the host group that contains the hosts that are to be clustered (for example, `Sydney\HypervHosts`).

> The Hyper-V hosts that are to be clustered must all be in the same host group. In addition, they must meet the OS prerequisites in order to be displayed under **Available hosts**.

7. In the **Available hosts** list, select a Hyper-V host that you want to add to the cluster and click on **Add**; you will see the hosts that you added moving to the **Hosts to cluster** column.

> You can press and hold down the *Ctrl* key and click on each host to select various hosts together, or you can press and hold down the *Shift* key, click on the first host, and then click the last host to select a series.

The following screenshot depicts the **Create Cluster Wizard**:

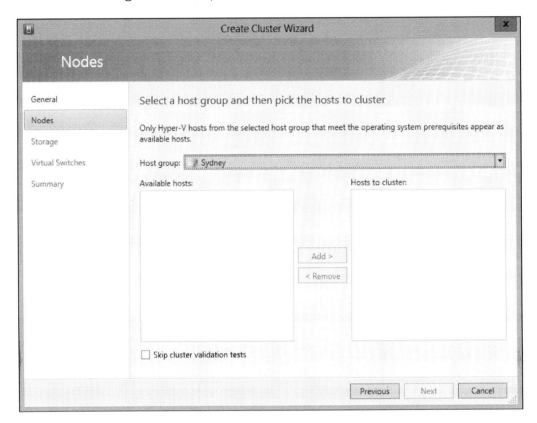

 If you select **Skip cluster validation tests** (not recommended), the cluster will have no support from Microsoft as there will be no guarantee that the servers meet the cluster requirements.

8. Click on **Next**.

9. The **IP Address** page of the wizard will be displayed if, among all the hosts, at least one physical network adapter is configured with a static IPv4 address and there is a physical network adapter on all other hosts that are assigned to the same subnet.

 VMM will display the list of associated networks for that static IPv4 subnet.

10. In the **Network** column, select the network(s) to allocate a static cluster IPv4 address to, and then do one of the following:

    ❑ When no static IPv4 address pools are associated with the subnet, type in the IP address of the selected network in the **IP Address** column.

    ❑ When static IPv4 address pools are associated with the subnet, you can choose one the following options:

    ❑ In the **Static IP Pool** column, select an IPv4 address pool for VMM to automatically assign a static IPv4 from that pool.

    ❑ In the **IP Address** column, type in an available IPv4 address within the same subnet, and make sure not to select an IP pool in the **Static IP Pool** column. VMM will detect if you type an IPv4 address in the range of the IPv4 address pool, and will not assign that to another host.

> If any host has a physical network adapter configured with DHCP that falls in the same subnet, you don't need to set up a static IPv4.

11. Click on **Next**.

12. On the **Storage** page, select the disk(s) to add to cluster and then configure these options: **Classification**, **Partition Style**, **File System**, **Volume Label**, **Quick Format**, and **CSV**.

> The list of available disks characterizes the logical units associated with the nominated host group.
>
> When assigning storage as out-of-band storage, as the disks are not managed by VMM, all disks will be selected and shown as available. You will not be able to change the selection.
>
> Additionally, *do not select clustered file system disks for the cluster when using a third-party CFS*; if you do this, the cluster creation will be unsuccessful.
>
> If the number of selected hosts is even, the smallest disk (>500MB) will be automatically chosen as the witness disk and will become unavailable for selection.

13. On the **Virtual Networks** page, select a logical network that is to be automatically associated with the external virtual network when VMM creates it on each cluster node.

> The logical network associated with a physical network adapter (including associated VLAN IDs) must be identical on all nodes.
>
> Logical networks already assigned to external virtual networks will not be displayed.

14. Type in a name and a description (optional) for the external virtual network.

15. If you want to allow the management of hosts through this network, select **Allow hosts to access VMs through this virtual network**.

> It is recommended to have a dedicated physical network card for host management instead of sharing it with VM traffic.

16. If you need to communicate with the hosts over a VLAN, select the **Hosts can access the VLAN ID** checkbox and then select the VLAN (defined as part of the logical network).

17. Click on **Next** and verify the settings on the **Summary** page, and then click on **Finish**.

How it works...

During the cluster-creation process, VMM verifies whether the hosts meet the prerequisites, such as the required operating system versions and the domain; for each host, VMM enables the Failover Clustering feature, unmasks the selected storage logical units, and creates the external switches (virtual networks).

The setup continues; VMM runs the cluster-validation process, and then it creates the cluster with the quorum and enables CSV for each logical unit designated as a CSV (Cluster Shared Volume). When managing a logical unit's assignment, VMM creates one storage group per host node by default. In a cluster configuration, it creates one storage group per cluster node.

> In VMM, a storage group binds together host initiators, target ports, and logical units (which are exposed to the host initiators through the target ports).
>
> A storage group can have multiple host initiator IDs, that is, it can have an iSCSI Qualified Name (IQN) or a World Wide Name (WWN).

For some types of storage, it is ideal to use one storage group for the entire cluster, where host initiators of all nodes will be restricted to a unique storage group. For this configuration, use VMM PowerShell to set the `CreateStorageGroupsPerCluster` property to `$true`:

```
$StorageName = @(Get-SCStorageArray)[0]
Set-SCStorageArray -StorageArray $StorageName -
CreateStorageGroupsPerCluster $true
```

You can force the storage format by using **Force Format**; on the **Storage** page, right-click on the column header and then click on **Force Format**.

 Use the **Force Format** option with extreme caution, as the current disk data will be overwritten during cluster creation.

When the cluster creation job is finished, verify the cluster status by clicking on the created host cluster and confirming that the host status for each node (in the **Host Status** column in the **Hosts** pane) is **OK**.

To view the detailed status information for the created host cluster (including the cluster validation test report), select the host and right-click on it, click on **Properties**, and click on the **Status** tab.

There's more...

Now let's talk about some other options.

Adding a Hyper-V host as a cluster node

Carry out the following steps to add a Hyper-V server to an existing cluster:

1. In the **Fabric** workspace on the VMM console, in the **Fabric** pane, expand **Servers,** expand **All Hosts**, and then select the host to add and drag it to the host cluster name.

2. In the **Add Node to Cluster** dialog, type in the credentials (for example, `lab\host-admin`) for an account with administrative rights on the host, or specify a Run As account.

3. Click on **OK**. VMM will then add the node to the cluster. In the **Jobs** workspace, check the job status.

 You can verify that the cluster node was added by going to the **Fabric** pane, expanding **Servers**, expanding **All Hosts**, and then locating and clicking on the host cluster. In the **Hosts** pane, confirm that the new node is displayed in the host cluster with a host status of **OK**.

See also

► The *Failover Clustering Hardware Requirements and Storage Options* page at `http://technet.microsoft.com/en-us/library/jj612869.aspx`

► The *Failover Cluster Step-by-Step Guide: Configuring Accounts in Active Directory* page at `http://go.microsoft.com/fwlink/p/?LinkId=213267`

Managing fabric updates in VMM

A VMM-managed fabric server comprises the following workloads: Hyper-V hosts and host clusters, the VMM library servers, Pre-Boot Execution Environment (PXE), the Windows Server Update Management (WSUS) server, and the VMM management server.

You can monitor the update status of the servers, scan for compliance, and update all or a set of the server's resources as well as exempt resources from the installation of an update.

You can also orchestrate update remediation on Hyper-V host clusters, in which VMM will place one node of the cluster at a time in maintenance mode and install the updates. If the cluster supports live migration, the Intelligent Placement feature will be used to live-migrate the VMs off the node; otherwise, VMM will save the state for the VMs and the host will start the VM after updating.

 After integrating the WSUS server with VMM, it is recommended that you manage it only through the VMM console (unless you have SC Configuration Manager sharing the same WSUS server). Do not use the WSUS administration console to manage the integrated WSUS server.

Getting ready

In order to use VMM to manage the updates, it is recommended that you install a dedicated WSUS server, but you can use an existing one or install it on the VMM Server if it is a small deployment.

As a prerequisite, install the WSUS administration console on the VMM management server before integrating WSUS with VMM (if the WSUS server is not installed on the VMM management server), and then restart the VMM service.

 It is neither a recommended approach nor a best practice to install the WSUS server on the VMM Management server unless it is a lab, POC, or a small deployment.

How to do it...

The following sections detail the procedures to configure WSUS integration with VMM.

Installing WSUS for VMM 2012

Carry out the following steps to install WSUS for VMM:

1. Install a WSUS role (which was covered in _Chapter 1, VMM 2012 Architecture_). You can use the following PowerShell commands:

```
PS C:\> Install-WindowsFeature -Name UpdateServices,
UpdateServices-Ui

## Assuming D:\WSUS is the update content folder

PS C:\> 'C:\Program Files\Update Services\Tools\WsusUtil.exe'
PostInstall CONTENT_DIR=D:\WSUS
```

2. In the Windows Start menu launch **Windows Server Update Services**, and in the **Configuration Wizard** configure the following:

   1. Microsoft Report View 2008 (not required if you installed the WSUS server on the VMM server).
   2. Upstream Server.
   3. Languages.
   4. Products (at least Windows OS, SQL, IIS, and System Center).
   5. Classifications (at least Critical and Security Updates).

6. Sync Schedule (manual).

 If you have installed the WSUS server on a server other than the VMM Management server (recommended approach), install the WSUS administration console on the VMM Management server and restart the VMM service.

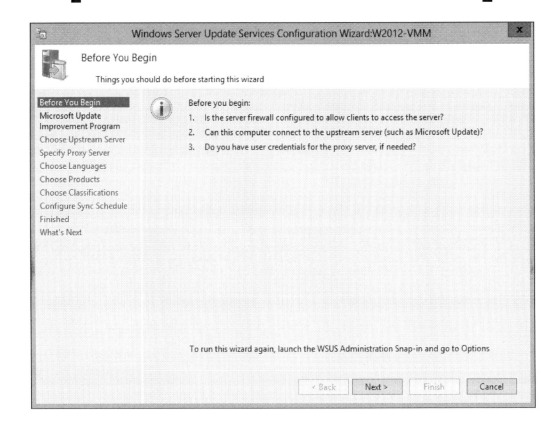

3. Click on **Finish**; then click on **Synchronizations** in the navigation pane to confirm that the initial sync succeeded.

Integrating WSUS with VMM

Carry out the following steps to add WSUS to VMM:

1. In the **Fabric** workspace on the VMM console, click on **Add Resources** on the **Home** tab in the ribbon.

2. Select **Update Server**, and on the **Add Windows Server Update Services Server** dialog in the **Computer name** field, type in the FQDN of the WSUS server (for example, `w2012-wsus.lab.local`).

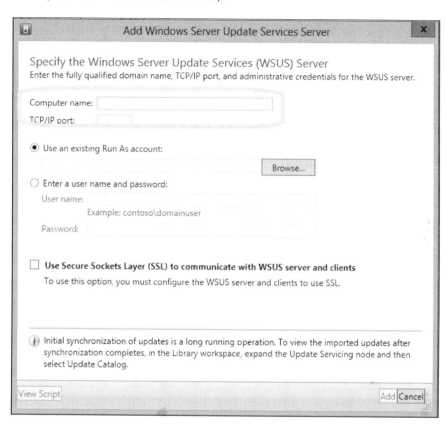

3. Specify the WSUS TCP/IP port (The default is 8530).

4. Click on **Use an existing Run As account** and then click on **Browse** to select the Run As account, or click on **Enter a user name and password** and then type in the user credentials (in the format `domain\username`; for example, `lab\wsus-admin`) for an account with administrative rights on the WSUS server, to connect to the WSUS server.

5. If required, select the **Use Secure Socket Layer (SSL) to communicate with the WSUS server and clients** checkbox, and click on **Add**.

These steps will add the WSUS server to VMM, followed by an initial synchronization of a collection of updates. This operation can take a long time as it depends on a number of factors such as the network, updates, bandwidth, and so on.

How it works...

VMM uses WSUS to send updates to managed computers, but in a different way compared to the Configuration Manager. VMM provides two inbuilt update baselines that can be used to apply security and other critical updates to the servers in your VMM environment, but you must assign these baselines to host groups, clusters, or individually managed computers before you start using them.

You can install WSUS on the same server on which you installed the VMM management server. Note that this is only recommended in small scenarios.

 The WSUS administration console is required on each VMM management server.

To check whether the WSUS server was successfully integrated into VMM, in the **Fabric** workspace, expand **Servers** and click on **Update Server**. In the results pane, you should be able to see the configured WSUS server.

In the **Library** workspace, expand **Update Catalog and Baselines** and click on **Update Catalog** to see which updates were downloaded through WSUS synchronization.

Subsequently, you should configure the proxy server for synchronization by clicking on **Update Server**, clicking on **Properties** in the **Update Server** tab in the ribbon, and adjusting the update categories, products, and supported languages that will be synchronized by WSUS.

There's more...

You can assign computers to a baseline. To do that, carry out the following steps:

1. On the **Library** workspace on the VMM console, in the **Library** pane, expand **Update Catalog and Baselines** and click on **Update Baselines**.

2. In the **Baselines** pane, select the baseline (for example, **Sample Baseline for Critical Updates**).

3. On the **Home** page in the ribbon, click on **Properties** and then click on **Updates** on the baseline dialog box.

 You can add/remove baselines from those that are listed.

4. Click on **Assignment Scope** and then select the hosts, hosts groups, and/or clusters that are to be added to the baseline.

5. Select the computers symbolized by the roles they perform in VMM, or click on **All Hosts** to apply the baseline to all computers. Note that all the roles that the computer performs will be selected.

6. To confirm, click on **OK**. This will save the changes.

Scanning servers for compliance

You can scan computers to check their compliance status for a particular baseline. You will be required to scan the servers again if the server was moved from one host group to another, an update was added/ removed from a baseline assigned to that server, or if it was just added to the scope of a baseline. To perform the scan, carry out the following steps:

1. In the **Fabric** workspace, go to the **Fabric** pane and click on **Servers**.

2. On the **Home** tab, click on **Compliance** and then check the compliance status in the results pane.

> Until you scan the servers for compliance, the compliance status will show **Unknown** and the operational status will show **Pending Compliance Scan**.

3. In the **Compliance** view, select the servers to scan.

> You must perform and complete the updates successfully in the **Compliance** view.

4. In the **Home** tab, click on **Scan**.

> When the task is completed, the compliance status of each update will change from **Unknown** to **Compliant**, **NonCompliant**, or **Error**.
>
> The **Scan** and **Remediate** tasks are available in the **Fabric Resources** view as well.

Remediating updates for a standalone server in VMM

To make noncompliant standalone servers compliant, you will need to carry out the following steps in VMM:

1. In the **Compliance** view, select the servers to remediate.

> Click on a specific server to display the baselines checked for it.

2. Select an update baseline or a single update within a baseline that is **Non Complaint**, and then right-click and click on **Remediate** or click on **Remediate** in the **Home** tab.

3. In the **Update Remediation** dialog you can optionally select or clear update baselines or specific updates, to limit which updates are applied.

4. If the update requires a restart, select the **Do not restart the servers after remediation** checkbox to manually restart the server after the update is applied.

5. Click on **Remediate** to begin the remediation process.

Remediating updates for a Hyper-V cluster in VMM

To make noncompliant servers in a Hyper-V cluster compliant, you need carry out the following steps in VMM:

1. In the **Compliance** view, click on **Remediate**.

2. In the resource list on the **Update Remediation** dialog, select the cluster to remediate.

3. If the update requires a restart, select the **Do not restart the servers after remediation** checkbox to manually restart the server after the update is applied.

4. Select **Allow remediation of clusters with nodes already in maintenance mode** to bypass maintenance mode for a particular node (which happens by default).

5. Select **Live migration** to move the VMs before starting the process, or **Save State** to shut the VMs down and then proceed with the updates.

6. Click on **Remediate** to begin the remediation process.

See also

▶ The *How to Integrate Fabric Updates with Configuration Manager* page at `http://technet.microsoft.com/en-us/library/hh341476.aspx`

▶ The *How to Update WSUS Settings in VMM* page at `http://technet.microsoft.com/en-us/library/gg710534.aspx`

▶ The *How to Create and Remove Update Exemptions for Resources in VMM* page at `http://technet.microsoft.com/en-us/library/gg710535.aspx`

Configuring Dynamic Optimization and Power Optimization in VMM

Dynamic Optimization (DO) is a new VMM feature that initiates live migration of VMs that are on a cluster, to improve load balancing among cluster nodes and to correct any placement constraint violations.

It can be configured with a specific frequency and aggressiveness on a host group, which determines the amount of load discrepancy required to trigger a live migration through Dynamic Optimization (DO).

Dynamic Optimization settings can be configured for the CPU, memory, disk I/O, and network I/O.

By default, VMs are migrated every 10 minutes with medium aggressiveness. You must take into consideration the resource cost (for example, the network) of extra migrations against the advantages of load balancing among cluster nodes, when setting the frequency and aggressiveness for Dynamic Optimization.

 By default, a host group inherits DO settings from its parent host group.

Power Optimization, a Dynamic Optimization optional feature, is enabled only if a host group is configured for live migration of VMs through Dynamic Optimization. It helps meet resource requirements and saves energy by shutting down hosts that are not needed by the cluster, and turns them back on only when they are needed.

Power Optimization settings comprise CPU, memory, disk space, disk I/O, and network I/O settings.

For Power Optimization, the servers are required to have a baseboard management controller (BMC) that supports out-of-band management. See the *Configuring host BMC settings* recipe in *Chapter 8, Managing VMware ESXi and Citrix XenServer Hosts*.

The rules of thumb for Power Optimization are as follows:

▶ For clusters created outside VMM and then added to VMM:

1. One node can be shut down on a cluster with five to six nodes.
2. Two nodes can be shut down on a cluster with seven to eight nodes.
3. Three nodes can be shut down on a cluster with nine to ten nodes.

▶ For VMM-created clusters:

1. One node can be shut down on a cluster with four to five nodes.
2. Two nodes can be shut down on a cluster with six to seven nodes.
3. Three nodes can be shut down on a cluster with eight to nine nodes.

Then for each extra one to two nodes on a cluster, one more node can be shut down.

Getting ready

For enabling Dynamic Optimization and Power Optimization, the VM must be running on a cluster.

Additionally, for Power Optimization, confirm the BMC supported protocol. See the *Configuring host BMC settings* recipe in *Chapter 8, Managing VMware ESXi and Citrix XenServer Hosts*.

How to do it...

We will carry out the steps in the following sections to configure settings for Dynamic Optimization and Power Optimization.

Configuring settings for Dynamic Optimization

1. In the **Fabric** workspace on the VMM console, expand **Servers**, expand **All Hosts** under **Servers**, and then select the host group to configure.
2. Click on **Properties** on the **Folder** tab in the ribbon, and then click on **Dynamic Optimization**.

3. If you don't want to inherit the parent host group settings, on the **Dynamic Optimization** page deselect **Use dynamic optimization settings from the parent host group**.

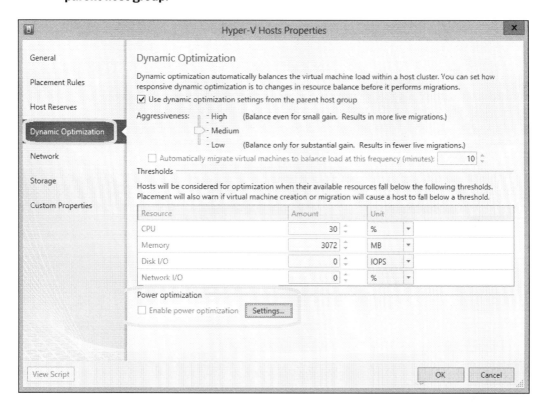

4. To set the **Aggressiveness** level, select either **High**, **Medium**, **Low**, or any value in between.

If you select a higher level of aggressiveness, the result will be more live migrations; on the other hand, if you lower the aggressiveness level, the end result will be less live migrations. The default value is **Medium**. Live migrations will happen based on the ratings determined by Intelligent Placement.

5. To run Dynamic Optimization from time to time, select the **Automatically migrate virtual machines to balance load at this frequency (minutes)** checkbox and type in a value to specify how often it will run.

> You can type in any value between 10 (default) and 1440 minutes (24 hours).

6. Click on **OK** to save the changes.

Configuring settings for Power Optimization

1. In the **Fabric** workspace on the VMM console, expand **Servers**, expand **All Hosts** under **Servers**, and then select a host group to configure (for example, **Sydney**).

2. Click on **Properties** on the **Folder** tab in the ribbon, and then click on **Dynamic Optimization**.

3. Select **Enable power optimization** to enable Power Optimization for the selected host group.

4. In the **Customize Power Optimization Schedule** dialog, configure the **CPU**, **Memory**, **Disk I/O**, and **Network I/O** resources settings, or leave the default values as they are.

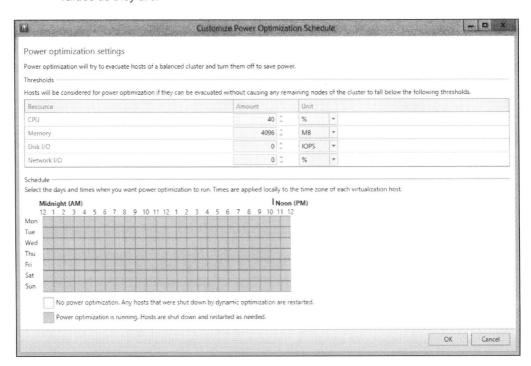

5. In the **Schedule** section, select the days and set the time you want Power Optimization to be performed.

6. Click on **OK** to save the changes.

 Power Optimization will be scheduled according to the time zone of each node in the cluster.

How it works...

Dynamic Optimization can be enabled only for clusters with two or more nodes and will only be performed on the clusters that support live migration, have shared storage, and are not in the maintenance mode.

 If a host group comprises standalone hosts or clusters that do not support live migration, Dynamic Optimization will not be performed on those hosts/clusters.

Also, VMs that are not highly available are not migrated during Dynamic Optimization.

Dynamic Optimization on demand is also available for host clusters, without the need to configure DO on the host groups, which can be done using the **Optimize Hosts** task in the **VMs and Services** workspace. When DO is requested for a host cluster, VMM lists all VMs that will be migrated and then requests for the administrator's approval.

In the Dynamic Optimization settings you can set the level of aggressiveness, which is a measure of how responsive Dynamic Optimization is to changes in resource balance before it starts migrating VMs. Be cautious in balancing the resource cost of extra migrations against the benefits of balancing load among nodes on a cluster, and always check the effectiveness of Dynamic Optimization in your environment for a certain period of time before increasing or decreasing the values.

When manually optimizing the hosts (using the **Optimize Hosts** option), for load balancing, VMM will suggest VMs for migration, with the current and target hosts indicated.

 The list excludes any hosts that are in maintenance mode and VMs that are not highly available.

By configuring Power Optimization (PO) for the host group to meet resource requirements, VMM will shut down hosts not needed by the cluster (migrating all VMs to other hosts in the cluster), and turn them on again when they are needed; VMM will perform the Dynamic Optimization process to live-migrate VMs and balance load within the cluster.

Power Optimization is only available when VMs are being live-migrated automatically to balance load, and the physical host has BMC settings configured.

Power Optimization settings specify resource capabilities that must be kept when VMM shuts down a node cluster. These settings make a buffer of resources available, to guarantee that oscillations in resource usage in the course of usual operations do not end in VMM powering the nodes of the cluster on and off unnecessarily.

It is possible to schedule the time (in hours and days) at which power optimization can be performed, according to the time zone of each host.

 By default, Power Optimization will be run continuously if the feature is enabled.

There's more...

Now that we have enabled DO, let us take a look at how it is performed on a cluster.

Performing Dynamic Optimization on the host cluster

1. In the **Fabric** workspace on the VMM console, expand **Servers**, expand **All Hosts** under **Servers**, and then select a host group.

2. On the **Folder** tab in the ribbon, click on **Optimize Hosts**. Click on **Migrate** to start the Dynamic Optimization process within the cluster.

 VMM will perform a Dynamic Optimization assessment to decide whether a VM should be live-migrated to improve load balancing in the cluster.

See also

▶ The *Dynamic Optimization of the Private Cloud Infrastructure* page at http://
blogs.technet.com/b/server-cloud/archive/2012/02/08/dynamic-
optimization-of-the-private-cloud-infrastructure.aspx.

Live-migrating virtual machines with VMM 2012 SP1

Live migration is a feature that got a huge improvement in VMM 2012 SP1 due to the following Windows 2012 capabilities:

- ▶ Live migration between two isolated Hyper-V servers (with no shared storage).

- ▶ Live migration within cluster nodes.

- ▶ Live migration between nodes of two different clusters.

- ▶ Live storage migration: You can migrate the VM files (for example, VHD/VHDX, ISO, and VFD files) to update the physical storage, or to address bottlenecks in storage performance. Storage can be added to either an isolated Hyper-V host or a Hyper-V cluster, and then the VMs can be live-migrated (moved) to the new storage.

- ▶ Live VSM: You can use live system migration (VSM) to migrate both the VM and the storage in a single action.

- ▶ Concurrent live migration: You can perform multiple concurrent live migrations of virtual machines and storage. The limit of concurrent live migration can be manually configured; the live migrations will be queued if the number of live migrations exceeds the specified limit.

 Note that the network usage for live migration might create a bottleneck.

Getting ready

Before you start performing live migrations, there are some requirements that you need to look at. These are discussed in the following sections.

Live migration requirements

The following are the requirements that need to be met before live migration can be performed:

- ▶ Two or more Hyper-V servers with processors from identical manufacturers (either all Intel or all AMD). This is because it is not possible to live-migrate from AMD to Intel processors and vice versa.

- ▶ Windows Server 2012. Live migration between hosts running Windows Server 2008 R2 SP1 or earlier and Windows Server 2012 is not supported.

- ▶ VMs should be configured to use virtual hard disks or virtual Fibre Channel disks, and not pass-through disks (physical disks).

Virtual Fibre Channel is not supported by VMM 2012 SP1. You cannot configure or add it to a virtual machine through VMM. However, you can configure it using **Virtual San Manager** under the **Actions** menu under **Hyper-V Manager**, and it will work perfectly as it is supported by Hyper-V.

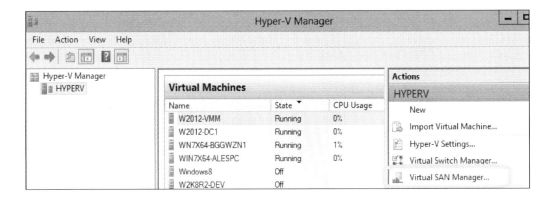

> ▸ A dedicated private network for live migration network traffic (recommended).

> ▸ Source and destination Hyper-V servers on the same domain, or on trusted domains.

> ▸ If the source or destination VM VHD has a base disk, it should be in a share available to the target host as well, as live migration does not usually migrate the base disk.

> ▸ Live migration among clusters is only supported for hosts running Windows Server 2012 with the Failover Cluster service and the CSV feature installed and enabled.

> ▸ If the source and destination Hyper-V hosts use shared storage, all VM files (for example, VHD/VHDX, snapshots, and configuration) must be stored on an SMB share with permissions to grant access on the share to both source and target computer accounts.

Live storage migration requirements

The following are the requirements for live storage migration:

> ▸ Live storage migration moves VM images (VHD, VFD, and ISO files), snapshot configurations, and data (saved state files).

> ▸ Storage migration is for virtual machines.

> ▸ Storage migration does not migrate parent (base) disks, except for snapshot disks.

Live system migration requirements

The following are the requirements for live system migration:

▶ The VM must exist in a location that is not visible to the destination host.

▶ For individual Hyper-V Windows 2012 hosts, the migration can happen among local disks or SMB 3.0 file shares.

▶ For Hyper-V Windows 2012 clusters, the VM can be migrated (moved) to either a CSV or SMB 3.0 file share on the target (destination) cluster.

How to do it...

Carry out the following steps to perform a live migration of a VM between two standalone Hyper-V Servers:

1. In the **VMs and Services** workspace on the VMM console, in the **VMs and Services** pane, expand **All Hosts**.

2. In the **VMs** pane, select the VM to migrate (for example, **W2012-FS01**).

 As this is a live migration, the virtual machine is running.

3. On the **Virtual Machine** tab, click on **Migrate Virtual Machine** to open the **Migrate VM Wizard** window.

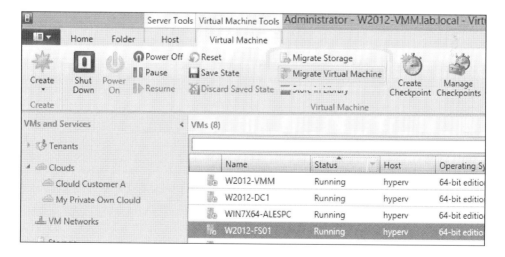

4. In the **Select Host** section, a list of possible destination hosts and their associated transfer types will be displayed.

 If both the Hyper-V hosts can access the same SMB 3.0 file share, the transfer type will display **Live**.

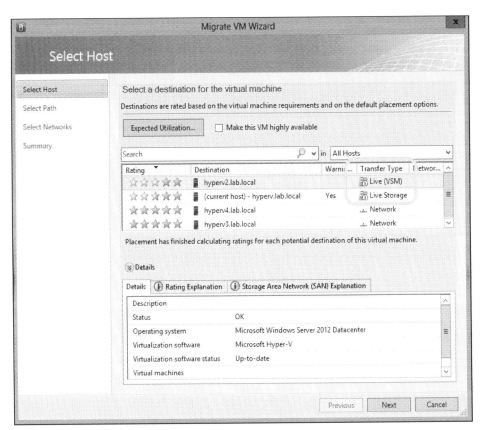

5. Select a destination host that shows a better rating and transfer type **Live** (for example, **hyperv2.lab.local**), and click on **Next**. Click on **Move** on the **Summary** page to start the migration process.

6. The **Jobs** workspace will open, showing the tasks being performed.

How it works...

There are a number of ways in which live migration can be used. You can live-migrate a virtual machine from one Hyper-V host to another keeping the VM files (VHD/VHDX, ISO, and VFD files) and configuration files in the same shared location (a CSV storage, an SMB share, and so on), move the VM files and the virtual machine together (live VSM), or move only the storage (live storage migration).

VMM reviews and validates the configuration settings of the target Hyper-V host before initiating the migration.

If the VM is running, the storage migration option enables you to live migrate the storage from one location to another without stopping/breaking the workload of the VM. Storage migration can also be used when you need to move, provision, maintain, or upgrade storage resources, or to move a standalone or cluster VM to another location.

Live-migrating a VM does not necessarily move the VM files (VHD/VHDX, ISO, and VFD files); keeping that in mind, you can perform the following actions:

- Configure the VM files to run on a file share that has access from both source and target Hyper-V hosts, and then run a live migration.
- Run a live VSM, which is a combination of live migration and storage migration, but in a single action.
- Run a separate live storage migration.

There's more...

As we have seen before, there are many types of live migrations available, especially with the SC 2012 SP1 version. Let's see how we can perform each one of them.

Performing live migration of a VM between hosts in two clusters

Carry out the following steps in order to perform live migration of VMs between hosts in two different clusters:

1. In the **VMs and Services** workspace on the VMM console, in the **VMs and Services** pane, expand **All Hosts**.

2. In the **VMs** pane, select the highly available VM to migrate (for example, **W2012-FS02**).

3. On the **Virtual Machine** tab, click on **Migrate Virtual Machine** to initiate the **Migrate VM Wizard** window.

4. In the **Select Host** section, review and select a destination cluster node that shows a better rating and the transfer type **Live** (for example, **ClustHyperv2**), and then click on **Next**.

To see the detailed rating, click on the **Rating Explanation** tab in the **Details** section.

5. Click on **Next**, and then click on **Move** in the **Summary** section.

6. To track the job status, open the **Jobs** workspace.

7. To check the migration status, on the **VMs and Services** pane in the **VMs and Services** workspace, select the destination host; in the **VMs** pane, you should see a VM status of **Running**.

Performing live storage migration between standalone hosts

1. In the **VMs and Services** workspace on the VMM console, in the **VMs and Services** pane, expand **All Hosts**.

2. In the **VMs** pane, select the VM for which you want to perform storage migration (for example, **W2012-FS01**).

3. On the **Virtual Machine** tab in the ribbon, click on **Migrate Storage** to open the **Migrate VM Wizard** window.

4. In the **Storage location for VM configuration** field in the **Select Path** section, select the default storage location or click on **Browse** to select the storage destination; then click on **OK**.

5. Select the **Add this path to the list of default storage locations on the host** checkbox if you would like to make this the default path for the VM's storage.

 Make sure you specify the FQDN of the destination file server in the share path if you specified an SMB 3.0 file share in the storage location field (for example, \\w2012-fs02.lab.local\vms).

The **Migrate VM Wizard** is shown in the following screenshot:

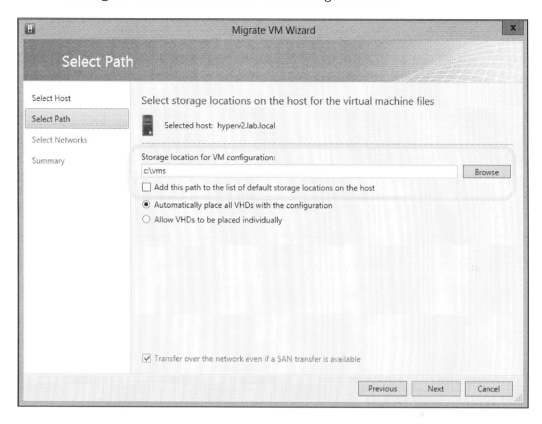

6. Click on **Next** and then click on **Move** in the **Summary** section.

7. Check the job status in the **Jobs** workspace.

Performing concurrent live migrations

When you perform more than one live migration per host at a time, VMM runs it concurrently. On the VMM console, it is not possible to select multiple VMs at the same time for the live migration wizard; instead, you will need to start the multiple live migrations one by one.

 VMM considers live VSM as one live migration and one storage migration.

Carry out the following steps to view the concurrent migration settings:

1. In the **Fabric** workspace on the VMM console, select the Hyper-V host.

2. Right-click and select **Properties**, and then click on **Migration Settings**.

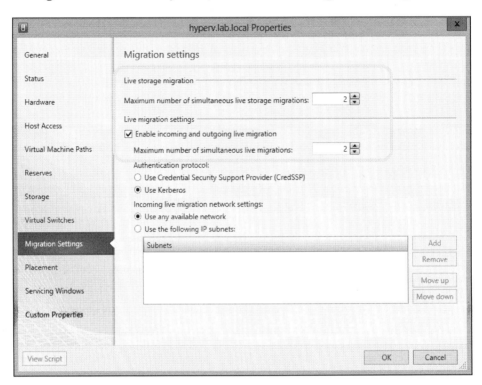

3. Change the concurrent live migration settings accordingly.

4. Click on **OK** to save.

 You need to perform this operation for every Hyper-V host.

See also

▶ The *Virtual Machine Live Migration Overview* page at `http://technet.microsoft.com/library/hh831435.aspx`

Linux virtual machines in VMM 2012 SP1

Linux-based VMs are now fully supported by VMM 2012 SP1, when hosted on a Hyper-V Server. This gives you the ability to add Linux-specific settings, such as OS specialization, when creating a Linux VM template, and additionally the ability to add that template to a service template that deploys a multitier application or service.

Getting ready

Before deploying Linux VMs, check whether Linux Integration Services (LIS) is installed on the VMs. VMM does not check whether a VM meets the LIS requirement. However, if these requirements are not met, the VM will fail to deploy.

[Some Linux distributions include LIS by default. But if LIS is not included, you must manually install it.]

How to do it...

Carry out the following steps to install the VMM agent for Linux on a Linux VM:

1. Log in to the VMM management server with administrative rights.

2. Click on the Windows key (▦) and type cmd. Right-click on **cmd** and select **Run as administrator**.

3. Type in the following command in the command prompt:

    ```
    C:\>cd "\Program Files\Microsoft System Center 2012\Virtual
    Machine Manager\agents\Linux"
    ```

```
Administrator: Command Prompt                           _  □  X

C:\Program Files\Microsoft System Center 2012\Virtual Machine Manager\agents\Lin
ux>dir
 Volume in drive C has no label.
 Volume Serial Number is 0010-2F99

 Directory of C:\Program Files\Microsoft System Center 2012\Virtual Machine Mana
ger\agents\Linux

16/11/2012  11:23 PM    <DIR>          .
16/11/2012  11:23 PM    <DIR>          ..
29/10/2012  01:25 PM             7,261 install
29/10/2012  01:25 PM         9,318,400 scvmmguestagent.1.0.0.544.x64.tar
29/10/2012  01:25 PM         8,509,440 scvmmguestagent.1.0.0.544.x86.tar
               3 File(s)     17,835,101 bytes
               2 Dir(s)  185,733,849,088 bytes free

C:\Program Files\Microsoft System Center 2012\Virtual Machine Manager\agents\Lin
ux>_
```

4. Copy the agent installation files to a new folder on the Linux VM, and then open it on the Linux VM.

5. If your Linux VM is a 32-bit version, run the following:

    ```
    #./install scvmmguestagent.1.0.0.544.x86.tar
    ```

6. If your Linux VM is a 64-bit version, run the following:

    ```
    #./install scvmmguestagent.1.0.0.544.x64.tar
    ```

How it works...

When creating a VM with Linux as the guest operating system, if the Linux distribution does not already have LIS, you must install it; after the machine starts, you will need to install the VMM agent for Linux as well.

The following will be created on the virtual hard disk when installing the VMM agent for Linux:

▶ A configuration file (scvmm.conf) containing the location of the logfile

▶ An installation logfile (scvmm-install.log)

▶ The logfile (scvmm.log) that will be generated at the next VM boot when the program starts automatically

▶ A default log folder (/var/opt/microsoft/scvmmagent/log)

▶ A default installation folder (/opt/microsoft/scvmmagent/)

See also

▶ The *About Virtual Machines and Guest Operating Systems* page at http://go.microsoft.com/fwlink/p/?LinkId=271219

▶ Installing LIS for Hyper-V on Windows Server 2012, on the *Hyper-V Overview* page at http://go.microsoft.com/fwlink/p/?LinkId=271220

▶ The *How to Install the VMM Agent for Linux* page at http://technet.microsoft.com/en-us/library/jj860429.aspx

Configuring availability options and virtual NUMA for VMs in VMM 2012 SP1

In VMM 2012 SP1, you can configure availability options for VMs that are deployed on Hyper-V host clusters, which include:

► **VM priority**: By configuring these settings, the host clusters will be instructed to start or place high-priority VMs before medium or low-priority VMs, ensuring that (for better performance) the high-priority VMs are allocated memory and other resources first.

► **Preferred and possible owners of VMs**: These settings influence the placement of VMs on the host cluster nodes. By default, there is no preferred owner, which means that the possible owners include all cluster nodes.

► **Availability sets**: By placing VMs in an availability set (to improve continuity of service), VMM will attempt to keep those VMs on separate hosts whenever possible.

You can also configure NUMA, which is a memory architecture that is used in multiprocessor systems. NUMA tries to reduce the gap between the speed of the CPU and the memory usage; its benefits include avoiding slow processor performance that is caused when various processors attempt to access shared memory blocks. A NUMA node is identified as a group of CPUs for each block of dedicated memory. For more NUMA concepts, see `http://msdn.microsoft.com/en-us/library/ms178144(v=sql.105).aspx`.

How to do it...

Carry out the following steps in order to configure priority for a VM or a VM template on a host cluster:

1. Open the VMM console and execute one of the following options:

   ❑ To configure a deployed VM, on the **VMs** pane in the **VMs and Services** workspace, select the VM, right-click on it, and click on **Properties**.

   ❑ To configure a VM stored in the VMM library, in the **Library** workspace, select the stored VM, right-click on it, and click on **Properties**.

   ❑ To configure a VM at the time of creation, click on the **Configure Hardware** section.

   ❑ To configure a VM template, in the **Library** workspace, expand **Templates** in the left-hand side pane, click on **VM Templates**, right-click on the VM template in the templates pane, and click on **Properties**.

2. On the **Hardware Configuration** (or **Configure Hardware**) section, select **Advanced** (you will probably have to scroll down to see this option) and click on **Availability**.

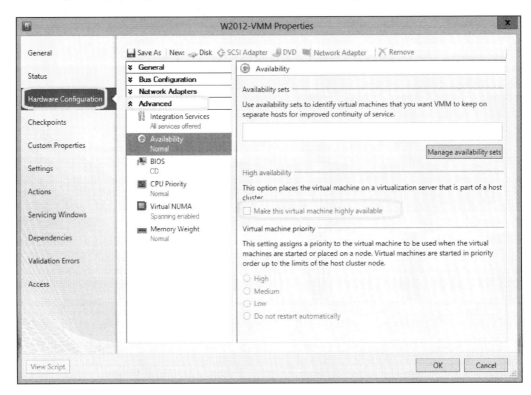

3. Select **Make this virtual machine highly available**.

On a deployed VM, this setting cannot be selected, as it depends on whether the VM is running on a host cluster or not.

4. On the **Virtual machine priority** section, select the VM priority as either **High**, **Medium**, or **Low**. However, if you want the VM to always start manually and never preempt other VMs, select **Do not restart automatically**.

5. Click on **OK** to save the settings.

How it works...

Availability options allow you to configure VM priority, preferred and possible owners of VMs, and availability sets. These options are configured by the VM and will allow you to refine the VM high-availability settings by prioritizing resources like CPU and memory as well as by influencing the placement of VMs in cluster nodes, all to improve performance and the continuity of service.

In case of a node failure, if high priority VMs (the VMs for which you selected the priority level **High**) do not have the necessary resources to start, lower priority VMs will be taken offline to free up necessary resources. The preempted VMs will later be restarted in the order of priority.

You can also use PowerShell for Failover Clustering to configure the **Availability sets** setting (**AntiAffinityClassNames**).

There's more...

Let's a have a look at more configuration options.

Configuring Availability Sets for a VM running on a host cluster

On the VMM console, do the following:

1. For a deployed VM, on the **VMs and Services** workspace in the **VMs and Services** pane, expand **All Hosts** and then select the VM in the **VMs** pane.

2. For a stored VM, in the **Library** workspace, in the library server where the VM is stored, select the VM.

3. Right-click on the selected VM and then click on **Properties**.

4. On the **Hardware Configuration** tab, click on **Availability**.

5. Make sure to select **Make this virtual machine highly available**.

 On a deployed VM, this setting cannot be selected as it depends on whether the VM is running on a host cluster or not.

6. In the **Availability sets** section, click on **Manage availability sets**.

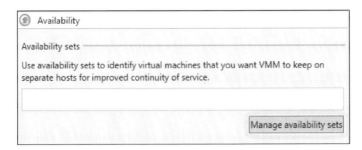

7. Click on an availability set, and then click on either **Add** or **Remove**.

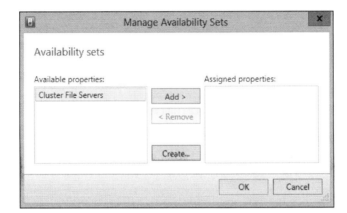

 To create a new availability set, click on **Create...**, type
the set name, and click on **OK**.

8. In the **Manage Availability Sets** dialog, click on **OK** to confirm.

9. In the VM properties sheet, click on **OK**.

Configuring preferred and possible owners for a VM

Carry out the following steps to configure the preferred owner for a virtual machine:

1. In the **VMs and Services** workspace on the VMM console, in the **VMs and Services** pane, expand **All Hosts**; then select the VM in the **VMs** pane.

2. Right-click on the selected VM and select **Properties**.

3. Click on the **Settings** tab and then do the following:

   ❑ Configure the preferred owners list if you want to control which nodes in the cluster will own the VM regularly.

❑   Configure the possible owners list and do not include the nodes that you don't want as owners of the VM, if you need to prevent a VM from being owned by a specific node.

4.   Click on **OK** to confirm.

Configuring virtual NUMA in VMM 2012 SP1

Virtual NUMA projects NUMA topology onto a virtual machine, which allows guest operating systems and applications to make intelligent NUMA decisions, aligning guest NUMA nodes with host resources. Carry out the following steps to configure virtual NUMA:

1.   In the **Advanced** section of the VM properties, click on **Virtual NUMA**.

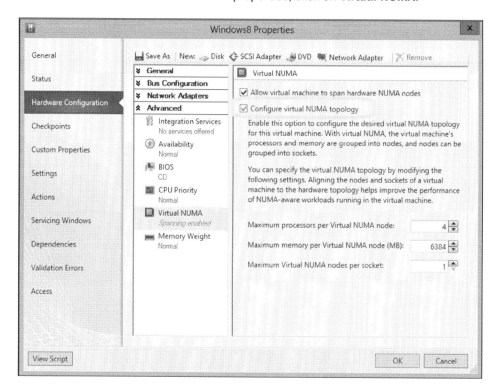

2.   In the **Maximum processors per Virtual NUMA node** field, specify the maximum number of VPs on the same VM that can be used simultaneously on a virtual NUMA node. The value should be between 1 and 32.

3.   In the **Maximum memory per Virtual NUMA node (MB)** field, specify the maximum amount of memory that can be assigned to a single virtual NUMA node. The value should be between 8 MB and 256 GB.

4. In the **Maximum Virtual NUMA nodes per socket** field, specify the maximum number of virtual NUMA nodes that are allowed on a single socket. The value should be between 1 and 64.

> To enable maximum bandwidth, configure different NUMA VMs to use different NUMA nodes.

5. To enable spanning, select the **Allow virtual machine to span hardware NUMA nodes** checkbox. Deselect the checkbox to disable NUMA spanning.

> Even if NUMA spanning is not enabled, based on the physical host topology, virtual nodes can still allocate memory from the same or different host NUMA nodes.

See also

▸ The *NUMA Concepts* section on the page at http://msdn.microsoft.com/en-us/library/ms178144(v=sql.105).aspx

Configuring resource throttling in VMM SP1

The additional features provided with the resource throttling feature in VMM 2012 SP1 include enhanced CPU (processor) and memory-throttling capabilities, which ensure that CPU and memory resources are allocated and used effectively. The ability to set the virtual processor (VP) weight to provide it with larger or smaller shares of CPU cycles ensures that VMs can be ranked when CPU resources are overcommitted.

Memory throttling helps to rank access to memory resources in situations where memory resources are constrained.

How to do it...

Carry out the following steps in order to configure processor-throttling:

1. On the VMM console, execute one of the following:

   ❑ To configure a deployed VM, on the **VMs pane** in the **VMs and Services** workspace, select the VM, right-click on it, and click on **Properties**.

   ❑ To configure a VM stored in the VMM library, in the **Library** workspace, select the stored VM, right-click on it, and click on **Properties**.

   ❑ To configure a VM at the time of creation, click on the **Configure Hardware** section.

❑ To configure a VM template, in the **Library** workspace, expand **Templates** on the left-hand side pane, click on **VM Templates**, right-click on the VM template in the templates pane, and click on **Properties**.

2. In the **Hardware Configuration** section, select **Advanced** (you will probably have to scroll down to see this option) and click on **CPU Priority**.

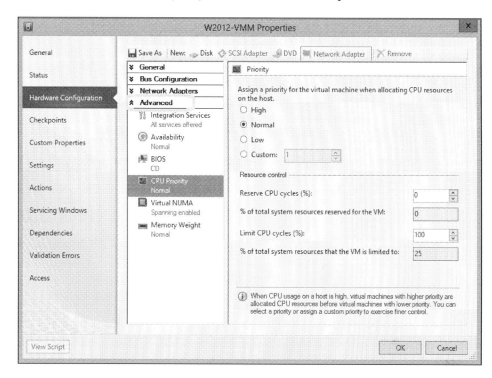

3. Select the VM priority, which specifies how the CPU resources will be balanced between VMs.

VMM Priority	High	Normal	Low	Custom
Relative weight value in Hyper-V	200	100	50	between 1 and 10000

4. In the **Reserve CPU cycles (%)** field, type in the percentage of the CPU resources in one logical processor that will be reserved for a VM.

 A zero value indicates that there is no reserve.

5. In the **Limit CPU cycles (%)** field, type in the maximum percentage of CPU resources in one logical processor that the VM will consume.

How it works...

In the **Advanced** section of the **CPU Priority** settings of the virtual machine, you can configure the weight of a virtual processor (VP) to make a share of CPU cycles available to it. You can configure the following settings:

▸ **High**, **Normal**, **Low**, or **Custom**, which defines how the CPU is shared when contention occurs, with VMs defined as **High** being allocated CPU resources first.

▸ **Reserve CPU cycles (%)**, which defines the percentage of CPU resources associated with one logical processor that should be reserved for the virtual machine; useful for CPU-intensive applications.

▸ **Limit CPU cycles (%)**, which defines the maximum percentage of resources on one logical processor that the VM can consume.

> The options to Reserve CPU cycles and Limit CPU cycles are only supported in Windows Server 2012 Hyper-V hosts.
>
> For highly intensive workloads, you can add more VPs, particularly when a physical CPU is near its limit.

There's more...

You can also configure the memory-throttling feature, which will help rank access to memory resources in situations where they are constrained, meaning that VMs that have a priority of **High** will be given memory resources before VMs with lower priority.

Note that defining a VM as one with a priority of **Low** might prevent it from starting when the available memory is low.

The memory priority settings and thresholds can be set to **Static**, in which you can assign a fixed amount of memory to a VM. They can also be set to **Dynamic**, where you can define the following settings:

▸ **Start-up memory**: Memory that is allocated to the VM when it starts up. The value will be adjusted as required by Dynamic Memory (DM).

▸ **Minimum memory**: Minimum memory required by the VM. It allows a VM to scale back the memory consumption below the start-up memory requirement (in case the VM is idle). The unbound memory can then be used by additional VMs.

▸ **Maximum memory**: Memory limit allocated to a VM.

▸ **Memory Buffer Percentage**: Defines the percentage of spare memory that will be assigned to the VM, based on the amount of memory required by the applications and services running on the VM. The amount of memory buffer is calculated as the **amount of memory needed by the VM/(memory buffer value/100)**.

Configuring memory throttling

Carry out the following steps to configure memory throttling:

1. In the properties of the VM, in the **Hardware Configuration** section, select **General** and then click on **Memory**.

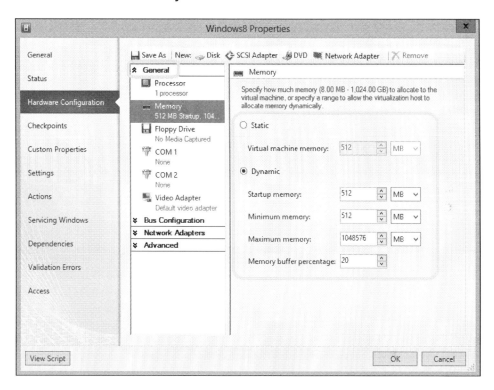

2. Click on **Static** to define the fixed memory that should be allocated to the VM.

3. Click on **Dynamic** and then do the following:

   ❑ In the **Startup memory** field, specify the memory for the VM for when it starts up.

   ❑ In the **Minimum memory** field, specify the minimum memory that the VM can run on.

   ❑ In the **Maximum memory** field, specify the maximum memory that can be allocated to the VM. For Windows Server 2012, the default value is 1TB.

   ❑ In the **Memory buffer percentage** field, specify the available memory that will be assigned to the VM (if it is needed).

Configuring memory weight

You can give priority to a VM when memory resources reach the limit. Configuring the VM with **High** will give it higher priority when allocating memory resources. On the other hand, if you set the VM priority as **Low**, the VM would not be able to start if the memory resources are reaching the limit.

To configure the memory weight for a VM, on the properties of the VM in the **Hardware Configuration** section, click on **Advanced** and then click on **Memory Weight** and configure the priority.

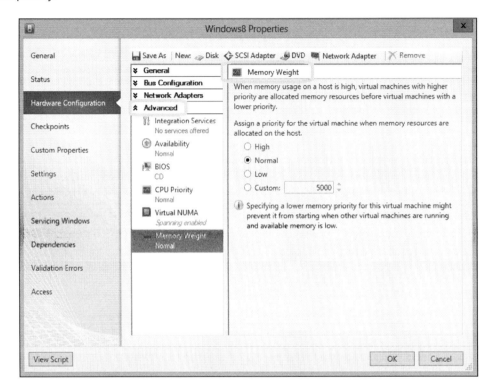

See also

▶ *Configuring availability options and virtual NUMA for VMs in VMM 2012 SP1*

Deploying SC App Controller 2012 SP1 for hybrid cloud management

App Controller (SCAC) is a replacement of the VMM Self-Service Portal. However, it is far from being just a replacement. It enables integration and management of VMM 2012 and Windows Azure services, meaning that it enables you to manage private and public clouds all together in a single console. You can, for example, upload Windows Azure configuration files, package files, and virtual hard drives from on-premises Hyper-V machines to Windows Azure.

 Check the terms of use and privacy statement for the Windows Azure service at `http://go.microsoft.com/fwlink/?linkid=236391`.

Getting ready

Before installing App Controller (SCAC), ensure that the system meets the hardware and software requirements and all the prerequisites are installed; see `http://technet. microsoft.com/en-us/library/gg696060.aspx`.

How to do it...

Carry out the following steps to deploy System Center App Controller 2012 SP1:

1. Log in to the server if you plan to install SCAC 2012 SP1 with local administrative rights, browse to the SCAC installation folder, double-click on the setup file, and click on **Install**.

2. On the **Product registration information** page, type in the product key and then click on **Next**.

3. Select **I have read, understood, and agree with the terms of the license agreement** and click on **Next**.

4. The server will be checked to see whether the prerequisites are met; if they are, you will have to type in the installation path in **Select the installation location** and click on **Next**.

5. On the **Configure the services** page, type in the user credentials (for example, `lab\svc-scac`, which is specifically designated for App Controller services) and either accept the default (`18622`) or type in a new port that will be used for communication between App Controller services.

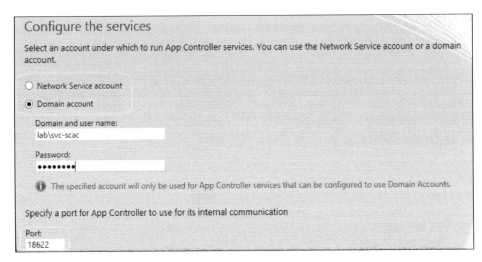

 You can enter credentials for either of these two accounts: **Network Service account** or **Domain account**.

6. On the **Configure the website** page, type in or select an IP address from the list of IP addresses that users can use to access the application.

7. Type in the **Port** field the port on which `HTTP.sys` must listen for requests made to this website (for example, `443` for **HTTPS**).

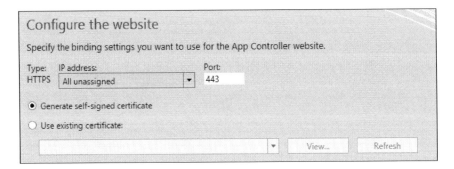

This assigned port cannot be changed without reinstalling App Controller.

8. Select whether to generate a self-signed certificate (which needs to be added to the Trusted Root Certification Authorities store of all computers that will access the App Controller website) or a previously imported SSL certificate and then click on **Next**.

9. On the **Configure the database** page, type in the **SQL Server** name and the **Port**, **Instance name**, and **Database Name** fields and click on **Next**.

 You can only have one SCAC database per SQL Server instance.

10. If you're using an existing App Controller database, like a highly available deployment of SCAC, on the **Configure encryption key** page, select the previously exported encryption key and type in the password, and click on **Next**.

 Use the `Export-SCACAesKey` PowerShell command to export the encryption key.

11. On the **Help improve App Controller for SC 2012** page, you can choose to either opt for the Customer Experience Improvement Program (CEIP) and use Microsoft Update or not, and then click on **Next**.

12. Click on **Install** to confirm and then click on **Finish**.

How it works...

Before you begin the installation of the App Controller server, ensure that you have checked all the prerequisites, as per the page at `http://technet.microsoft.com/en-us/library/gg696060.aspx`.

In order to install the App Controller server, you must be logged in as a domain user with local administrative rights. Also, the account must have a DB owner on the SQL Server.

During the process, you will be required to provide the database connection, and if the SCAC database already exists on the SQL Server, you can provide the exported encryption key. This process is required when deploying an HA SCAC.

Be careful when selecting the SCAC website port as the assigned port cannot be changed without reinstalling App Controller.

At the end of the installation process, you have the option to start the SCAC website. Note that Silverlight is required in order to open it.

If you face issues while installing SCAC, you can check the logfiles located in the `%LOCALAPPDATA%\AppController\Logs` folder.

There's more...

To connect to SC App Controller, open the SCAC URL (for example, `https://w2012-vmm.lab.local`) on a web browser. Provide suitable credentials and click on **Sign in**. If Single sign-on is enabled, you will not be prompted for credentials.

Connecting to private clouds: integrating with VMM 2012

Open the SCAC website and carry out the following steps to connect SCAC to SVMM:

1. On the **Overview** page, click on **Connect a Virtual Machine...** under **Private Clouds** (or click on **Clouds** and then **VMM Server** in the ribbon).

2. In the **Connect** dialog, type in the **Connection name**, an optional **description**, and the **FQDN** and **port** of the VMM management server.

3. Select **Automatically import SSL certificates** to allow files and templates to be copied to and from VMM cloud libraries, and then click on **OK** to create the VMM connection.

Connecting to public clouds

Open the SCAC website (for example, `https://w2012-vmm.lab.local`) and carry out the following steps to connect SCAC to a Windows Azure subscription:

1. On the **Overview** page, click on **Connect a Windows Azure...** under **Public Clouds** (or click on **Clouds**, then **Connect**, and then **Windows Azure Subscription**, in the ribbon).

2. In the **Connect** dialog, type in the name and an optional description and the subscription ID that can be found on the Windows Azure Management Portal.

3. Click on **Browse** to import the management certificates, and then click on **OK** to create the Azure connection.

See also

▶ The *How to Connect to a Hosting Provider in System Center 2012 SP1* page at `http://technet.microsoft.com/en-us/library/jj605416.aspx`

▶ The *Managing Windows Azure Subscription Settings* page at `http://technet.microsoft.com/en-us/library/hh221354.aspx`

▶ The *How to Delegate Users* (to Public or Private Clouds) page at `http://technet.microsoft.com/en-us/library/hh221343.aspx`

Index

V

Thank you for buying
Microsoft System Center Virtual Machine Manager 2012 Cookbook

About Packt Publishing

Packt, pronounced 'packed', published its first book "*Mastering phpMyAdmin for Effective MySQL Management*" in April 2004 and subsequently continued to specialize in publishing highly focused books on specific technologies and solutions.

Our books and publications share the experiences of your fellow IT professionals in adapting and customizing today's systems, applications, and frameworks. Our solution-based books give you the knowledge and power to customize the software and technologies you're using to get the job done. Packt books are more specific and less general than the IT books you have seen in the past. Our unique business model allows us to bring you more focused information, giving you more of what you need to know, and less of what you don't.

Packt is a modern, yet unique publishing company, which focuses on producing quality, cutting-edge books for communities of developers, administrators, and newbies alike. For more information, please visit our website: www.PacktPub.com.

About Packt Enterprise

In 2010, Packt launched two new brands, Packt Enterprise and Packt Open Source, in order to continue its focus on specialization. This book is part of the Packt Enterprise brand, home to books published on enterprise software – software created by major vendors, including (but not limited to) IBM, Microsoft and Oracle, often for use in other corporations. Its titles will offer information relevant to a range of users of this software, including administrators, developers, architects, and end users.

Writing for Packt

We welcome all inquiries from people who are interested in authoring. Book proposals should be sent to author@packtpub.com. If your book idea is still at an early stage and you would like to discuss it first before writing a formal book proposal, contact us; one of our commissioning editors will get in touch with you.

We're not just looking for published authors; if you have strong technical skills but no writing experience, our experienced editors can help you develop a writing career, or simply get some additional reward for your expertise.

Microsoft System Center 2012 Service Manager Cookbook

ISBN: 978-1-84968-694-5   Paperback: 474 pages

Learn how to configure and administer System Center 2012 Service Manager and solve specific problems and scenarios that arise

1. Practical cookbook with recipes that will help you get the most out of Microsoft System Center 2012 Service Manager.

2. Learn the various methods and best practices administrating and using Microsoft System Center 2012 Service Manager.

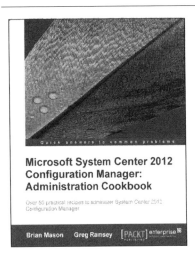

Microsoft System Center 2012 Configuration Manager: Administration Cookbook

ISBN: 978-1-84968-494-1   Paperback: 224 pages

Over 50 practical recipes to administer System Center 2012 Configuration Manager

1. Administer System Center 2012 Configuration Manager.

2. Provides fast answers to questions commonly asked by new administrators.

3. Skip the why's and go straight to the how-to's.

4. Gain administration tips from System Center 2012 Configuration Manager MVPs with years of experience in large corporations.

Please check **www.PacktPub.com** for information on our titles

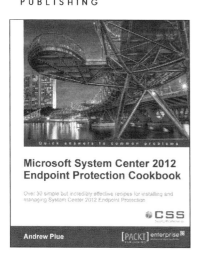

Microsoft System Center 2012
Endpoint Protection Cookbook

Over 30 simple but incredibly effective recipes for installing and
managing System Center 2012 Endpoint Protection

⬤CSS

Andrew Plue   [PACKT] enterprise 🞩

Microsoft System Center 2012 Endpoint Protection Cookbook

ISBN: 978-1-84968-390-6   Paperback: 208 pages

Over 30 simple but incredibly effective recipes for installing and managing System Center 2012 Endpoint Protection

1. Master the most crucial tasks you'll need to implement System Center 2012 Endpoint Protection.

2. Provision SCEP administrators with just the right level of privileges, build the best possible SCEP policies for your workstations and servers, discover the hidden potential of command line utilities and much more in this practical book and eBook.

Windows Server 2012
Hyper-V Cookbook

Over 50 simple but incredibly effective recipes for mastering
the administration of Windows Server Hyper-V

Leandro Carvalho   [PACKT] enterprise 🞩

Windows Server 2012 Hyper-V Cookbook

ISBN: 978-1-84968-442-2   Paperback: 304 pages

Over 50 simple but incredibly effective recipes for mastering the administration of Windows Server Hyper-V

1. Take advantage of numerous Hyper-V best practices for administrators.

2. Get to grips with migrating virtual machines between servers and old Hyper-V versions, automating tasks with PowerShell, providing a High Availability and Disaster Recovery environment, and much more.

3. A practical Cookbook bursting with essential recipes.

Please check **www.PacktPub.com** for information on our titles

22102341R10182

Made in the USA
Lexington, KY
12 April 2013